SIMPLIFYING
THE ROAD TO
WHOLENESS

SIMPLIFYING THE ROAD TO WHOLENESS

Nancy Stewart Ging

To order additional copies of this book, contact:
Xlibris Corporation
1-888-7-XLIBRIS
www.Xlibris.com
Orders@Xlibris.com
To contact author: e-mail: nancyging@aol.com
12790

CONTENTS

SECTION II

SECTION III

DEDICATIONS

To Jan Flyte, Kay Noreen and Manny Jackson

To my children, Tracey and Kevin for enduring and participating in miracles

To Jade Mikayla, an angel in our midst

To my mother and sister, Edna Stewart and Sally Lanzi, amazing women, both, and Joe Buck, my late, great and delightful Dad

To Union Church of Hinsdale, Illinois (U.C.C.), the Taize community of Ascension Church of Oak Park, Illinois (R.C.C.) and the Brothers of Taize, France

To my clients, one and all

ACKNOWLEDGMENTS

We are called to do what we cannot do without the help of others.

With gratitude for "the others"—

Kris Berry Cromwell, for her cover art, rich intuition and friendship

Carrie Miller, for converting my hand-sketched hand-outs into computer graphics

Tracey Trendler and Beth Lanzi for offering editorial assistance

Rev. Richard Nye and Rev. Paul Stiffler for their clergy-support, their love and faith in me

Dr. Sandra Alcorn and Dr. Stanley Krippner, professionals in academia who inspired me over twenty-five years by living what they teach

Miriam Reitz, Ph.D. for her supervision, consultation, and steady support over the past twenty years

For those colleagues who expressed enthusiasm for my ideas before I put them into print and, therefore, motivated me to finally get out of my own way: Daniel Freedman, Richard C. Schwartz, Carolyn Myss, and several academicians of the Society for Spirituality and Social Work especially Hesook Lee and Dona Reese

For my elders, the women of substance in my prayer group with whom I met weekly for many years who kept me connected to my roots: Louise Barnard, Lou Jacobs, Charlotte Shipley, Vivian Peterson, Marietta Long, Teddy Vincent, Betty Oostenbrug, Carol Jacus, Ginny Monroe and Doe Peters Simerson

For those friends who made a big difference by seeing what I sometimes forgot to see in myself: Toby Berkun, Cindy Bouman, Bob Burby, Dan Cherry, Beverly Grall, Angela DeMaio, Jeanne Dickerson, Anne Firestone, Bonnie Hawes, Annette Hulefeld, John Kudella, Nancy Leonard, Barbara Marseille, Barbara Michels, John Naughton, Mary Parker, Marsha Riskin, Liz Schoeberlin, Barbara Schuppe, and Susan Willenbrink and for Jim Lavin who serves the Creative Forces with joyful humor, dance and song

For the Sisters of the Warrenville Cenacle for creating a place of profound peace

And especially for every session with every one of my clients for each has given me the opportunity to practice presence, expand my heart and know wholeness myself

INTRODUCTION

It is my desire to pass on to others the benefit of what I, a psychotherapist, have learned the long, hard way as a survivor of cancer and other frightening diseases, as one who has known depression intimately, and as an adventurous and intent observer of and participant in the Life Process.

From the angles on reality which I now enjoy, I feel that the length of my journey to wholeness could have been much less costly in terms of time, money and struggle. I'm eager for more of us to get to the place of knowing wholeness and joy sooner and have plenty of time to play! It's my heartfelt belief that we are to have fun, enjoy the earth and our senses, fully participate in love and the dance of life *at least* as much of the time as we spend working, striving and taking care of business. May the perspectives and guidance in this book bring you this opportunity.

The stories, techniques, theories and perspectives in this book can be helpful to anyone. They are written for people seeking wholeness and for therapists looking for new and faster ways to help themselves and others find it.

This book is comprised of three main sections. Section I is an easy overview of a formula for wholeness by simply inviting greater awareness of the perspectives **1, 2, 3,** and **4.** These viewing points of life are described briefly in the first seven chapters of Section I. Each chapter is a steppingstone to the next; the basic premises are gathered along the way.

Section II is a more detailed description of the perspectives presented in Section I. It also includes comparisons of two polar opposite paradigms of Reality (both *real* enough), ideas about balancing Realities, paradigm surfing, partnering polarities, sex along an intimacy continuum, paradigm bigotry, mixing-up paradigms, body-focused awareness of energies, roots of addictions, relationship attractions, family energy connections and many other aspects of life on the road to wholeness. Section II also contains examples and stories of the usefulness of the perspectives 1,2,3, and 4. It contains self-help suggestions as well as original theoretical material and practice techniques and exercises for therapists, healers, and coaches to use with their clients. The theoretical material may be useful to those who teach in the various fields of the helping professions.

A number of guided imagery exercises and body-focused self-healing techniques are found throughout Sections I and II.

The conclusion of Chapter 23 includes a list of 36 basic concepts of this book. I choose not to offer them at the beginning of the book because it may be more pleasurable and practical for the reader to come upon them as each chapter unfolds. The first ten chapters are intended to be read sequentially.

A few themes and concepts re-appear in several chapters. This is intentional. New ideas can be integrated more easily if repetition is part of the process.

The poetry and diagrams in this book are my own except where otherwise stated. May the poems and diagrams help you shift from one brain hemisphere to the other as you move through these chapters. Throughout the book I have capitalized words and phrases that represent aspects of the highest energy we can attempt to hold.

Section III is a story of my personal experience as a therapist-on-the-mend, portions of the tale of my extensive, expensive, often "off-beat" and long process of healing, finding selfhood and wholeness.

At the end of the book the reader will find Notes and hopefully, useful Appendixes such as "Ten Strategies for Holistic Counseling" and an extensive book list for bridging paradigms.

I have included, as Appendix D, a lengthly personal log of educational experiences in which I have participated; I feel immensely grateful for having had the means to partake in such learning and healing adventures that have brought me to a place of full health. It includes listings of many of the spiritual healing sessions and psychic readings I had during the years when my health threats loomed large. The commitment to my full integration and well-being was fueled by the fact that I hoped to one day be able to share the fruits of this quest with others in need. For years I have wanted to publish a synthesis of what I have learned from a wide variety of people and what I have also discovered inside my own mind **in order to help others who may not have had the healing and learning opportunities I have had.** It is my hope that many of my conclusions and the health I now enjoy may be yours as well.

SECTION I

CHAPTER ONE

THE ESSENTIALS

Let us simplify. The behavioral sciences have created enormous complexity, leading therapists and clients alike to lose sight of what is *most essential.* It is time to expand our consciousness while, at the same time, reducing complexity in how we think about ourselves and our lives. The essential concept of this chapter is that there is more confusion about being a person than there needs to be. We need to discover, experience and remember our essence. This is not a terribly time-consuming endeavor. It is essential that we know who we are. Life is often problematic, however we have lost sight of what is most essential about ourselves and this has made our journey through life more arduous.

HOLISTIC COUNSELING WITH SPIRIT AND SOUL

Whether you want to help yourself find wholeness, or you are looking for a holistic counselor or hoping to become one, these approaches will help you.

Holistic, alternative or psycho-spiritual therapists need not become confused about imposing their own values on clients in the process of including Spirit and Soul in psychotherapy. Spirit and Soul are ALREADY included in whatever we do. Spirit is our *essential connected aliveness* and Soul is *our very BEING.*

I'd like to offer some perspectives which I've arrived at during the past 20 years in private practice as a holistic therapist for individuals, couples and families.

NO CONFLICTS

These ideas should not be problematic for therapists or clients. They are not religious ones, yet they "work" with all religions, all traditions and with agnostic and atheist individuals as well.

In my twenty years of full-time private practice I have never had a client suggest to me that I was imposing a point of view upon them. The concepts I have included in my sessions as a therapist are concepts about Reality, about the way life seems to work for me and for most people who are awakening to their wholeness.

This book and the theoretical material is also my story, my cosmology, a world view which is expansive and inclusive. These chapters include new findings about the heart, the brain, the New Sciences, and some ideas which have occurred to me as I have done a dance of synthesizing many fields—biological, psychological, theological, religious, metaphysical—that have been helpful to me in my own personal journey as a passionate seeker of truth on a quest for consistent psychological balance, physical health and spiritual wealth.

As a psychotherapist and healer, the theories, perspectives and processes with which I have worked have energized me as I have delighted in the dramatically rapid and lasting shifts into well-being on the part of many of my clients. The healing and growth has been mutual, mine taking longer than many of my clients. Had I waited until I had arrived at thorough-enough integration of my own personality before entering into in- depth, full-time clinical practice I would have missed my calling altogether. As a therapist and human-being-on-the-mend, my own healing and my arrival at these perspective has been a linear process, one drama of my life leading to the next mode of my practice, like building blocks. It has also been a non-linear process with sudden flashes of the whole of things.

A DANCE WITH NUMBERS

The "how to's" of wholesome, holistic therapy, with ourselves or clients, may be as simple as **1-2-3 and 4.** Humanness is a complicated condition. To be a person in the world is difficult. We can make it less so by shifting our stance, using a formula for living life which simplifies and keeps us attending to basics. I call this formula:

"1-2-3-4 Wholeness "

The numbers 1, 2 and 3 represent qualitatively different perspectives on who we are and how we are experiencing life at any given time. It is liberating to awaken to where we are standing, to know which stance we are operating out of, and to flow from one realm to another with a high degree of consciousness. Living in this way becomes a dance, a dance of different stances. Number four represents four quadrants or compartments within our greatest healing resource.

CHAPTER TWO

ONENESS

ONE represents "a pre-existing condition" of whole-ness. Every individual has this, no matter how unbal-anced he or she may seem to be at the level of physical and/or psychological self. **ONE** represents our spiritual condition, the depth, breadth and balance or wholeness of our Soul. The Soul is that which embraces and holds all our potential and all that we experience in our fre-quently fragmented human condition. The Soul ex-panded is the dimension which connects us with and in which we may actually experience The One. In addition to the number *one* representing the Soul of an individual, ONE also represents The Holy Whole, Grand Container of All That Is, whose image we reflect.

PRIMARY IDENTITY AS SOUL

To the questions "Who am I?" or "What am I?" the most wholesome answer is "I am all that I have ever experienced in my life, the whole of it and that which holds it!" or "I am my Soul." When we identify ourselves as our Soul first and foremost, all wounds and alleged pathology will pale by comparison.

Healing and integration within the personalities of people in therapy happens much more rapidly when therapists remember who their clients are at the most essential level, the Soul.

Something is true for everyone: if we were to divest ourselves of our roles in life and temporarily put aside our personality patterns, we are left with the best of us, our Soul. It is our Soul which endures beyond its period of residence within our body, at least in the memories of those whose lives have been touched by our in-spirited presence in the world. Our Soul is also the best place out of which to live our lives when we are incarnate, when we are wearing a physical body. Our most empowering identity and how we may best think of ourselves is as the wholeness or Soul that we are. When we become conscious of who we are and experience ourselves at this level, our acceptability is not in question. With this perspective we recognize that we are quite enough. Within our soul we already know *balance*, dark and light together. Nothing is excluded from the **one**ness that we are. Our Soul is, among other things, the sum total of all that we are and all that we have experienced and will experience. This Soul is also that which *holds* all that we are. It is a grand container.

A BETTER, BRIGHTER VIEW

As we see the Soul as our primary identity and reflect on the totality of our lives from this vantage point, we frequently perceive that a balance of pleasure and pain has been experienced in our lives. As I have observed the lives of hundreds of clients, life seems to be compensatory for those who seek consciousness expansion. Persons who have known particularly painful early lives find happiness of a commensurate degree in later life which balances the previous pain *if* they choose to awaken to the unity of their Soul's perspective. Difficulties can more easily be accepted as simply "aspects" of one's totality when we look at our life through the largest picture frame possible, through the eyes of the Soul. Unfortunately, for those who resist and refuse to awaken into greater consciousness, history keeps repeating itself. The repetition compulsion of which Freud spoke is a painful fact of life which therapists see played out in the lives of clients who have been afraid to grow. The dramas and patterns in love and work occur over and over again until they are brought into the bright light of consciousness.

STORY OF A SHIFTED STANCE

I described this perspective to a 30 year old client who had over-identified with her wounds and symptoms. In other words, she considered her wounds and symptoms to be who she was, to a large degree. Her parents had divorced, she had a very disturbed mother and an alcoholic father. Reasons for concern. During our second session I shared my cosmology with her. Although highly intelligent and educated, this "yuppie" had no world view which could serve her growth.

One of the first things I noticed 20 years ago when I embarked on my holistic practice was that many clients had no way of thinking about life in general, or their own lives in particular, from which they could get to any place that was more comfortable. Like many, my client simply sought symptom relief. This is what clinical training had taught me to provide but it did not seem sufficient; I wanted to share with clients a *way to comprehend Reality*. During the second session I shared with this young woman my perspective of the psychological self (the lesser self) and the Soul (the Greater Self). I suggested that she consider thinking of herself primarily as a Soul—her *fullness of being*, that which she really IS. "We HAVE a personality, just as we HAVE a body, but who we REALLY ARE is our Soul; it is our BEING, our IS-ness," I said. I encouraged her to try on this perspective for a few weeks and see how this stance served her. That night she dreamt about exploring a 12 million dollar house, and noticed a cracked tile in one of the bathrooms; she then continued through the house. After this dream's message was understood the client needed very few sessions as she shifted into identifying with her wholeness. Our Soul is indeed a mansion, a castle containing our wounds, mere cracked tiles to simply notice and accept (and repair if necessary) and move beyond. In one of her major works, *The Interior Castle*, (1577) Teresa of Avila wrote of the Soul as a beautiful mansion in which God resides in the centermost place.[1] Healing happens once we get the spacious picture. My muse spoke of it this way:

Oh spacious Soul,
My grand container
Which heals and holds this life's sum total,
You nurture possibilities within—
As waves you flow
Beyond the fleshy boundaries of my skin.
You fold within your arms my personality;
You hold and yet you set me free
For as I'm conscious of YOUR energy
I AM expanded, grandly
Connecting, then, with **ONE,** with All
And listening, may hear "the call."

WE ARE "*ONE*derful"

We can recognize that we are in the mode of **one-ness** by the sense of wonder, peace, completeness, safety, fullness and trust which we can actually sense physically. Our body has a vast capacity to feel the *ONE*derful, *WONDER*ful, **one**der*FULL* **ONE**ness.

> WOW!
> W-O-W
> Whole Only Whole
> Only, for that is All there is
> ALL THAT IS:
> THE Wholeness
> Our wholeness
> W.O.W.
> Wonderful One, Wholeness

The sense of balance and integration is actually palpable. There is a particular quality of openness, spaciousness to this perspective which one can learn to recognize and experience bodily. This unity consciousness of the stance of **ONE** reflects "All That Is." Yet it is not the *only* stance there is. The human condition carries with it a vast capacity for experiencing life in **TWO**'s.

CHAPTER THREE

DOUBLE VISION
FOR A UNIFIED SELF

In the context of this formula for living, **two** represents two things: 1) **two** different views of reality with a qualitatively different self to go with each reality AND 2) **pairs** of opposites balancing each other as polarities (described in later Chapter Sixteen).

Mythologist Joseph Campbell said, "The world is divided into two kinds of people: those who see the world in two's and those who don't."[2] With this I doubly agree.

TWO DIFFERENT REALITIES

We experience life in two qualitatively different realities. The often painful work of life on earth is more manageable as we learn to dance between these **two** realities with growing awareness of the choice to raise or lower the volume on one dimension or the other, seeking balance between the **two** dimensions, the **two** realities. As we live out of this intention, balance in our lives can be found, within both our inner experience and in our interaction with the environment.

A sign in my office depicts these two dimensions: it shows a storm above a man at sea in a rowboat with the words "Pray to God but row toward shore." I changed the "but" to "AND," for we live in *both* of these two realities—the reality of the unseen forces (the mystery of prayer) and the reality of more concrete matter (solid shore). The Arabs say "Pray to Allah and tie your camel." During a talk introducing a meditation session, one of my teachers, Ram Dass said, "You have to remember your zip code even when you're in the middle of inter-galactic bliss."[3] Indeed.

OUR GREATER SELF

The Greater Self of each of us "gets," or can sense, the big picture. This Greater Self is something we each already have. As a microcosm of All That Is, it feels a connection with the compassionate nature of The Grand Container Which Holds The Holy Whole, The Super Self, The Macrocosm, Over-Soul[4]. Therefore, our Soul/ Greater Self has a sense of trust. The Soul is actually boundless and flows into the whole of things, the Universe, yet our concrete minds need to be able "to get our head around it" so I describe it in a more concrete way, as arms embracing the personality or lesser self.

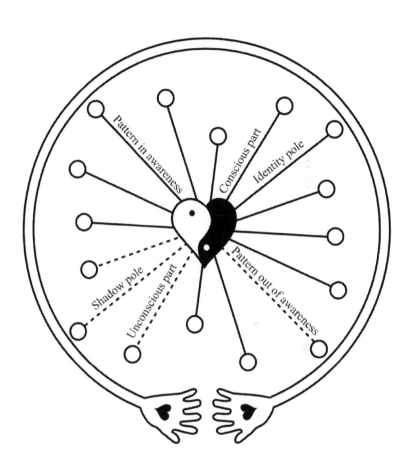

What can be conceptualized by one side of us as "a container" which holds all of our human experience is known to the other side of us not as a container but as energy that cannot be contained, continues into infinity and has no boundaries. This is the container/not container paradox of the Soul.

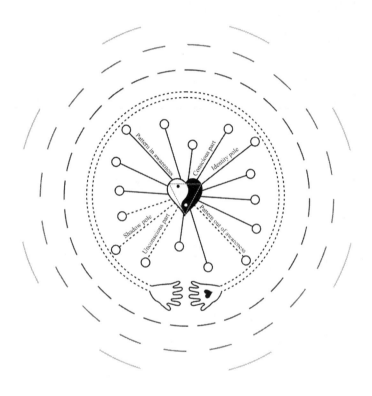

TO TRUST AND TO THRIVE

The more moments of consciousness expansion a person accrues, the greater grows the capacity to trust. Trust-ability is often difficult to achieve for the lesser self of our human nature. Whether or not we are conscious of it, some degree of fear is a fairly constant companion for all but the most enlightened humans beings. Our human nature is intricately involved with the issues of physical and psychological survival.

When we feel that life is a challenge to be mastered, which indeed it is, we are living out of our lesser self, our "human nature." When we experience life as a banquet to enjoy, which indeed it *also* is, we are living out of our Greater Self. The Soul or Greater Self knows that our BEING is infinite and is not burdened by the motives of survival. "Thrival," were it a word, is of the Soul's realm. The Soul or Greater Self knows that it is here for the duration of Eternity. Its experience is one of safety.

BIG AND LITTLE SELF

The following oft repeated words (of Anonymous) are an example of the trusting consciousness of the Great Self: "If you love something, let it go; if it's yours it will come back to you. If not, it wasn't meant to be."

On a T-shirt rack I once saw a shirt with a slogan, the essence of which was this: If you love something, let it go; if it comes back to you it's yours. If not, hunt it down and kill it! This T-Shirt was displaying the consciousness of the lesser self of our human nature which can be needy, desperate, possessive, and even capable of being vindictive. We need to get acquainted with both dimensions of our personhood, with all our capacities, great and small. Let us accept our glorious power to love ourselves and others, as well as shine the Light of our consciousness on the darkest corners of our humanness. The more we know of ourselves, the larger and more powerful we feel; accepting the dark and petty pieces of our human nature can actually serve us by bringing us to our wholeness. Wholeness requires both the dimness and the brightness of our personhood.

REPRESSION ROBS US OF ENERGY

It is easier to accept the less than sublime aspects of our character when we think of these qualities as simply *energy*. Indeed, from the perspective of the Energy Paradigm, *everything* is energy. The more of ourselves we know and accept, the more qualities of energy we embrace. Then a greater quantity of energy is available to us. We waste a substantial amount of energy keeping aspects of our personality repressed or buried; the process of repression takes energy that we could be using far more pleasurably. Obviously we have also lost access to the energy of the repressed emotions themselves.

THE REPRESSION CALLED DEPRESSION

Consider depression as an example: is it any wonder that we feel tired when we are depressed? Very often depression is related to anger that is repressed or buried beneath our awareness. It takes a tremendous amount of energy to keep strong anger or rage buried. Anger and rage are highly charged emotions, buried or not. Seeing and accepting the anger is an extremely energizing, often exhilarating experience.

NOTHING MUCH TO FEAR

Once we know of our Greater Self and feel the love for ourselves which already exists in that larger dimension of our wholeness, there is no longer a risk in looking at aspects of our personality. Without the perspective of our Greater Self as our primary identity, we resist seeing all the faces of our humanity and may even feel ashamed of who we are. Shame ceases to be a burden once we know that we are, first and foremost, a Great Self.

SAINTED AND CRAZED ONES

A saint may be someone who has become acquainted with and is accepting of the darkest aspects of his/her nature. As a result of facing and embracing the contracted energies of uncomfortable emotions and human fear-based capacities, the saint's Spirit is spacious and able to be accepting of and compassionate toward all people, even those individuals who are still being taken over by fearful, enraged and desperate aspects of their personhood.

FEAR OF CRAZINESS

Once a person *accepts* that a potentially chaotic, wild and crazy aspect of human nature may exist internally, fear of going insane subsides and responsible behavior ensues. For some people, that responsible behavior may include taking medications. When we stop running from our own potential craziness and get to know it as a pattern of energy that exists within the human family and therefore each of us "owns it" to some degree, more inner peace is possible. At the same time, much of the fear we feel about people who are acting out of their craziness will simply evaporate.

MASTERING THE HUMAN CONDITION

As we move into the consciousness of our Greater Self we accept all that we are; here we can become masters of the human condition, expanding our capacity for compassion. Compassionate love and the ability to accept others who are in extreme states of mental and emotional disarray may be the greatest quality we homo sapiens can find in our repertoire of capacities. Perhaps optimal mental health is the degree of self-knowledge and personal integration which brings one to the place of willingness to accept all individuals, even those of little integrity. Perhaps optimal sanity amounts to the degree to which we take care of every aspect of who we are.

We can be *monsters* with the human condition; this condition can be an affliction. Better that we become the *masters* of the human condition that is a reflection of our higher, holy nature.

OUR CONDITION(S)

The human condition includes immense richness in its diversity. Our capacity for beauty and ugliness walk side by side within our psyche. As we seek to know and accept our darker qualities it is important that we remember that our human nature with its lesser self is not to be devalued in relation to our Greater Self. Our human nature is simply more of a problem for us. "Tweaking" the human condition is a worthy pastime and we may choose to "work on ourselves" endlessly throughout our life. However, we are already WHOLE at the level of our Greater Self; when we remember this there may be less urgency about "working on" our personality issues. Our Soul/Greater Self actually heals and transforms our personality when we bring all that we are into conscious awareness. We may not need so much therapy or fixing as much as we need to remember who we are. A new perspective, a new cosmology can help.

Our Greater Self and lesser self are simply two very different dimensions of who we are—one aspect of our personhood for each of the two different realities in which we reside. The "lesser self" has less spaciousness, less expansiveness. Let us suspend judgment about our lesser self. Lesser in this context does not mean "worse than;" it means "less than." (Some might prefer to think of the lesser self as "the little self", a more endearing term perhaps). Each of us has to make peace with our "human condition" and each of us needs to discover that we have a super-human condition within and beyond our lesser, little human nature. Our Soul or Greater Self has existed within us all along but our human condition can be so noisy that we can't hear it, or so distracting that we can't see it. It wishes to be seen and heard.

OUR SOUL IS OUR OWN

Our Soul is always our own. To some degree our personality is our own personal "human nature" which we were born with, but to a significant degree we become who we are as human beings in response to the energies and behaviors of our parents and their relationship with each other. Our Soul, however, is neither damaged or enhanced by the behavior and energies of others. Our Soul grows and evolves from our very own choice to be more conscious.

MOTIVATIONS ARE TELLING

Our motivation will indicate where we are coming from at a particular time. When our behavior is motivated by anything other than the spacious acceptance and love coming from our wholeness, we are significantly separated from our Greater Self and are operating from our lesser self. A desire to receive love and approval is a demand which our human nature may never get beyond. Our Greater Self or super-human nature is connected in its expanded state with THE **ONE**ness, All That Is, The Holy Whole. Our Greater Self knows that it IS love. It IS compassionate acceptance and peace. This level of who we are is beyond human need.

A STORY OF TWO MODES

A client who made an appointment for hypnosis to help with a nail biting habit had something additional on her mind. For the past two years she had been estranged from her best and oldest friend. This friendship had been of thirty years duration and my client was hoping to hear from the woman on her rapidly approaching birthday the following week. My suggestion was that she let herself move into the consciousness of her Greater Self as she was falling asleep at night and imagine that she was sending a message to the Greater Self of her friend, encouraging the friend to reach out, making contact by sending my client a birthday message.

Three days after my client began doing this, two days after her birthday, she received a lovely birthday card on which her "friend" had hand-written a kind and warm message. This gave my client hope that there might be mending ahead—a meeting of their minds, healing to their friendship. My client felt her own heart opening wider and felt that her "prayer" had been answered. Great Self to Great Self communication had possibly occurred between these two woman. Then my client unfolded an enclosure inside the card, a long typewritten letter from her estranged "friend." She found it full of insulting comments, saying that my client "had limitations as a friend," etc. The typewritten enclosure was filled with all manner of defensive and competitive comments.

The little self and very human nature of her former friend had revealed itself, just as the Greater Self had also shown itself in the handwritten, warm note. The perspective of Greater Self and lesser self was helpful to my client. It gave her hope that her estranged friend would respond out of the higher nature of personhood as my client was envisioning that dimension of her "friend." As we become increasingly aware of the stance we are living from in our thoughts, emotions and behaviors, we will notice that in nearly every moment we have a choice to lead with our higher nature or our lower one. Exercising this power of choice is strengthening to both aspects of Self/self.

BALANCING REALITIES—AND LOOKING FOR THEIR "LAWS"

Just as there are the natural polarities of the created world—night/day, dark/light, Earth/Heaven, female/male, North/South, East/West—we, the people, experience life in *two qualitatively different realities.* We become more adept at **balancing realities** when we recognize that *for each of the two realities a separate set of "laws" apply.* Our physical-material reality follows the laws of Newtonian Physics, the scientific paradigm of our western world. The reality of Oneness or what I shall call the Energy Paradigm follows laws that are closer to Quantum Physics and metaphysical laws. We have a brain hemisphere for interpreting each of these two realities. Without becoming experts on physics or metaphysics we can begin to balance realities and balance our selves. This will bring us to greater degrees of integrity.

Integrity is synonymous with mental health; it is the integration of all that we are, dark and light forces in partnership. Wholeness and integrity need not be so hard to find. The rigors of living are easier when we move into this perspective of double vision and get to know the ways that each reality presents itself to us. This perspective also enlarges and ennobles us.

POLARITIES, EVEN REALITIES, ON A CONTINUUM

Polarities are pairs of opposite energy patterns which are at the end of a pole, a continuum. The mid-point between a pair of energy patterns is the point of balance and partnership of these opposites. As we look at our life from the perspective of **two**'s, seeing our life as being comprised of many pairs of opposites, we can more easily find the balance points in the many and varied aspects of living.

NUMBERING THE DUAL REALITIES

The reality of interconnected waves of energy I call Reality # 1. The reality of separate forms and patterns of behavior I label Reality # 2. The realities themselves are best seen as polarities on a continuum. Consider this continuum of reality to be a spectrum of energy going from the most spacious (Reality #1) to the most dense material (Reality #2). The place where these realities meet in the middle I acknowledge as Reality # 3.

*S*pacious, Transpersonal, Soul

(Reality #1)

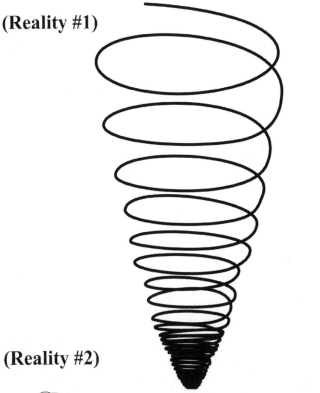

(Reality #2)

*D*ense, Identity, Personality

NEW CREATION AND BLESSINGS

Just as the whole is greater than the sum of its parts, the meeting place of opposites is greater than the two poles coming into proximity. The meeting of poles can bring the gift of a new creation, Reality # 3. Unexpected blessings occur when and where the lion lies down with the lamb. At those meeting places, where Spirit infuses matter most fully, we find wholeness, Unified Selfhood.

A UNIFIED THEORY OF THE SELF/self

This is, essentially, a practical, usable Unified Theory of the psychological self **and** Soul, or a Unified Theory of Self/self. It brings the conventional paradigm of science into partnership with the emerging new paradigm: the energy paradigm. We ARE a Great Self (i.e., soul) and we HAVE a psychological self.

A SIMPLE SUMMARY OF "TWO," SO FAR

Two by **two. Two** realities, **two** perspectives or angles, **two** scientific paradigms. There are also **two** qualitatively different dimensions of our personhood: primarily, we ARE a **Great Self** (our spacious, gracious Soul, our wholeness, wholeSelf, our consciousness, our connected aliveness or Spirit) and secondarily, we HAVE a **lesser self** or little self (our human nature, personality). The harmony and wholeness found at the meeting place on the continiuums of opposites poles can bring peace, health even magic to one's life.

The degree to which we balance these Realities is the degree to which we experience emotional health and spiritual wealth, Unified Selfhood.

This simple perspective of **two,** at its most basic level, is *in itself* helpful for seekers of wholeness. For some, this short description may suffice in giving a framework from which to navigate toward full-bodied selfhood. However, curious minds may what to know more, so I will elaborate in Section II.

CHAPTER FOUR

MANY "TWOS": PERSONALITY PARTNERS

In addition to the **TWO** realities, and **TWO** ways of experiencing ourselves, another level of **TWO**'s exists. These are the duos, pairs of opposites within our personality, our human nature.

ENLARGING OURSELVES BY ACCEPTING BOTH SIDES

Like light and shadow, or the two sides of every coin, there are two sides to our personality patterns or parts. And we all have a wealth of coins in our personality nature!

Polarities are pairs of opposite energy patterns, variations of nature's Yin and Yang magnetically attracted to each other. Unities of opposites. Ideally, we can grow in self-knowledge and hold both sides of our many polarities in awareness with an equal degree of respect for the energy they represent. We may even observe them with awe and wonder. Rather than feeling pulled in opposite directions, our acceptance of these polarities of energy as a fact of life moves us to the place where they meet, a place of peace and balance. This balanced, healthy and mature psychological self we will call the lesser self to distinguish it from our Greater Self, or soul. Awareness of our opposite ways of feeling and thinking actually enlarges our internal world when we have the courage to accept the less appealing side of the polarity, the side which we often hide from ourselves and others, leaving it in the shadows of our mind where it may drain our energy.

DEMONSTRATE, DRAW, DESCRIBE

If we demonstrate, with our own arms, the "arms" of the soul's wholeness embracing, encircling the totality of one's more concrete life experience at the biological, human level, we are able to sense how our soul holds and contains our many personality polarities. This gives us a kinesthetic, or physically felt, experience of the inclusive vision. To make it even more concrete we can draw on paper a large soul- circle, adding smaller personality circles inside of it. Just as we feel comforted by the song, "He's Got The Whole World In His Hands," we feel relieved and restored to our right relationship with ourselves when we see our soul warmly and compassionately holding our human condition. And a double condition it is.

ACCEPTANCE AND AWARENESS NEED NOT MEAN ACTION

Having a feeling and ACTING out of that feeling are quite different phenomenon. Once we know this we are not afraid to accept the feelings which could get us into trouble *if* we allowed intense or primitive feelings to mutiny the ship, take over and take charge of our actions. We can own and simply notice all feelings; we need not be at the mercy of any of them. Certainly acting out of destructive feelings or expressing all negative thoughts would not serve us or our mental health. But AWARENESS of the wide range of human experience within ourselves expands us and makes us more compassionately accepting of others. Better still is the awareness that each personality pattern has an internal partner, an opposite energy pattern to balance it if we take a look inside and have a willingness to feel both.

CARETAKER-TYPES, TAKE NOTE

Many will recognize within themselves, for example, a nurturing, care-taker pattern balanced by a needy inner child (which may sometimes be outside of conscious awareness). Professional caretakers, the people in the helping professions and healing arts, are frequently the last people to assume responsibility for their own self-care. It is a common behavior pattern among helping professionals to deny ourselves the awareness that we may have an emotionally hungry child within and give to others the attention the starving part of us needs. Speaking in terms of concrete observable behavior, something that we consider to be "good" or caring is occurring; we may call this altruism, selfless service. From a perspective of subtle energies however, we serve others best once we have brought our own energies or personality patterns into balance. The first steps in this process include the uncovering, discovering and befriending of the many pairs of personality parts within.

PERSONALITY PAIRS HAVE EQUAL DEGREE OF INTENSITY

Another example of a pair, or polarity of personality energies, would be a pattern of worthlessness or unworthiness being compensated for, or balanced by, an opposite energy of equal intensity such as perfectionism or arrogance, etc. Another example: an exhibitionistic aspect of the personality may be balanced by an ashamed pattern which wants to hide; one side or the other of that "coin" may be buried in the unconscious, but the energy exists nevertheless. One of the important factors to keep in awareness is this: at each end of a particular polarity, an opposite personality pattern with an equal degree of intensity can be found. Aware and self-accepting people are able to welcome both sides of many of these coins into consciousness.

PAIRS OF OPPOSITES: YIN AND YANG

Becoming familiar with the properties of the feminine-passive-receptive principle (Yin) and it's partner, the masculine-active-penetrating principal (Yang) can help us set more specific intentions for wholeness which is balance between these two. This balance can give birth to something new, something greater than balance. (This will be explored in depth in Section II). The ancient Chinese perspective does not speak of Yin AND Yang, but of YinYang which is all one piece. Western minds may not be ready to grasp this degree of integration just yet. First we need to become acquainted with ourselves as containing many pairs of opposites.

A WIDE VARIETIES OF PAIRS

The scope of the various themes of pairs of energies, partners in polarity, is very great. They will be described in more detail in a later chapter. In this chapter it will simply be noted that looking for opposites in life and honoring those opposites is a perspective which broadens and deepens our experience of living.

Making our life a balancing act is not only health giving, it is fun. It is fascinating to look for and look AT the many pairs of opposites which make up our lives, our physical, mental and emotional natures. The very act of looking for these pairs is an experience which expands our consciousness, our capacity for awareness.

If we are feeling uncomfortable and, without denying the bad feelings, remember a time when we felt comfortable, our energies will balance each other and we'll feel better.

There are neutral polarities occurring in physical reality such as right and left, East and West, North and South, smooth and rough, up and down. There are polarities to which judgment is added: good and bad, right and wrong, pleasure and pain. There exist polarities which pertain to the processes and stages of our human existence such as birth and death, young and old.

THE BODY'S PAIRS OF OPPOSITES

As we become accustomed to observing ourselves as living in duos, we notice that even our physical bodies contain opposite processes, opposite elements and properties of nature, pairs of opposite systems—such as two types of nervous systems, one an accelerator and one a brake.

A wholesome diet needs to have pairs of minerals in balance, such as calcium and magnesium, copper and zinc. For optimal health a balance of chemical qualities in the body is needed, such as the acid and alkaline balance in the digestive system. As we look for it we can find nature seeking balance by coming into harmony with its opposite, its mate. In a multitude of ways we need to find our most harmonious, healthy center-point between pairs of opposite energies. **It is time for us to balance our realities, partner our polarities, honor our opposites, dance with our dichotomies and play with paradox.**

CULTURAL AND LIFESTYLE POLARITIES

We may notice sociological and cultural polarities. For example, an individual or group may be totally of and for "The Establishment" or may be the opposite, living closer to a counter-culture, alternative lifestyle. Obviously there is affluence and poverty, the economic polarity.

There have been periods of history when men have been expected to be totally masculine in their behavior and women totally feminine. We may now be moving to a time where more individuals are androgenous, having a combination of many qualities of the opposite gender. There is a sexual preference continuum with totally heterosexual inclinations at one end of the continuum, totally homosexual inclinations at the other end, and an either/or bi-sexual inclination in the middle of that polarity. Sexuality will be discussed in greater detail in Chapter 19.

We may look at our *desires* in polarized ways and say that "the grass is always greener on the other side." Life may be more consistently comfortable when we have no preferences, yet most of us experience some definite likes and dislikes and these help define us as individuals.

PERSONAL POLARITIES

There are a multitude of polarities which relate to mental and emotional conditions or qualities of observable behavior. To name just a few examples, we might think of the polarities such as expressive and inhibited, "hyper" and mellow, confident and insecure, generous and stingy, sloppy and fastidious ("anal"), flexible and rigid. While we may place a judgment on generous as being a good quality, there is a time to contain and limit one's generosity.

OF LESSER SELF AND GREATER SELF IN CONTEXT

The context is important in choosing whether to tip the scales of one's behavior toward the generous side of the polarity or to move toward the opposite end of the scale. Consider the polarity of self care/self love on one hand and love for others/serving the collective of humanity on the other. When we are coming from an imbalanced place on a continuum of personality polarities, we may be very concerned with survival and self-interest, missing the joys of service to others. If we are at the other end of the continuum, swimming in a sea of self-less service, we may lose our concern for the practicalities of self-care, such as taking time to rest or planning for retirement.

At a centered place on this continuum of polarities, the concern for self and others may be equal. As we move into the consciousness of one's Greater Self we can begin to feel at one with everything. The balanced human personality/lesser self connects at the heart with the consciousness of the Soul/Greater Self. Here human wholeness meets holiness.

OPPOSITES WHICH *COMPLETE* (NOT COMPETE WITH) ONE ANOTHER

The word opposite may connote opposition. Opposites have opposed each other in our prior thinking. It is time to try on another way of thinking about opposites. Complementary opposites, opposites which complete each other through their partnership can become the predominate way we think of "opposites" in the 21st Century. Monday night football will still happen. But competition and contests with winners and losers can be relegated to fun and games. Corporate America can evolve into a culture which allows an individual to lead with his or her Greater Self.

ABC IS AS EASY AS 1, 2, 3

The Aware, Balanced, Cohesive/Connected (ABC) personality or lesser self is our healthy human reflection of our Greater Self. (The personality may be fragmented or split; the Soul is always whole). ABC is as simple to remember as 1, 2, 3.

IN SUMMARY:

Every energy has its partner, its complementary opposite. Everything in nature is Yin or Yang or YinYang, a marriage of the two. Whether we are observing life in abstract or concrete ways, or noticing our own individual personality patterns or "parts," there is a complementary opposite energy to be considered. Quite **simply**, to feel balance in our life more often, we need only remember an opposite energy or an opposite perspective whenever we are feeling something strongly. The word opposite in this context does not mean to oppose but to sit opposite from the other, exchanging energy with one's complementary energy, each energy *completing* the other. There is no reason to do this except when we are feeling extreme in any way, feel uncomfortable or out of balance within our bodymind or in our relationships.

CHAPTER FIVE

FULL-BODIED BEING

The duo of *consciousness and the body* is the **two**some that brings us to the fullness of our humanity. Body and soul are the duo, the two on which to hold our intention for the marriage of the **two** realities.

BODY AND SOUL TOGETHER

"Keeping body and soul together" is a wise response to the question, "How are you?" In the very masculine Western world wherein the focus is on DOING rather than on BEING, the question often is "How are you DOING?" However, the underlying question is: "How ARE you?" And, "Keeping it together" is a response that connotes well-being if "it" applies to the duo of our body and consciousness.

CONSCIOUSNESS

While remaining somewhat ineffable and mysterious, *consciousness* is akin to our Soul energy, the depth of awareness and acceptance. The One, or God, has often been referred to as the Super-Conscious or the Di-

vine Mind. I enjoy thinking of it as The Holy Whole
That Holds ALL That IS.

Just as our body is our own personal, portable, plot
of Earth, our consciousness is our own spark of the Eternal One, our own spacious sky and light. It is a spark
that can exist in every cell of our body when we invite
consciousness, our soul energy, to take up residence
within our physical body.

Our consciousness is not our mind's thinking. Consciousness is a mystery which has not been defined because it cannot be defined. It is entirely of the realm of
Reality #1. It is entirely spacious. It is beyond words,
beyond understanding of the mind's kind. Consciousness is akin to spaciousness. "Amazing Space," we may
sing. Grace and space, graciousness and spaciousness
may be identical twins, or nearly so. The scientists who
are living from a polarized place on the spectrum of
Reality, the solid, mechanical realm of Reality #2, like
to think of consciousness as something produced by
the brain. "The kidney's produce urine and the brain
produces consciousness; or consciousness is the steam
arising off the macaroni, the brain."[5] But from the perspective of Reality #1, Consciousness is vast and vastly
different from what the metaphors of the Reality #2 scientists convey. A medical school professor said to his
students, "Only half of what we teach in medical school
is true, the problem is we don't know *which* half."

CONSCIOUSNESS CLIMBING

In recent years, one of the heartening occurrences in two separate arenas—science and business—has been an annual conference which brings each of these two fields into the light of consciousness. The Conference on Consciousness and Science and a separate happening, The Conference of Consciousness and Business, are attended annually by hundreds of people wanting their particular field of expertise to include this mystery called consciousness. It is a word which will be increasingly in our thoughts during the coming years. Becoming more aware, awake and making more conscious choices is what this new millennium calls us to do and to be.

WELCOMING THE SOUL

In this chapter, we will concern ourselves with infusing our own physical body with consciousness. Of course, our body is already alive, filled with life force, with spirit. Yet welcoming our soul into our physicalness brings far greater aliveness and vision.

Of the many, many modes of healing, personal growth and therapy which I have used in my own evolution, by far the most important aspect was inviting my soul to take up residence in my body. The many thousands of dollars spent on my education, in therapy (conventional and alternative) and on transformational seminar and workshop attendance, ecclesiastical studies, meditation retreats, sessions with all manner of spiritual healers, energy workers, intuitive, psychics, astrologers, acupuncturists, etc., has been money well spent. Perhaps all the various help I've received has had a cumulative effect, nurturing me to the point where I was ready to embody more of my soul. However, I might have saved myself a small fortune had I spent my time and money on body-focused work and in opening to more fully receive consciousness or "light." This has been the most important piece in the long process of healing and moving toward enlightenment that I have experienced.

EMBODYING SOUL IS A PROCESS

What is important to note is that embodying soul is a process. It starts with knowing that we have to ask and invite our Greater Self to take up residence to a greater and greater degree within our physical body. The duo of body and soul may be something that we have sung songs about but many have not been informed about the importance of this marriage. And many have not been shown how this embodiment can be achieved.

GRADUAL GLISTENING

The body cannot take in the soul all at once. Energy Medicine experts tell us that we would "blow our neurological circuits" if we were even *able* to fill up with more "light" than our body had been prepared to receive. Nature protects us here. The metaphor of Moses protecting his eyes by not looking directly at the burning bush (God's presence appearing to Moses)[6] because of its brightness is a fine metaphor for this process. We must fill with this energy gradually. However, we would be wise to take into our physical form as much of this "light" as we can as soon as we can do so. Radiant living requires this.

DISSOCIATION

Many highly-spiritual people seem to be what therapists call "dissociated" from their body. I have had many clients who are professional psychics with very real gifts of "seeing."These clients have come to me for therapy when they have heard that I respect and relate to their unusual ways of perceiving life. Conventional medical-model psychology and psychiatry sees much of the behavior of psychics as "symptoms" of mental illness. Actually, these people have simply been living with an imbalance of "right-brain" perception. I have also noticed, however, that many of these clients with gifts of the spirit have "dissociative disorders." These disorders can range from being slightly out of touch with one's emotions (which are located in the body) to a full-fledged multiple personality disorder (now called Dissociative Identity Disorder in the DSM-IV, the Diagnostic and Statistical Manual-IV which categorizes mental illnesses, developmental disabilities and personality disorders).

Dissociation happens to many people, to one degree or another, when we have been frightened or traumatized during our early childhood. It is actually a very marvelous psychological defense mechanism when used in moderation. A frighted child splits its consciousness off from the body so the emotions (which are always located in the body) are not experienced. Some people do this so often that they develop a pattern of living from a place outside their body, often making those people extremely perceptive or hyper-vigilant to danger.

Many people who think of themselves as very spiritual are not anchored in their body. If we are not well-grounded and have lost our connection to the earthy realm of reality we are not whole. Transcending our pain or fear by moving away from our feelings, out of our body may be a temporary respite from trauma. It does not, however, bring us to a place of wholeness.

ONE WOMAN'S STORY

A client I saw for several months had been traumatically abused throughout her childhood. She was born into an affluent, educated family but one in which she saw her father frequently strip her mother of her clothes and brutally beat her. All of the children, including my client, were beaten as well. Life had compensated this woman with physical beauty and a brilliant mind. She left home and went on to complete a very fine education giving her a pedigree as impressive as her parentage was pathetic. As one would expect from such a background, she had a significant amount of dysfunction in her relationships. Like many highly intuitive, even psychic people with whom I have worked, this woman had coped with her childhood ordeals by disso-ciating or splitting off her consciousness from her body and emotions. This was a great escape. Having fallen into this technique of lifting her awareness to a level beyond her body, she continued to use this defense in adulthood. She, like many other gifted psychics had developed this talent because of great terror in child-hood. Fortunately such perceptiveness, protective para-noia, can be useful in adulthood. However, the strong intuition arrived at through trauma has its price.

This client was certain that her hypoglycemia was an entirely physical malady. She vehemently disagreed with me when I suggested that there was a chance it could clear up as we did the work of recalling and re-leasing from the body memories of childhood traumas. Within a time-span of only a few months, she and I were able to experience great appreciation for the healing process that happened for her as her bio- chemical im-balances decreased and her hypoglycemia disappeared and stayed away.

THE BODY KNOWS

My own unpleasant, disruptive symptoms of hy-poglycemia in the early 70's disappeared by the end of the 70's as I became more aware of my feelings. Having personally experienced this change in the output of my endocrine glands, I have encouraged clients to work through their childhood memories with guided-imagery used in a body-focused way. Happily, the hypoglycemia symptoms of many clients have fallen away as intense, repressed emotions have been released and/or integrated. There is a time to release and a time to integrate, incorporate and embrace. The body and the soul seem to know which needs to happen and when.

FIBROMYALGIA AND PHYSICAL PAIN

Fibromyalgia is another body mind condition which can be greatly lessened in severity with the release of emotional pain. As we pay close attention to our own body's signals we become aware that body-mind is one entity. Wounds to the psyche can certainly show up in the body as chronic physical pain. It is never a mistake to clear out the chaos in one's memory bank. The pay-off can be a more flexible physique and freedom from physical pain. Bringing consciousness into the body with the intention to heal, as mysterious as it may sound, has very concrete results.

SOMETIMES THE BODY HAS DUALITIES

While it is true that the body does not lie, it is also true that many people have an inner body that is the polar opposite of the outer body. When a person has not released painful emotional experiences and the psycho-physical defenses around those painful emotional experiences, a person may have an inner body that reflects one side of their experience and an outer body that reflects the adaptation to the experience. Here are eight possibilities as described by Stanley Keleman:[7]

A rigid outer body	and a collapsed inner body
A swollen outer body	and a dense inner body
A dense outer body	and a collapsed inner body
A swollen outer body	and a rigid inner body
A collapsed outer body	and a swollen inner body
A swollen outer body	and a collapsed inner body
A dense outer body	and a rigid inner body
A Rigid outer body	and a dense inner body

Bioenergetics master, Keleman writes, "Life makes shapes."[8] The energy of emotions and thought can manifest as physical form. Keleman writes of four basic structures.[9]

* rigid-obedient-controlled
* dense-defiant-shamed
* swollen-invasive-manipulative
* collapsed-compliant-compromising

BODYWORK AND BODY FOCUS FOR FREEING THE MIND

My experience has convinced me that many people can outgrow their need for medication if painful memories, negative patterns and traumas are worked out of the cellular memory of their bodies with body-therapy, body-focused psychotherapy and/or the more subtle energy work with various forms of energy medicine. Initially, medication can put a person in enough balance so that blockages of emotional energy stuck in the body can be more easily released . Eventually, with enough time spent in body work or energy healing, medication may be decreased or eliminated. However, many individuals do not have the time or the money to spend on these most effective avenues to liberation: body-focused therapies and energy work. Many people do not know that they can learn to do some of this healing work for themselves, at home in their spare time. Tapping on acupuncture points can change things. Instead, millions are currently choosing to use medication alone.

MEDICATION MAY BE IN ORDER

Correctly prescribed drugs certainly offer relief from suffering and may have only minimal side effects. There are significant harmful effects to physical health when we allow ourselves to live long with anxiety or depression, not to mention the damage which may occur to relationships as a result of "faulty wiring" and bio-chemical imbalances. All things considered, taking medication makes more sense than remaining miserable. However, one may grow beyond the need for medication as more consciousness is infused into the physical body and we learn to listen to what our body is telling us. Alas, not everyone is interested in awakening to greater levels of consciousness quite yet.

WHY ARE MILLIONS ON MEDICATION?

Many have been critical of the extensive use of medication, especially of the millions of Americans on antidepressants. Rather than suggesting that medical doctors and their patients are over-using drug therapy, psychopharmacology or drugs for depression and anxiety, I would suggest that these medications are a necessary blessing for most people who take them.

It is my feeling that the human brain has not been able to evolve fast enough to deal with the enormously stressful way of life in urban and suburban America. The human brain is probably better suited to life in a tribe, a small community of people enjoying sacred rituals, much dancing and singing and mutual sharing of the care for those in need of extra care. Our nervous systems would probably not require medication so often if we lived in small communities, if we worked less, played more. However, since we are not able to turn back the clock to times of greater simplicity, many must take medications to enhance the functioning of the nervous systems. Medication makes up for the evolution the nervous system has not yet had time to accomplish. Simplifying our lives is the wisest choice but many are unable to accomplish this change to a slower pace. The extreme stimulation of "life in the big city" may be creating a need for chemical help within our brains and endocrine systems. We are lucky that such help is available at a time in history when many energy sensitive people simply need it.

PREJUDICE AGAINST MEDICINE

There exists a prejudice against medications for the mind. This narrow-mindedness is hurting people whose resistance to drug taking is deterring them from taking well- prescribed medications which could improve the quality of their lives immeasurably. Many clients with whom I have worked have expressed remorse that they did not discover the helpful effects of medications earlier in their lives. Medication has given them access to healthy selfhood and a much better quality of life.

HERBS, NOTIONS AND POTIONS

Certainly, the many alternative therapies—herbal combinations, nutritional supplements such as amino acids, essential oils, flower remedies, etc.—are well worth trying. They are very helpful for many and have few or no side effects when used correctly. However, many people use them without proper guidance and can create imbalances and get into difficulty, particularly with herbs. For others, the natural, alternative therapies are simply not as effective as medications. Some people are bothered by the necessity for taking many of the natural remedies several times in one day.

GROUP ENERGY

While altering one's bio-chemistry with medication is the conventional paradigm path taken by millions, many others are also experiencing the wonders of "energy medicine," individually or in large group experiences. And these approaches to well- being are by no means mutually exclusive.

Group energy can foster the experience of embodiment of one's soul, if this is part of the intention of the group members. Perhaps this is an alternative to the tribal experience our bodies and souls may long for. I am most grateful for having attended many extended meditation retreats, such as a week in Taize, France with hundreds of other people. I've benefited by several week-long energy medicine training programs that included hours of body-focused meditation. It is the power of the collective energy of a group of kindred spirits, sharing the intention of opening to more consciousness, that has been most significant in my own process.

HEAVEN AND EARTHINESS

Spiritual practices that neglect the earthy aspects of life as we know it are shallow compared to those that include the denser reality of our physical form. Such practices may be useful up to a point, but true wholeness is found as a full-bodied experience at the place where the two realities meet and marry. In Section II, body-focused therapy and ways to invite and welcome soul energy into the body will be discussed in greater detail; a description of ways to experience the different textures of energy of the two different realities will also be explored.

CHAPTER SIX

BE A TRINITY

Two hemispheres and one heart
Meet to make a trinity for living;
Two perspectives of reality from mind
May find their greatest advocate in giving
Sovereignty to a heart awakened.
Once this heart-brain triangle we know
Lives will link with Grace, toward calling's flow.
As we activate and honor this grand trine
Lives become more humane, more Divine.

HEART-BRAIN PARTNERING

Number **three** in the formula for wholeness may be most important energetically. The Scarecrow, the Tin Man and The Lion of The Wizard of Oz provide symbols for this trio. There is a gift of three, a precious triangle in the body mind; becoming aware of it can have a powerful effect. Adding information about the heart to the masculine and feminine modes of the brain has "rounded out"or "triangled" this formula for living.

Essentially the same trinity is expressed somewhat differently with the words: body-mind-spirit. These three are often depicted as points on a triangle. More accurately this trio should be depicted as three concentric circles. The outermost circle, Spirit, holds and infuses the mind and body with life force, aliveness and consciousness. The physical body is the densest or most material aspect of our nature and would be placed in the centermost part of the circle. The energies of our mind are in between the spiritual body and the physical body.

Whether we think of this threesome as a triangle or as three concentric circles, we need to remember that we are, at our best, a trinity.

THREE DIFFERENT PROCESSES

In speaking of these **three**, we refer to their processes as: the brain's thinking, the heart's way of knowing , and "gut feelings". The feminine principle, Yin, or so-called "right brain" phenomenon, includes the whole-body sense which is close to the "gut feelings." When we speak of "thinking" we are generally referring to what is commonly referred to as "left-brain" logical, analytical phenomenon or Yang. Therefore, the trinity of Yin Brain, Yang Brain and Heart is essentially the same as Body, Mind and Spirit. Whichever way we choose to conceive of it, we have a threesome inside that calls for our awareness. Attending to this trinity empowers us.

LONGING FOR ITS PARTNER

"If I only had a brain," sings the Scarecrow who represents the earthy bodysense. "If I only had a heart," sings the Tin Man who represents the hard, cold, calculating brain. We may benefit from giving attention to the opposite energy we are feeling when we are feeling strongly, for this "partner" will bring balance to our energy field and we long for balance.

HEAD, HEART, HARA PARTNERING

The "hara center" is the Japanese name for "the gut," the lower abdomen where our vital life force is said to be stored. In Chinese traditions this area is referred to as the Dentien (sometimes spelled Tan Tien).

Head, heart and hara center, then, is another way to label the participating energies in the magnificent three. Putting one's attention on the lower abdomen while standing flat footed on the earth (or on the floor) fortifies us by giving us a bodily felt sense of solidifying strength. It is strength of a different sort than the gentle, yet also powerful strength of the heart. To go out into the world with an open heart can leave one vulnerable to harsh and aggressive energies. To be prepared for life in the world, one also needs an alert, clear head and a connection with one's "hara."

TALE OF AN UNPROTECTED HEART

A sensitive man with whom I was acquainted attended a meditation weekend for men only, a spiritual retreat. This man was a sensitive person with a great deal of feminine energy. He was married to a woman who carried much male energy, a very aggressive woman. One Sunday evening, after a weekend of meditation and fellowship in a psychologically safe and nurturing setting, this man went out into the world with a tender, loving, open heart. He went home to his wife who was experiencing Premenstrual Syndrome or carrying an energy pattern akin to it. She was not particularly happy about having been left with their three young children for the weekend. This apparently physically healthy man of 40 years went to bed and died of a heart attack in his sleep that night. Perhaps an awareness of the hara center and attention to it might have balanced his very open and tender heart. This story may illustrate and admonish us to remember and to honor the trinity of head, heart and hara.

TRIANGULATION

Triangulation is a term used in Family Systems Therapy to describe various dysfunctional patterns. Two people, a dyad, may focus on a third person as a way of avoiding feelings which need to be addressed within the dyad. Or family members may "play one against the other." Triangles happen in a number of ways in families and are usually problematic. The triangle for wholeness within the 1-2-3-4 perspectives on this book is a positive one. It is the triangle of head, heart and hara.

THE HARD WIRING: THE HEAD

Getting to know and love our own particular brain enhances our movement toward wholeness and health. Wise are those who acquaint themselves with the peculiarities of their unique brain. No two are exactly alike. In any reasonably healthy person, brain- functioning has its unique combination of strengths and weaknesses. To whatever degree of technicality we are comfortable, we need to become more intimately acquainted with our computer-like brain. The more we befriend our brain and make our relationship with it a conscious aspect of living, the more motivated we are to take care of it with exercise and brain-healthy foods. Discovering damage done by long-forgotten head injuries, through various pictures of the brain and its functioning, can add compassion and a desire to adapt to life in new, improved ways. After all, the creative forces of life are always on our side, always working for us when we open our minds to this notion. Brains can evolve and heal.

HEALING THE HARDWARE

In March 2000, I attended a workshop entitled "Healing the Hardware of your Soul," led by Daniel Amen, M.D.,[10] a neurologist and psychiatrist, who said, "You can't fulfill your soul's purpose unless your brain is working properly!" To the question, "How do I know who the real me is, if I take medication?" Amen replies, "The real you is who you are when your brain is functioning normally."[11] Amen, Amen.

To navigate our way through life we need our brain to be as balanced and healthy as it can be. Many people may benefit from the wise use of medications, or "better living through chemistry." Optimal brain functioning need not be a luxury item; increasingly we can acquire it. Lost minds can be found.

Dr. Amen, of Fairfax, California, is an expert in Attention Deficit Disorder or A.D.D. He recommends a SPECT brain scan for those who are finding life particularly challenging whether they have A.D.D. or a different brain arraignment. This scan, one of several different types of brain scans available, shows a picture of brain *functioning*, rather than the physical *structure* of the brain. These functions, blood flow and metabolism to various parts of a brain, can indicate much about personality, behavior and patterns of thinking.

Amen prescribes medication when needed and also recommends alternative approaches to holistically inclined patients. In addition, Amen recommends various forms of psychotherapy and techniques such as eye-movement therapy (EMDR)[12]. In my practice of psychotherapy, I have used Eye Movement Desensitization and Reprocessing Therapy in combination with Energy Medicine, "parts work," and body-focused therapy with great success. It is good to find informed psychiatrists and neurologists who are aware of these modes of therapy. Doctors exist who have been adventurous enough to move beyond the conventional approaches, without abandoning sound, sensible, established treatments for mood and mental problems. When it comes to knowing the brain, Amen and doctors with his attitude and training can be a great help to therapists and clients alike.

SOME NERVOUS SYSTEMS CAN'T BE TRUSTED

The bio-chemical and neurological aspects of our human condition is immensely important for the experience of psychological health. Many a client has been frustrated when an idealistic therapist says, "Trust yourself!" What self is it of which the therapist speaks? Clients who suffer from bio-chemical imbalances or neurological deficits know that they cannot entirely trust their personality self which is intimately entangled with their brain and/or endocrine system.

ATTENTION DEFICITS AND CONSCIOUSNESS

As a clinician who was formerly a special education coordinator and therapist to children at a therapeutic school, I've seen a great many children and adults with Attention Deficit Disorder. I have been impressed by the level of consciousness, the awareness of more dimensions than members of our main-stream culture generally address; people with deficits in paying attention are often tuned in to multi-dimensions, even in the midst of their often overwhelmed states. The distractibility may be the result of these people's natural tendency to live in more than one dimension concurrently. I have never met a client with A.D.D. who was anything less than fascinating because of this depth of perception (despite the difficulty with focus). A polarity with depth and height of perception at one end, and inability to focus at the other end seems to be present here. Ironically, many people with deficiencies in their ability to focus may be gifted at seeing "the big picture." It is unfortunate when a child who is diagnosed with A.D.D. thinks of it as something is "wrong" with him or her. There are gifts that often go with this condition. Multiple realities present themselves to people with A.D.D., frequently. This gets confusing and overwhelming. It makes for more comfortable living if a person can shift quickly back and forth between the two (and possibly more) different realms. That is, unless the person gets to the place of enlightenment where all realms converge.

TWO DIFFERENT REALMS

Fortunately, there is another domain, another organ that is ever-ready to provide us with the experience of trust, courage, compassion, joy. To me, *the heart* leaps out as the most precious, sweetest, softest "hardware of the soul." The heart and the brain are of two different realms, even developing separately in a young fetus (the heart starts beating before the brain begins to form), eventually connecting through the vagus nerve and the thalamus gland. Recent research on the heart-brain relationship is immensely liberating news.

The heart is more than a metaphor for healing love. It is, indeed, the place where we can physically experience both our soul's realm of interconnected energies, the harmony of the "quantum" whole, compassion, acceptance, *and* the place where our personality polarities meet in balanced personality selfhood. Within the heart we *find ourselves*, Great self and lesser self, both.

FOR LOVE OF A LIVER

A client came to my office for pre-surgical hypnosis for a liver transplant which she was scheduled to have the following week. She had a life-threatening liver disease and was told that the surgery could not be put off any longer. At the time of her liver diagnosis, this client was the age her mother was when her mother died. For this reason, she had asked her doctors to postpone the surgery until she had her next birthday, getting her past an ominous chronological age. During the months of waiting she had several additional tests to check on the condition of her liver. It was in a very serious state of ill-health.

The time had come for surgery. She had told me of her Christian background which had been a positive orientation for her. Fortunately, heavy emotional baggage from an oppressive version of Christianity had *not* been her experience. My usual protocol includes asking a client to visualize anyone who represents unconditional healing love placing their hands over the area where there is an energy blockage, pain or disease. Because of her positive feelings about Jesus since her childhood, I suggested that she visualize Jesus' hands over her liver and I asked her to speak to her liver, thanking it for its years of service, saying good-bye to it. (This might sound ridiculous before one realizes the aliveness and consciousness of every organ, every cell). Tell your liver to "be a love sponge, "I continued. Using a series of pre-surgical hypnotic suggestions, I prepared her body to cooperate with the surgery. One of the suggestions given before surgery is that there will be very little bleeding during surgery. (I am always amazed when clients tell me after their surgery that the doctor reported that there had been little bleeding, for there is a skeptical part of me that doesn't entirely believe these techniques can work!)

As I relaxed more deeply along with her, I asked her to imagine the image of the sacred heart of Jesus, with fire's flames flickering out of the heart; I suggested she see this sacred-heart superimposed upon her own heart. We then both visualized and intended for the healing Light of the heart to fill her liver, while at the same time I had her do eye movement as I had been trained to do with the EMDR technique.

At the end of the session, as she was leaving my office, she said she could actually feel warmth flowing out of her hands into her liver. Two days later she was told she no longer needed the liver transplant, a rather miraculous happening. Three years later she continues to do well without surgery. Something had happened that was more than mere therapeutic techniques. Miracles with the energy of healing love happen all the time in a holistic therapy practice. I have experienced them in my own life. (Section III includes these stories). This woman's miracle was a larger than average miracle. It is a blessing to participate in such mysterious happenings.

THE ENERGY OF THE HEART

All clients I have worked with in a body-focused and/ or heart-centered way, including a few diagnosed with schizophrenia, have been able to actually FEEL the experience of the heart's realm. I state that the heart is the place where past and future meet in the present moment, the eternal now, the energy of eternity. And the heart is the place where our soul's wholeness and the Spirit of Heaven meets our own personal, portable, plot of Earth, our body. Quickly, we can move to an experience of courage and love emerging from our own heart. HeartMath describes how the brain will actually entrain with, or move into alignment with, the heart's particular soothing and healing rhythms when one focuses on and breathes into the physical heart while remembering a time or place of harmony, gratitude and appreciation.

Sweet simplicity—it's bliss,
Only the heart can know this,
For bliss is not the province of the brain
Wherein complexity does reign.
Come quiet revolution,
Internal evolution,
Come heart-head marriage.
I welcome now this union
A holy whole communion
My body is the carriage.

A DIFFERENT "TAKE" ON PERFECTION

To the thinking mind of "left-brain" Reality # 2, the word perfection means something quite different than what the heart hears. To the linear mind where judgment is active, "perfection" means doing something without any flaws, doing a good job, an absolutely exquisite job. To the heart's realm of Reality # 1 there is no judgement, there is acceptance. Perfection, to the heart, may simply mean what is so. Whatever happens is "perfect" or somehow "fitting" with all else that is true, with all else that is happening.

SELF IMPROVEMENT AND THE URGE TO GROW

A drive for self-improvement frequently includes or implies self-rejection, at least unconsciously. Some people strongly oriented to the Reality #2 paradigm believe that with too much self- acceptance a person would become complacent and not grow. In the Reality #1 experience of spacious acceptance there is an abundance of the energy of " flow" and the urge to grow is ever present. Growth energy is more available to us when we have quieted the chaos of internal self-rejection.

Many years ago when I was busily involved in the Human Potential Movement, going to personal growth workshops rather continually, a friend told me that she thought I was addicted to growth! She said, "It's like if you don't have your quotient of growth each day you get nervous." This would be an example of operating out of both paradigms—but leaning to the Reality #2 "Self-improvement to combat self-rejection realm." The spacious energy engendering growth was genuine enough but the pushiness that was behind the flowing growth realm was perhaps more dense, judgmental.

CRITICISM

If we habitually lean more to the Reality #2 realm and are therefore rather concrete and judgmental, rather than accepting, it would obviously be more difficult to hear and mull-over criticism for the grain of truth that is often included in it. If, however, we inhabit the spacious openness of our heart and have a balanced heart-brain partnership it will be far easier for us to receive and grow from criticism. The mind's criticism needs to be in partnership with the heart's compassion.

THE SANCTUARY OF THE HEART

The brain, with its fear of separation and survival-based orientation, is brought to greater levels of peace when one's attention goes to the heart. Free of the survival issue, the heart holds the Quantum perspective of no-separation, interconnectedness and eternal love. The heart is never confused; the brain's hemispheres and other portions of neurology frequently experience confusion. This chaos can be abated by the particular healing electricity of the heart. Like firelight, the energy of the heart is transformative when we bring our consciousness to it. The power of our attention, putting our

consciousness on a place within our body or a personality pattern, transforms as fire transforms. We live in
an age of Laser Surgery. We need to be aware that we
can take laser love to ourselves by paying attention to
that which needs and deserves it.

Teilhard de Chardin, the enlightened Jesuit philosopher and visionary, said,

> "The day will come when, after harnessing space,
> the winds, the tides and gravitation, we shall
> harness for God the energies of love. And,
> on that day, for the second time in the history
> of the world, we shall have discovered fire."[13]

We must "hatch our hearts" and help others to hatch
theirs. Within our hearts we can find the pure gold of
our transformative fire.

The hatching of the heart[14]—
So ripe, this phrase is haunting me.
How good, indeed, it would be for the world
If each of us would HATCH our HEARTS this year,
Allowing hardened shells surrounding these
To slowly crack and fall away,
Releasing Light and Love with wings
So all within the orbit of our field
Could feel the flow
And somehow know
That love of every kind
Comes from the heart, not mind.
There is a circle here:
The mind informs the heart,
The heart illumes the mind
Which then, again, informs the heart—
And so it goes; with Grace the process flows.
Celebrate anew, each day, your best of parts:
Your tender and courageous heart
And start to HATCH that HEART today;
Tomorrow, someday, set it free
Then feel your Essence, fully BE.

NEW FINDINGS, NEW PROGRAMS

The emotions, located in the body, below the heart, are also soothed and become less extreme when one is settled in one's heart. Both The HeartMath Institute[15] and Paul Pearsall[16] have produced computer programs, with a pulse sensor for a finger, which actually demonstrate the power of the heart upon the brain! According to HeartMath research, the level of anti-aging hormone DHEA increases significantly and a hormone of stress, Cortisol, decreases significantly when the heart's realm is activated.

A SUMMARY OF ONE, TWO, THREE

The heart, with its sense of the whole—ONEness, must be the place where the experience of the body/mind's duality or TWO meet, creating a powerful trio, trine or triangle. I call this Heart-Brain Partnering. The *essentials* of this formula can be as easy to remember as **1-2-3.** I suggest that these numbers and the perspectives they represent be kept alive in the background of our minds in the hopes of keeping what is *most essential* in the foreground of our living:

* 1) Each of us is *primarily* a wholeness, a soul. Our essence or soul experiences reality as a oneness; our soul is a unity. It is a reflection of the Holy Whole, or God/Goddess/All That Is.

* 2) Our human condition and brain experiences reality as duos, pairs of opposites; our human nature is dualistic. The ABC self, Aware, Balanced, Cohesive/Connected self of the healthy personality is a reflection of the Soul.

*3) The awareness of our inner trinity brings together the unity of our soul with our dualistic human nature; this trinity is called by many names:

Head-hara-heart.
Mind-body-spirit.
Brain-bodysense-heart.
Yin brain, Yang brain and heart.

Tin Man (mental), Scarecrow(earthy-physical), Lion (heart).

The heart is where the Greater Self and the many pairs of opposite personality energies meet in harmony giving us the experience of a Unified Self/self. Here the best of our human nature—our compassionate heart—meets with our own Soul which flows into the very heart of Heaven.

*4) When both the Greater Self and an ABC self exist, we are brought to an enlightened state.

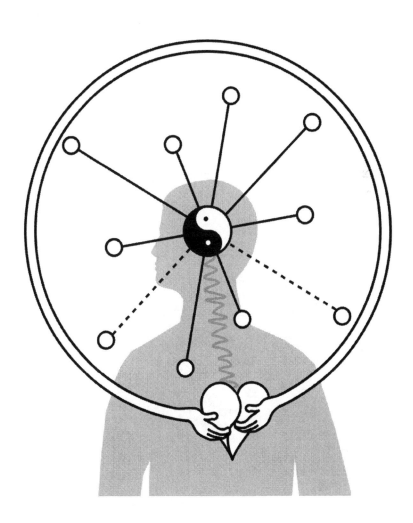

CHAPTER SEVEN

A HARMONIOUS QUARTET

Four compartments has the heart
Housing all its qualities;
Two Yin, two Yang chambers apart
Meet Soul at their interstices.

There is a unique place in the United States known as The Four Corners area where four States meet. The area in and around the point where Arizona, Colorado, New Mexico and Utah touch corners is considered by Native Americans to be a particularly sacred place. Similarity, our pump, the physical human heart has four chambers which meet and connect at one place. This place, the heart of the heart, is a very rich image which we can think of as representing our soul, our high wholeness, a marriage of the highest energies of the feminine and masculine principles.

Since all of nature is either Yin or Yang, the four chambers of the physical heart must be two yin and two yang, containing and giving forth these energies. We can liken them to the four directions, North, South, East and West which are honored by indigenous peoples. A quartet, a foursome connotes stability, constancy.

TWO SOFT-HEARTED CHAMBERS

Two main chambers of Yin (easily remembered as feminine, with which it rhymes), the *soft*-hearted receptive energies, can be seen as The Chamber of Compassionate Love and The Chamber of Trust. Yin is the principle of nature which is receptive, open and yielding. Other heart qualities which seem to reflect the Yin Principle are faith, hope, acceptance, willingness, surrender, welcoming, expectancy, following, release, forgiveness, grace, inspiration, awe, wonder, learning, openness, awareness, patience, tenderness, beauty, under-standing and flexibility.

TWO STOUT-HEARTED CHAMBERS

Two Chambers of the Heart are the domain of the *stout-hearted*, male energies of the Yang Principle. There are many qualities of the heart which reflect Yang. I have chosen to lift up The Chamber of Courage and The Chamber of Joy as two heart qualities which may be seen as representing primarily high-Yang or masculine prin-ciple qualities. Yang is the principle of nature which is active, giving. Besides courage and joy, other Yang heart qualities may be strength, playfulness, sparkle, exuber-ance, enthusiasm, humor, efficiency, delight, clarity, power, purpose and responsibility.

YIN AND YANG, AND YINYANG

There are qualities of the heart which seems to be a marriage of Yin and Yang. These YinYang energies can be seen as the Whole Heart Energy of Gratitude. Other YinYang heart qualities may be appreciation, peace, truth, honesty, balance, harmony, integrity, synthesis, love, simplicity, purity, freedom, abundance, sister/brotherhood, communication and connection.

CLASSIFICATION IS NOT THE WHOLE PURPOSE

We need not get caught up in a precise classifica-tion of heart qualities. A linear categorization of qualities is not of great importance. One of the problems with psychology, which arose from the medical model of the conventional paradigm, has been an over-emphasis in classifying and categorizing traits which has caused clinicians to loose sight of the *essence* of who people really are. Many institutions fall apart or gradually lose their effectiveness because of the excessive use of the principles, approaches and techniques which initially brought them into being. Psychotherapy needs to evolve into something beyond its conventionally taught approaches. The paradigm which would serve holistic therapists best is a marriage between the Energy Paradigm and the conventional Paradigm of science. We ought not be distracted from our client's essence by categorization or trying to "figure out" in a left-brain way whether a heart quality was Yin or Yang or a combination thereof. What is most important is to move our attention to our heart and stay with its healing power.

NOT A MERE "STRENGTHS-BASED" APPROACH

What I suggest is not merely what is called a "strengths-based approach" in psychological and social service fields. Looking at what is right with a person rather than what is wrong with that person is an improvement over how psychotherapy was once practiced. While focusing on our strength is always helpful, the "strengths-based" approach has come from the conventional paradigm which looks at concrete behaviors more than from the paradigm of energy. A balance of paradigms is now necessary.

SEEK FIRST THE HEART'S MAGIC

To psychotherapists and self-help book readers who have been fascinated by complex theories of personality and psychopathology as I have been for many years, this heart-focused perspective may seem too simple, even simplistic. I do not deny that the rich and complex theoretical material in which therapists have been schooled has great validity. And certainly the many therapeutic techniques that have emerged out of conventional psychology will continue to be useful. Yet, if clinicians have been overlooking the healing power of the greatest resource human beings contain within themselves, a resource which can quickly move our clients into their personal power, capacity to love and sense of wholeness, then we have been misguided. First things first. "Seek ye first the kingdom of God, and all things shall be added unto you,[17]" said Jesus. The heart within the body is that kingdom. We need to be aware that everyone already has wholeness and healing power in the heart; connecting with these gifts is the first order of business. After those primary resources are lifted up and felt, we can then go on, if necessary, and do fine-tuning of personality quirks or serious pathology using what conventional training has provided. Medication is a blessing to those who are severely out of balance. With many, however, the heart connection is the experience which can fully lift us out of our previous identity as a mentally or emotionally disturbed person. To *first* feel wholeness by LEADING with the HEART gives us access to our healing power.

FEELING WELL = FEELING THE WELL, THE HEART

Our heart center, when focused upon, brings us to a place of fullness. The heart is a well, a spring of ever-flowing soft, warm, expanded energy giving us the experience of well-being. When we allow our heart to become the sovereign leader of our life we feel very *full*. A feeling of emptiness that plagues so many people can become an experience of the past when we move into our heart's feeling of fullness. Some dense or intense thoughts or emotions may need to be addressed and transformed before we can experience the heart as the haven that it is. But we can all be certain that this well of love for ourselves exists at the heart level for anyone and everyone. When we say we are "feeling well" we are speaking of our well-being which includes a sense of inner peace, compassionate acceptance, trust and gentle joy. The source of these feelings is the well of the heart—the fulcrum and fountain—with its abundant supply of comfort and trust and love.

A HEARTLESS WOMAN—WHO WASN'T

Even in the early days of my practice, I believed fervently that everyone contained goodness within, but on rare occasions that belief was challenged and I was concerned that this idea might be merely a *hope* of mine rather than a fact. One client made me doubt my faith in people for a time. This was a woman who experienced feelings of abysmal emptiness and emotional discomfort. She needed a great deal of attention from others to fill the emptiness she lived with and she did all manner of dishonest things to get her emptiness filled. Her lack of care for and empathy with her many children was painful to witness; she seemed to have no desire to begin to meet her children's needs. For many months we worked together, making some progress, but she continued to show little concern for anyone in her family except herself—so great was the experience of own neediness. I decided to do hypnosis and guided imagery with her and as soon as she relaxed deeply into a hypnotic trance I began to talk with her in her altered state. Immediately, deep and loving concern about her children was expressed with warm feelings of sorrow about their neglect and a desire to get herself "well" so that she could truly nurture her children. Though it was twenty years ago, I recall the moment *well*, how real the loving kindness was within the depths of this woman who had seemed so cold and careless in the defended state which had cut her off from her heart. Our physical heart with the well-spring of warmth we can feel when we honor it is the greatest treasure trove we have. And we all have one waiting to be found!

CHANGE THE CHAMBERS' NAMES

I have often chosen to name the heart's four chambers,: 1) Compassion, 2) Trust, 3) Courage, and 4) Gentle Joy for these seem to be the primary Yin and Yang compartments of the heart into which others fall. A soft-heartedness and stout-heartedness combination-quality I lift up is Gratitude. However, we may wish to name these chambers differently. Sometimes the psyche of a particular person will seem to call for the highlighting of another heart quality. At those times, during imagery and heart- focusing work, I will name one of the chambers after a quality that person particularly needs to recognize as existing within their core (or coeur, the French word for heart, or in Spanish, corazon). It may be useful to consider balancing the chambers with **two** tender, vulnerable, receptive, soft-hearted, Yin qualities of the highest feminine principles of nature WITH **two** stout-hearted, strong, giving-forth, Yang qualities of the highest masculine principles of nature.

ATTEND TO THE HEART

Taking our attention to the heart's compartments deepens intimacy with this four-chambered, splendorous organ. And attention to the meeting place of those chambers, the heart of the heart, deepens our experience of heart sovereignty even further. In the process of attending to the pump within our chest, possibly even exploring it for Yin and Yang qualities, we make closer contact with the unique energy of that *whole* treasure trove. By attending to our heart we honor it as that jewel which give us the highest of human qualities.

MEETING PLACE FOR ALL DIRECTIONS

We can visualize our heart as the meeting place, of East, West, North and South and all that these directions represent in Earth Based traditions. It is the place where Heaven and Earth and all their energies can be available to us.

A WOMAN IN NEED OF HEART

Quite fresh in my memory is a client, a young woman, age 30, with a teaching career she loved. She had never been married and she was very pretty and noticeably obese. Her weight gain had occurred in the last two or three years. The reasons she expressed for coming to therapy were poor self-esteem, feeling depressed when she wasn't at work, not having ever really found herself, a desire to lose weight and the most pressing symptom she said was current pain from unrequited love, or unrequited "commitment-ability." She loved a man who was in her life, a truck driver in his mid-30's, who had been her good friend for at least a decade and they had shared intimacies during the past four years, off and on. Although they were involved in a sexual relationship, he made it clear to her that he didn't intend to really "date" her or anyone and a committed relationship was out of the realm of possibility.

The young woman said it was a mystery why she had suffered from low self-esteem since adolescence, a time when she entered into some risky and serious drug usage with peers who had little self-respect. She felt some shame about that earlier chapter in her life. Her family sounded unusually healthy and wholesome—parents who were relatively strict yet loved her dearly, with meaningful teaching careers, who loved each other, and also had two happily married older children. This client knew of no past traumas and suspected no traumas (but she had not always been sober as a teenager). Her past boyfriends had not been her equal in terms of accomplishments and aspirations. With 15 minutes remaining in the first session, I asked her how she thought of herself in relation to Life, inquired about her world view, whether or not she had a philosophy or notion about the way the Life Process works or **who she thought she really was**. I asked if she had a way of thinking about herself that made her feel better. She reiterated that she didn't really know who she was, felt insecure in the world and had little self-worth. I told her I wanted to connect her with her personal power, her heart and soul and assured her it was going to be easier than she expected to find herself, for she had never really been missing. She had just been unaware. Drawing for her my diagram, I first and foremost drew the arms of the soul Self, and then included within that circle the personality self as the meeting of the polarities of the personality energies, again stressing the embrace of the soul, the container. I said that her insecurity, the parts of her personality which had contributed to her excess weight, her depression, and her anger at the man she loved, were just experiences within her wholeness—the soul— which had been holding her personality without her knowing. I presented the heart as the center of the personality where all traits and qualities meet, where past and future meet in the present moment and where we connect with our Spirit and our eternal Soul power. I then invited her to close her eyes for an exercise that could connect her with self-love and her soul's energy— resources that have been within her all along. She simply had never been shown a way to access this kind of power and harmony.

A GUIDED IMAGERY EXPERIENCE FOR WHOLENESS

The exercise went something like this:

"Simply close your eyes for a few moments or you can even leave them open and simply focus your attention inward. Allow yourself to tune in to your body-sense and the subtle energies inside yourself. Let yourself remember that you are a child of the Earth, a daughter of Mother Earth. You are made up of the same energies, the same elements of which the Earth is made and your body flows to the same rhythms the Earth enjoys. You sense that your body is your own portable, personal, plot of earthiness. Let your heart exhale gratitude into your Mother Earth as you inhale the Earth's energies up into the soles of your feet. Take your attention down into the heart and core of the Earth and connect, with gratitude, to the Earth's center. Inhale the Earth's deepest energies, the Earth's Spirit, up into your feet and legs, into your tailbone and spine, receiving this energy, this red vibration of energy into your body like a red light. Take your attention to your heart and from your heart move your awareness upward through your head, out the opening crown of your head and take your attention to the Heavens or the Sky. Allow yourself to call upon and connect with the fastest, finest vibrations of Light, the purest energies you can invite into your mind-body.

You may wish to call upon any Master Teachers, guides, angel-energies or spirits of loved ones in the realm of Heaven.

Taking your attention to the crown of your head, imagine it to be a lotus bud or rose bud. Imagine now that you see a ball of light eight to ten inches above the crown of your head; you may sense this to be the star or essense of your soul. Invite it to come down toward the crown of your head while the petals of the flower opens. Simply receive this infusion of your soul's energy of wholeness, letting the pattern of your wholeness and the harmony and balance of all that you are take up residence in your body. This may even feel like honey or nectar entering your head and flowing into your body.

Imagine that you are looking at a beautiful sunrise or sunset over the ocean. You sense your heart self to be on the horizon, where earth and sky meet.

Now focus your attention on your heart in your chest and imagine a huge, vertical infinity symbol crisscrossing in your heart[18], a vibrating figure eight with one loop going deeply into the Earth and the other loop going high into the sky connecting with spaciousness and light.

Notice again that your heart is the place where Heaven and Earth meet. Consider that your heart is the place where you have access to the resources of both Heaven and Earth—the spaciousness and inspiration of the Heavens and the nurturing and nourishment of the Earth.

Now envision another infinity symbol, this one a small horizontal figure 8 that goes across your brain hemispheres with the crossing of the loops being at the corpus callosum of the brain, the part of the brain that connects the right and left brain hemisphere. This one is something like a pinwheel on top of a baseball cap! Simply set your intention to have the two brain hemispheres enter into a rich, respectful, relationship with one another as you see energy flowing along the lines of this "pinwheel" figure eight symbol. As you bring your brain's male and female principles into reconciliation, enjoy their responsiveness and respect for each other. Let the master glands of the endocrine system, the endocrine glands in your head, be energized and filled with light and brought into perfect harmony and order. The other endocrine glands in your body will come to order in response to the harmony and order of the master glands. Whenever you meditate you can re-call these thoughts and thus re-set your intention for full health and balance.

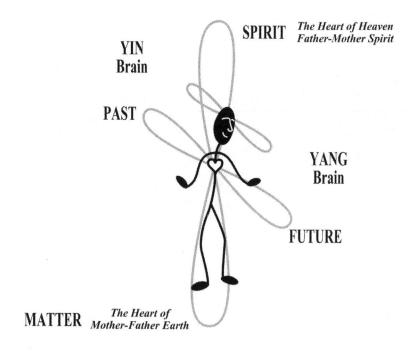

And now create in your visionary mind a third figure eight, and this one is another horizontal one, crisscrossing in your heart with one loop going out behind your heart, behind your back, connecting you with your past and the other loop going out in front of your chest connecting you with your future. Take your attention to your heart, the place where past and future meet in the place of timelessness, the Now, the "Eternal Now,"[19] the Energy of eternity, where the past and the future neutralize each other in the power of the present moment, the Now. Honor your heart, now, as the most precious jewel within your body, with the highest qualities which your humanity is capable of experiencing and sharing. Take your attention to the physical place in your heart where the four chambers of your heart meet. There is one such place in your heart and try to locate it with your attention, or **imagine** that you are locating this special place. Breathe with gratitude into this core of you, this heart of your heart.

Consider the four chambers of your heart. Consider the chamber of courage, courage that has been within you all of your life, the courage which has gotten you through all challenging episodes of your life experience. Notice that this courage is always there and will always be there because your heart has access to all the resources of strength from Heaven and Earth.

Now take your attention to the chamber of your heart which is the chamber of compassionate love. Breathe into this compassion for those others you care about, and feel the compassion within your heart for YOU! (Note: At this point tears began to flow down my client's cheeks. I asked her what she was experiencing and she said she knew she had to let go of the man in her life, she knew he would never be available as the true and committed mate she wanted. I let her stay with this compassion for herself around the loss she knew she had to experience; the tears began to dry up in a few minutes, and then I continued).

Take your attention to a third chamber of your heart, the chamber of trust, and feel the trust of which only your heart is capable. Nothing else within your being is capable of this degree of trust that all will be well. (I could sense her energy growing lighter).

And now take your attention to the fourth chamber, the chamber of joy. Recall a time when you felt child-like delight and joy. As you recall that natural joy of aliveness you might feel that every cell in your body is receiving a spark of the electricity of the heart's joy; imagine that every cell in your body is a voice in a gigantic chorus suddenly bursting into the Hallelujah Chorus. (She became radiant and began to smile and glow! She actually exclaimed, "I feel so HAPPY, I've never felt so HAPPY!") Now let all the energies of your heart (and I named several)—grace, freedom, clarity, peace, simplicity—all the qualities of the heart, tender and strong in balance, become the place from which you live your life. Your mind will be your consultant, informing your heart as your heart illuminates your mind; but your heart will be your leader. And now come back and open your eyes."

AN ALTERED STATE

I had lost track of time, since I was speaking from the timeless place of *my* heart during this exercise. We had gone slightly over-time and my next client was waiting. The young woman who sat before me was radiant and glowing. She was very energized yet calm. Gratefully, the young woman exclaimed that her friend (my former client) who had referred this client to me, was right. I could help her find herself! Certainly there was more work we could do if she wanted to do more inner work. Certainly I could help her come to know and love the various parts of her personality (and their polar opposite parts) which had been involved in her weight gain. Certainly we could do some work to heal her adolescent "parts" which had encouraged the dangerous drug and alcohol excesses in her past. But our first session moved this client into the richness of her heart. This is probably the most and best we can do for any client. Clearly, I felt it was the most important work I could do for this client. It was all she really needed, but she wanted to set up another appointment. As she departed I felt like a mid-wife of sorts, having helped this client give birth to her heart's sovereignty. My own heart was singing that I may have the best job in the world.

A month later this woman returned for another appointment, expressing much gratitude for her newfound heart connection. In the time since our first appointment she had made several positive changes in her life. She had also remembered and wished to share with me some ordeals which she had experienced in her adolescence, events which had left her with a substantial amount of shame. She was well aware that her connection to her heart had provided her with the container wherein she could hold and heal these past memories. Working through the feelings she had buried was much more easily accomplished because this young woman's heart was providing her with self-love, compassion and forgiveness. Perhaps the mind is not capable of forgiveness; perhaps peace is only possible through the heart, the place where we meet grace.

BENEVOLENCE IS WHO WE ARE

Our heart's the greatest treasure trove
The bodymind may hold
Compassion is its healing balm
For others to enfold.

And we as well receive this love
As often as we give it.
Benevolence is who we ARE;
Remember, then, to live it.

And NOW's the time, the only place
From whence the heart can flow;
Eternity's the here and now—
The heartspace whole, a'glow.

Let's honor now the organ—
Four chambered, splendid thing,
The meeting place of Mother Earth
With Heaven's beckoning.

So clear away the discontent
And set your ticker free!
Celebrate your choice to love,
Embrace humanity!

SECTION II

INTRODUCTION TO SECTION II

Life can become a little less difficult as we become aware that there are different ways of looking at life, even different brands of physics for the two realities in which we live. This section helps us find comfort in each of our two homes—our eternal home of invisible forces interconnecting as waves of energy AND our earthy home, this world of physical matter, of particles and molecules, separate objects and forms.

Only two realities? There may be many more realities, many levels of consciousness, many ways of comprehending reality. I present two realities because we have two brain hemispheres which provide us with two ways to comprehend reality. Most of what is referred to as "left-brain" thinking seems to interpret reality in one way and most of what we call "right-brain" thinking seems to interpret reality in another way. Just as the YinYang symbol has a small round area of the Yin's dark way within the Yang half of the symbol, and a small round area of the Yang's white way within the Yin half, there are some right-brain styles of thinking within the left-brain arena and vice versa. The important factor here is that male and female aspects of our brain seem to interpret reality in two different ways, just as the two different modes of physics—Newtonian Physics and The New Physics (or Quantum Physics) describe reality in different ways. Our heart's ways of knowing are akin to the perspective of Quantum Physics. This is my theory, or part of it. Partnering our polarities is another aspect of the theory. Unifying the personality self of conventional psychology with the realm of the soul, or Greater Self, is also a central component of this theoretical framework. Integrating the two paradigms into our living, and into psychotherapy and family therapy is another aspect of this material.

It is useful to consider that the realities which have emerged from science are reflections of different aspects of our human, physical, neurological nature. Brain, heart and whole bodysense—each has its own cosmology or world view.

The heart experiences the synchronistic, mysterious oneness, but the rest of life seems to call for more concrete answers to our questions and a more linear understanding of the stages of our development and the phases of our relationships.

This section will explore and embellish the angles on Reality I and II set forth in Section I. May the simplicity and essence of those perspectives not get lost in the more detailed material that follows.

CHAPTER EIGHT

SISTER/BROTHER CAN YOU PARADIGM?

Several years after receiving a degree in psychology, some mysterious happenings occurred in my life which could not, in any way, be explained in terms of my formal education. Was I, was our whole culture, to deny or pretend certain occurrences did not really happen? Occurrences of dream telepathy and mysterious healings. I went out in search of a world view that could accommodate some of the most amazing aspects of living that I had ever experienced. While I had been captivated with the personality theories I had learned in school , it seemed that the paradigm or world view out of which the science of psychology had come was simply not the whole story.

The psychology of C.G. Jung was most helpful, accommodating many of the mysteries of life.[20] Given the compelling nature of my quest (to be described in Section III) I explored still further, and further out. Shirley MacLaine was taking a beating in the press so, given my professional aspirations, I chose to be discrete.

AN ADVENTURE IN EDUCATION

While exploring the emerging new models of science in circles respected by the establishment, I also encountered people far outside the established areas of science and religion. Fascinating and sometimes peculiar people with unusual gifts of the spirit, sensitivities beyond anything I had known before, became part of my life. Besides receiving help and an off-beat education from these people in unorthodox ways, I also did a great deal of observing. I noted that spiritual healers and psychics (and other people I refer to as triple P's, or Primary Process People) had certain personality, relationship and cognitive peculiarities. One of their proclivities was seeing the world as "energy in motion."

AN ANCIENT PARADIGM

Often referred to as "the new paradigm," this perspective describes the interconnectedness of everything, with nothing being entirely separate. All is ONE wholeness. This ONEness or wholeness is comprised of intermingling energies. This world view describes a reality of energy in motion, everything being waves of energy of one kind or another. Referred to as a "new paradigm," it is actually ancient; primitive cultures have long honored the interconnectedness and aliveness of everything.

PARADIGM OF THE WESTERN WORLD

The conventional paradigm of science fathered by Isaac Newton is known as "Particle Physics." It describes a world made up of separate particles, things with molecular form, boundaries. Modern science is based on Newtonian Physics, but this perspective or science, it seems, is only half the story. It has been and will continue to be a useful paradigm for many aspects of life, but it is not sufficient for where humanity is going.

WHAT ABOUT "WOO-WOO" PHENOMENON?

The workings of subtle energies and spiritual experience cannot be explained or well-studied out of the paradigm of Particle Physics. Reportedly, 70% to 90% of all people have numinous, supernatural, spooky, "woo-woo" experiences which cannot be explained or even described in terms of the conventional scientific paradigm. The paradigm of Quantum Physics helps. Yet those who write about Quantum healing and the vision that "all is one" aren't presenting the most practical perspective for psychological differentiation, for moving into (lesser self) selfhood or individuation. In the greater, all-embracing reality, everything seems to be interconnected waves of energy and we are all one interconnected family of humanity. On another level, in the reality of form, molecular structure, of which Particle Physics teaches, we are separate individuals. In one "we are all in this together." In the other reality, "We are all in this. . . . alone" (said Lily Tomlin as a bag-lady in

"The Search for Signs of Intelligent Life in the Universe"[21]). Both perspectives are true. Developing " double vision" can create balance and health.

A MARRIAGE OF TWO PARADIGMS

I propose a paradigm which is a marriage between *the reality of spaciousness, a oneness comprised of interconnected waves of energy*, with *the reality of the concrete, material world of separate objects, molecules coalescing into form*; not a merger but a mutually respectful partnership of two realities which may be seen as being on opposite ends of a continuum. Balancing realities by living from the place where the two realities meet allows us to become the best that we can be as individual human beings and as energy-wave-citizens of the universe. This heartful living happens from the "place" of Reality #3, which is born when Reality #1 and #2 meet with respect for their differences.

SIMPLY STAY WITH THE ESSENTIALS

The basics of the double vision perspective of **TWO** realities in partnership are simple to grasp, simple to remember. One need not go beyond the basics of this "formula" for living to make life easier. The experience of wholeness and symptom relief is often felt with the overview of this world view alone. Yet, if our thinking minds demand more intricacies and embellishments, they may be included in our understanding but they are not essential. **Essentials** are what individuals in search of wholeness and holistic therapists need to keep lifting up at this time of rapidly multiplying therapeutic forms and techniques with which we can become distracted.

A STORY OF A SHIFT

A woman arrived at her first session in the midst of a variety of personal crises, family crises and what appeared to be hypo-mania, a low-grade manic condition of extremely high energy, exuberant mood. I felt great joy in working with this 40-year old wife-mother-grandmother-teacher, and looked forward to many months of sorting through her concerns and complaints. I presented to her my perspective of Greater Self, lesser/little self and the two realities through which we navigate, also teaching her body-focused exercises so she could actually experience this perspective. By the 3rd or 4th session she came bouncing into my office saying, "I've got it! I'm cured. I mean I KNOW there will always be crises, and I know life is one thing after another, and there are more things I'd like to work on in therapy and I love coming here. . . . but money is a big issue and I don't have insurance and I feel like NOW I can handle anything that life throws my way."

She thanked me profusely and said she'd be back if she needed to have more sessions and I supported her in her decision to wrap up our work together. I was terribly sorry I wasn't going to be seeing her regularly because it was pure joy for me to work with this client who had virtually *no resistance* (which is unusual) to discovering and *remembering who she REALLY IS.* My Soul told me she knew herself, now, to be truly complete and well, while my clinical mind tossed me the thought, "Maybe she'll be back sooner than she thinks." As time went on she referred many clients to me, sent me wonderful letters annually with Christmas cards thanking me for the perspective I gave her which was "still working" and insisted I write the book I said I wanted to write. She stopped in my office, ten years after we had first met for those small number of sessions, with a gift of book plates with angels and my name imprinted on them to encourage me to write a book about the perspective I had taught her. A few days later she died suddenly of an aneurism, within weeks of her 50th birthday. Just days before her death she called to wish me a Merry Christmas and reported that she felt wonderful, was happier than she had ever been in her life, happier with her marriage than she ever dreamed she could be, happier with her children, grand-children and with her expanded career. She reported that she was having fun, felt thoroughly at peace and "one with everything." She had mastered and married together the two realities.

CHAPTER NINE

TWO REALITIES IN CONTRAST

The fact that everything is in motion all the time is comforting as we consider difficult behavior in this "moving" way. As we gradually adjust the way we look at our lives according to these two realities, movement and change become our expectation, for in reality much more movement is occurring than the conventional paradigm had suggested.

Grasping the contrast between the two realities is most easily done by thinking of one reality as a wholeness holding mostly open space with intermingling waves of energy; let's refer to this as Reality # 1—easy to remember because this reality relates to the *"oneness"experience of our "Greater Self."* The other reality which is the reality of the physical, material realm (forms and observable behaviors, etc.), we will call Reality # 2—easy to remember because it relates to our "human nature" with its "lesser self," the *second best aspect of who we are.*

BREATHING AND THE SPACE BETWEEN

Let us look at breathing. The actual in-breath and out-breath is something we **DO**; it is concrete observable behavior. We can put this physical experience in the column of Reality # 2. The space between the in-breath and out-breath is simply BEING, nothingness, empty space, befitting of Reality # 1.

Wayne Dyer has reminded us that empty space is as necessary as notes are in the composition of music. Music is a useful example of two realities in a harmonious partnership. Consider the spaces (Reality # 1) and notes (Reality # 2) that comprise music; like Yin and Yang they are partners creating/producing together a score of music—both necessary aspects of the whole of music.[22]

MORE OR LESS ROOM FOR MOVEMENT

The Reality # 1 of Quantum Physics is a reality of waves of energy and mostly empty space; the emphasis with this paradigm is on the empty space. Lots of space to move around in, lots of space in which to flow, in which to change and grow. In contrast, reality as Newtonian Physics, also called Particle Physics, explains it to be is a reality of particles coalescing into forms and structures.

Everything is energy in motion. According to Quantum Physicist David Bohm, "There are no nouns, only slow verbs."[23] This page isn't paper, it is "papering," he would say. In other words, separate "things" do not really exist because *everything* is energy in motion; those "things" which seem to our eye to have form are only energies moving at a slower pace, like molasses, hence those energies have more density.

We welcome this fact when we are confronted with patterns of behavior or strong emotions in ourselves or in others. For as everything is viewed as merely energy, and that energy is in motion at all times, we can feel much more hopeful about patterns changing the way we want them to. Nothing is totally fixed, even the behavioral patterns of the most dense spouse!

Bohm referred to the world described by Quantum Physics as the "Implicate Order" or the "enfolded." He called the world described by Newtonian Physics as the "Explicate Order" or the "unfolded."[24]

A HUMAN AND SPIRITUAL EXPERIENCE

We are humans experiencing our spirituality *and also* souls noticing our human experiences. During the 90's, in the circles of spiritual seekers, it became fashionable to say that we are not human beings having a spiritual experience, we are spiritual beings having a human experience. Since the Quantum Reality or spiritual energies of life enfolds and holds our humanness, this statement is quite apt. Yet, as spiritual beings having a human experience, we often feel more densely human than spaciously spiritual. BOTH REALITIES are *real enough* in the experience of physical human beings. We experience ourselves in BOTH ways, as "human beings having a spiritual experience" AND "spiritual beings having a human experience." Sometimes our essential spiritual experience is in the foreground of our awareness. Other times our humanness takes over and moves into the foreground, and the sense of our selves as interconnected to the **One**ness Reality receeds into the background. "It's what's up front that counts" or shows us which reality is our primary point of perception at any one time.

EITHER/OR, BOTH/AND AND EITHER/OR-BOTH/AND

In the realm of Reality #2, evaluations and comparisons are made and something comes out on top as the winner as the other loses; it is the paradigm of "either/or." In the Reality #1 paradigm, all is ONE. This spacious, embracing paradigm is about inclusiveness and acceptance and therefore "both/and" is its perspective; it's a "win-win" proposition. In Reality #3 where both paradigms exist as truths of their own particular Reality we can speak of "either/or" AND "both/and" perspectives existing together. This is what happens when we shift back and forth often between awareness and experience, as discussed in another chapter. It may require much expansion of consciousness to be able to have the doubly inclusive perspective of Reality # 3.

However, we can learn to become aware of whether Reality #1 or Reality #2 is in the background or the foreground at any particular time and we observe this background-foreground configuration from the place of Reality #3. "It's what's up front that counts" or shows us which reality is our primary point of perception at any one time.

ALL SEEMS "REAL ENOUGH"

The Reality of the Energy Paradigm is the higher and larger Reality and is the container for the more dense reality of physical experience, yet the reality described by conventional science and known as "the real world" is indeed real to our five physical senses. Who can forget the Philosophy 101 professor who tried to convince us that the desk really didn't exist apart from our experience of it? To the eyes of the students the desk seemed real enough! With our physical senses we experience the material reality as being very *real*. It does not seem to be an illusion as some spiritual systems would teach. The desk is not experienced as merely an illusion when we are standing in the paradigm of our current culture, the Western World's paradigm of reality—the mechanistic, material paradigm of Newtonian Physics. Many spiritual perspectives will deny that anything other than Spirit is *real*. We need to remind ourselves that each reality is real enough to the dimension of our body mind that is interpreting it.

Contrasting these paradigms or realities in the following way may be helpful in getting a "feel" for these two different worlds:

ENERGY PARADIGM	"Real World" PARADIGM OF THE WEST
Reality # 1	Reality # 2
Reality as waves of energy	Reality as particles (parts)
Energy in motion	More dense fixed patterns
Reality as Quantum Physics knows it to be	Reality according to Particle (Newtonian) Physics
Focus is on the WHOLE Spaciousness, mostly open space	Focus is on PARTS Particles coalescing into form, structure
Spiritual	Material (Physical-Mental-Emotional)
Vague, amorphous, abstract, random	Concrete and more easily measured
Invisible	Visible
Known through intuition, or 6th (vibrational) sense	Known through 5 physical senses
Mysterious	Understandable
Power of a mysterious kind, Awe inspiring power	Power of a more concrete kind as in power over something
Honors the mystery	Seeks mastery of human life and nature
World of imagination	World of information;

is boundless		material reality has limits
"Implicate order"		"Explicate order"
"Enfolded"		"Unfolded"
The spaces between the notes		The notes themselves
The spaces between *the in-breath and out-breath*		The action of breathing the in and out breaths
Infinite		Finite
Oneness *"All are One"*		Separateness, differentiation we are separate individuals who can achieve mature interdependency
We're all in this together		We're all in this alone" (Lily Tomlin)
Concerned with BEING		Concerned with DOING
Primary Process	(Freud)[25]	Secondary Process
Unknown to the ego *Known through* *soul consciousness* *(Primary Process)*		Experienced with the ego (Secondary Process)
The Liquid of Life	(Alchemy)	The Philosopher's Stone
Spirituality *Seeking experience of* *ALIVENESS* *a whole-body experience*		Spirituality: Looking for MEANING in life, a more mental phenomenon

(The above is from the author's 1995 Internal Family Systems Conference Presentation and her Society for Spirituality and Social Work 1996 Presentation)

DIFFERENT WAYS OF KNOWING

While everything is energy, we "know" about the two realities in different ways. The energy which is mostly open space is known through intuition, the 6th sense—our sense of subtle energies or "vibes"—vibrations. This is the invisible reality which very spiritual people often refer to as the "true" reality, with the suggestion that the physical-material reality is a false reality, Maya, illusion.

The reality of the energy paradigm known through our "inner eye" and "inner ear" is the invisible reality referred to as the " Oneness." It can be amorphous, so subtle we might not relate to it much at all if we are the type of personality that inclined to think of life in concrete ways.

The physical, mental and emotional areas of life described in terms of the conventional scientific paradigm are more easily measured than the phenomenon of subtle and healing energies. Reality in the conventional paradigm is known through the five physical senses and "secondary process" which is the ego's process of navigating through life. This reality is understandable and understood. This is the world of concrete information rather than imagination. The material reality has limits; it is finite. An individual ends at the boundary of his or her skin in Reality # 2. In this prevailing scientific paradigm of the Western World, Reality # 2, consciousness might be seen as steam rising off the grey matter in the cranium, nothing more; since consciousness is not material and cannot be measured it is largely ignored. In Reality # 2, we human beings are separate individuals who can differentiate from one another and achieve mature interdependency. In this paradigm thoughts of one person cannot impact upon another.

MASTERY AND/OR MYSTERY

The paradigm of the physical-material reality places a high value on the *mastery* of human life and nature. In the energy paradigm coming from the Quantum perspective, the *mystery* of life is honored far more than mastery. Power in the conventional paradigm is of a more concrete kind; it is often thought of as power over something. Power in the energy paradigm is power of a mysterious kind, an awe inspiring power, an ineffable power like the power of love. The reality of the energy paradigm is known through soul, consciousness and the heart, while the reality of the Western World's predominant world view is experienced mostly with the ego.

We are human BEINGS in Reality # 1 and human DOINGS in Reality # 2. Actions, even the act of thinking and the experience of emotions, arise out of the physical body and the personality and are therefore of Reality # 2.

It is interesting to note that the ancient practice of Alchemy speaks of two kinds of elixir: 1) The Liquid of Life, connoting movement through fluidity and 2) The Philosopher's Stone, connoting the density of form.[26]

Spirituality can be seen as Reality # 1 and religion, with its structure and form, as Reality # 2. Yet spirituality itself can be broken down (or lifted up!) in the way that mythologist Joseph Campbell did: spirituality can be the seeking of the experience of ALIVENESS, a whole-body experience (Reality # 1) and/or spirituality can mean looking for the MEANING in life, a more mental phenomenon.[27]

SUMMARY IN POETIC FORM

You see,
We live in more than one reality.

We've been shown a world that's dense
Made of objects, separate parts,
Things, like nouns, contained within their skin
Or boundaries of another kind,
Edges making particles distinct.
This realm we know so well within the culture of the West,
The male's "left-brain" approach
May interpret it the best.
Newton's physics teaches well,
A reality of separate, individuated objects,
Parts or particles, and molecules
Yet tells us nothing of the whole.

There is another science for ALL this:
Quantum Physics brings us a Reality so Holy
Showing us that in this world there is nothing solely separate;
All is One in Quantum's world;
'Tis a world of energies which mingle
There are no distinctly single separate parts
But waves, like ripples, intersecting;
In THIS realm all are connecting
Waves of energy, lively, dancing
So alive is life, the Chi advancing,
And evolving, ever onward, never ending.

Yet not the same is so within the solid realm.
We see that bodies die;
For those who lose a loved one to its death
Will surely feel the loss was real;

Yet energy remains, somehow.
We speak of Spirit, Soul, forever and Eternity.
Feminine "right-brain" knows this Reality so well;
Sensing, dreaming, loving, trancing
Not of logic is this way,
Nothing here to solve or figure out;

Here, AWARENESS is the key,
To BE
And to begin to see the MYSTERY
To live in it, at any rate;
In this vast realm we do not problem solve—
                                          but we PARTICIPATE !
"Right-brain" Quantum world is, you see
That spacious, Light Reality,
That realm where ALL is One;
Of vibrations, energies here we sing;
As Buddhist to the hot dog vendor:
"Make me one with everything."
All connected as with heart
Clearly, heart's the place to start.
To know about the Whole,
The symphony of waves
Like sound vibrations, colors, smells
Giving off their energies, mingling into ours
Love is of this realm;
The metaphor of wind's another way (as its effect's we see)
To comprehend WAVE Reality
Wind and quantum's waves are not the things we see,
Although, we know their power.
Vibrations, even of the flowers
Give us much besides their beauty;
Finally we are learning of the ways of energy.
But let us not negate old Newton's world.
Our mind, at least, our "left-brain" knows of objects.
There, in my mind at least, exists a world of THINGS.
An architect of Quantum Physics, David Bohm said,
No nouns exist, only slow verbs,
For all is PROCESS in the Quantum way of being led.
I know, that both these sciences are so,
Within the living of our lives,
As we experience being human, and divinely so.
To have a body here on Earth
We feel our density
And cannot always see
Our life as Quantum's WAVE Reality.
For just as real as girl and boy are different,
So it is with life WITHIN our bodies,

Separate, dense, they seem to be—
And yet we're also energy
Intermingling.
It may now seem confusing
To consider living in two world's at once,
And yet we all are doing simply that,
Yet not so simply do we live
Without a framework of these two perspectives
And how we move so fluidly between them.
To bridge these paradigms
Has been the goal within my soul,
A theme, this dream for nearly 40 years
More clearly it is coming for me now,
As I have learned to live my life, I make this vow
Within this body dense
Where Soul has taken up its residence.
To practice being present is the key
To learn to live a life that balances realities.
To separate what's meant to be a partnership
Makes us broken, lost in "sin."
A formula for living life may start
With rules : YOU MUST BE PRESENT TO WIN !
Then dance and balance two realities,
And partner personal polarities,
Gain awareness of a trinity of male and female minds with heart !
Yet more than presence is required in this life;
We also must take action.
Again, again, the key
    For you,
    For me,
To EXPERIENCE our dense body matter and to DO
And also be AWARE, which is to BE.

CHAPTER TEN

YIN AND YANG REVISITED

Essence and form, nearly polar opposites on the continuum of the two different realities, may be conveyed by the words "spirituality" and "religion." "Spirituality" may be experienced at the esoteric and essential level of religious (and even non-religious) traditions and seems to relate to the energy paradigm. The word "spirituality" seems to convey the heart or essence, the *energy* of a system of beliefs. "Religion" is more about form and structure. These separate structures allow individual religions to be known and identified by their names and practices; the word "religion" is about a tradition itself, the form a system of beliefs has taken in the material world. It is most interesting to study and compare the world's religions. In doing so we discover that all truths ultimately converge, at their esoteric level, into the energy of the heart of compassion, oneness. Teilhard de Chardin taught that all things that rise in love converge.[28] Higher, faster, finer vibrations of energy meet in the Oneness. However, at the level of form and structure—the exoteric level—the separate religions look, and indeed may be, very different.

TWO PRINCIPLES OF NATURE

It is helpful in getting acquainted with our dualities to get a sense of the two different aspects of all of nature. Traditionally, Asians have described Yin and Yang in the following ways:[29]

YIN (Feminine):	YANG (Masculine):
Receptive/receptacle	Penetrating/instrument
Yielding	Controlling
Allowing things to happen	Making things happen
Gentle	Forceful
Soft, flexible	Hard, firm
Dark, wet, cold	Light, dry, heat
Weak, vulnerable	Strong
Passive, resting	Active, striving
Cooperative	Competitive
Moon	Sun
Earth, Physical	Heaven, Spirit
Inward, downward	Outward, upward
Imaginative	Logical
Diffuse	Focused
Circular	Linear
Abstract, vague	Concrete, specific

IN ADDITION

In addition to these conventional Asian descriptions of Yin and Yang, here are other ways to compare these opposite principles of nature:

THE FEMININE PRINCIPLE	THE MASCULINE PRINCIPLE
Dominant mode of "primitive" cultures	Main mode of "advanced" Western civilization
Life as mystery: (Gabriel Marcel)[30] participation in the mystery	Life seen as problems and solving of problems
Attitude of "Let it be,"	Attitude of "Just do it !"
God as preposition ("The Great WITH") That which connects; or as verb, a process, God as PRESENCE throughout Her-story	God as noun, more concrete particular figure or The Creator God as acting in *his*tory
God as "Spirit"	God as "The Spirit"
Soul cannot be contained; it is boundless energy merging with the Divine	Soul as container, that which holds our experience
"Human Beings" Being present	"Human Doings" Taking action
Our *IS*-ness nature	Our *business* nature; busyness
Reflects by looking forward With dreams, fantasies, patterns	Reflects by looking backward Using data, opinions
Sees and Accepts the whole Without placement	Analytical, evaluative, judging hierarchical
Awareness and Consciousness; Experience from Greater Self And "whole body" sense	Experience From 5 senses, action, emotion thought, specific body feeling
Trust based behavior	Survival based behavior
Process	Content

Far more useful than categorizing our experience as yin or yang is learning to *become more conscious and recognize WHICH REALITY we have been unconsciously living out of at a particular time or where on the bi-polar reality continuum we are.* It matters not so much whether the way we are looking at life falls into column A or B, Yin or Yang. What makes mastery of our lives more likely is recognizing that everything we experience can be experienced as: 1) subtle energy in motion *and also* 2) as something more concrete, something "you can get your head around." When we take a moment to discern which principle or which reality might be reflected in a way of experiencing the world or one's own life at a particular time, our awareness is heightened and our aliveness is enhanced.

Some things are not clearly Yin or Yang, but they are important to *contrast* with one another. For example, it is paramount for us to make a distinction between EXPERIENCE and AWARENESS of experience. Experiences of both Yin and Yang qualities occur, so "experience" cannot be put into one category or the other. Helping ourselves discover the difference between 1) the experiences and 2) the awareness of our experiences may be one of the most important things we can do for ourselves. When this difference is discerned and grasped a giant step toward mastery of living has been taken. These two words present us with two different ways of living, both necessary for being complete persons.

Awareness is discussed in greater depth in the chapter entitled, "Being Present To Ourselves."

EQUAL TIME

We are most complete as products of Heaven and Earth when we give equal time to the two realities, when we see the two realities as balancing each other, and as we dance along the continuum of realities comfortably. Without fear of being redundant, this perspective needs to be continually noted, as it is in this book, in order for us to internalize the patterns and the numbers. Once integrated it provides the internal experience of balance and the harmony of greater degrees of peace.

CHAPTER ELEVEN

METAPHORS FOR TWO REALITIES

Metaphors come from the land of symbols, "right brain" experience. They seem to slip past the density of the left-brain's preference for didactic, factual information.

BE A LIGHT BULB

A light bulb is a useful metaphor demonstrating life in two paradigms. Simply close your eyes and/or focus inward. Imagine that you are a clear glass light bulb shaped like your own body and plugged into your source of electricity, your spirit, your aliveness. Feel yourself sending forth your light, spreading your sunshine, sharing your energy with others. Your light is intermingling with light from other sources, other light bulbs. This sharing of your aliveness and light cannot be quantified or kept track of, unless you are the only light bulb in the room. Notice that you're sharing your light without losing your shape, without losing your identity as a separate light bulb, without giving yourself away, or losing yourself as a separate individual.

While light is both particle and wave in physics, in this metaphorical light bulb experience the light or energy we share represents our wave-like, flowing quality; the form or shape of the bulb represents our concrete aspects of our nature.

RE-PARENTED BY EARTH AND SKY

Another experience of the **two** qualitatively different realities which can help us **re-parent** ourselves is the image and physical experience or *feeling* of being sandwiched between Earth and Sky. While it is an obvious enough *fact* that we live between Heaven and Earth, many individuals have never let themselves feel this at the sensual, physical level. The expression, "Come to your senses," no longer means to me that one should "wise up" or get more sensible, mentally. Coming to our physical senses can bring us into an intimate mother-child relationship with the earth, allowing us to receive, energetically, the bounty of nurturing available from our primary mother, Mother Earth. We can consciously receive these resources from the perspective of the paradigms partnered, as *vibrations of energy* **and** as the more concrete blessings such as rain from the Heavens, food from the Earth. While Earth may have male and female properties, and sky may be thought of as having male and female qualities as well, it is useful to see them as a pair of parents, one mother and one father. As we receive nourishment and strength from the beautiful Earth Mother who is there *beneath our feet* to support us (ex-

cept during earthquakes) we can also open our consciousness to the Sky and, with awareness, receive Father Sky's spaciousness and Light (and all that the Heavens might include for particular individuals such as specific spiritual sources of guidance).

Whenever I hypnotize clients, I always suggest that
they experience their relationships with Earth and with
Sky as very personal, intimate, alive. Indeed, these are
our primary parents. Re-parenting, soothing oneself with
conscious awareness of these good parents in partnership, can occur at any and all times; the opportunity for
renewal of body and spirit is abundantly and ever
present.

SKY AND CLOUDS

Another useful metaphor which helps us get a sense
of the two different paradigms out of which we can operate more consciously is the metaphor of the sky and
clouds seen through a round window; roundness, or zero
is a symbol for our oneness, a symbol for the nothing/
everything paradox. Bringing our attention to this symbol lifts our consciousness to the Soul's wholeness.

SYMBOLS

Symbols have an impact on all of us, whether or not
we are aware of this. I was heartened many years ago by
a discovery I made about symbols, ones which I had
unconsciously chosen to live with. I decided to follow

my own advice and do the assignment I was giving to
students in a class I was teaching on the use of nocturnal dreams as a way to wholeness. I had suggested to
the class that they observe what symbols they had acquired in artwork, jewelry and even fabric adorning their
homes and in their clothing , taking care to notice any
recurring symbols. This was in the late 1970's when I
was still very fragmented at the personality level and
struggling to find myself/Self, my wholeness. To my
amazement, I discovered in my own home that nearly
every work of art on my walls—watercolors, batiks,
weaves, prints—was in the form of a circle! This gave
me great hope that I indeed had a Soul that had been
trying to show itself to me though my unconscious se-
lection of art. The other side of the coin emerged when
I realized that patchwork designs in many of my clothes
and in the print fabric covering my chairs seemed to
speak of the cacophony and fragmentation within my
personality and chaos in my personal life at that time.

SKY AND CLOUDS IMAGERY EXERCISE

Guided imagery of sky and clouds seen through a
ROUND window can be extended as follows:

Allow your eyes to close and imagine that you're
looking up at the inside of your forehead. You see a
round window in the center of your forehead and as you
look through that window, out beyond your forehead,
you see the clear, blue sky. Like the sky, your essence,

your Great Self or Soul is spacious, clear, bright, sunny and connected to All That Is.

Your sky-ness is sometimes dark like the nighttime sky but daylight always rolls back around revealing to you your spaciousness and clarity. And as you look out the round window in the center of your forehead you may see a cloud or two moving across the sky. The clouds are more dense forms of energy and may be symbols of your emotions or thoughts; some are pleasant feelings or thoughts, like attractive fluffy, white billowy clouds. Some clouds are grey, stringy, less appealing—like feelings or thoughts we may not particularly enjoy. Feelings or thoughts of any variety are like clouds— energy more dense than the sky's spaciousness; the clouds arise in our experience the way emotions and thoughts arise at times. As we watch them, simply noticing them, they move on through our experience. The clouds change and move across the background of the sky of our BEING. The clouds are temporary, transitory, fleeting aspects of our experience, like the experiences of our thoughts, emotions and bodily sensations. What remains a constant, however, is our skyness, the Great Self, the Soul holding our experience. The sky of our BEING is the background which is always present when the more dense energy of our clouds moves on through the scenes of our lives. In this imagery experience, clouds can be seen as concrete, having form. The background, clear sky, is simply energy, the energy of spaciousness connected to All That Is.

If only we remembered
How GOOD God is,
How Holy is the Whole, the "All That Is."
If only we remembered how we're loved
By Spirit, "All That Is," in Heaven above,
Heaven within, around and through
Heaven in me, Heaven in you;
The joy within our soul
Is clearly a reflection of the Whole;
The "All That Is" holds dark and light;
How is it that the total is so bright?
If only we remembered that bright spark,
The joy that Heaven holds, when all is dark;
We're not at all alone, we're always loved
The Whole holds us, we're known above;
We're fed, we're nurtured, calmed by Earth below
This Mother Planet Earth her gifts bestows;
All we need is here for us to claim;
She wants us to RECEIVE.
            Release the pain!
If only we remembered in our drought
The resource, love and joy that's all about.

CHAPTER TWELVE

BEING PRESENT TO OURSELVES

Presence is powerful. When a person is said to have presence, that individual is richly connected to the **ONE**ness dimension, the energy of their Soul, to the resources of energy from Heaven and Earth. Such people are noticed and taken seriously. Mahatma Gandhi, The Dalai Lama, Martin Luther King, Bishop Tutu, Nelson Mandela come to mind as people with presence. We can all think of people we have personally known who are not famous who we feel have presence.

PRESENCE IS NOT THE SAME AS CHARISMA

The distinction between charisma and presence may be a subtle one. Dynamic people are often highly polarized in their internal energies and this creates power of a kind somewhat different from presence. (Some people have both charisma *and* presence). Charismatic individuals are people with intensity which is born out of the tension between opposite energies. Creative people usually have great tension between the creative and destructive polarity within and this makes for dynamism or charisma. We feel stimulated and excited when we are around charismatic people.

PRESENCE UPLIFTS OTHERS

When we are in the midst of people with presence we are energized and enlivened in a deeper way. We are uplifted and nourished by people with presence. Maya Angelou[31] comes to mind as a woman with powerful presence. I heard her speak to several hundred people in a college auditorium several years ago where she spoke about her own power. She said that people often say to her, "Maya, you're such a powerful presence!" As she stood on an empty stage she shared how she replies to such comments: "I'm not standing up here on the stage all by myself. Everyone who has ever been a rainbow in my life is up here with me, standing right behind me. I take them with me. So, take ME with YOU." It was a powerful moment of presence. Presence seeks to share itself. The nourishment is available from such powerful people because of their strong connection with Heaven and Earth. People with presence are compelling. Their aliveness, Spirits and Souls are felt by others as is their integrity. One arrives at a place of integrity when one is very honest with oneself; with knowledge of oneself and acceptance, personality integration is possible for anyone when judgment is tamed. All human beings are lifted up by people such as Maya Angelou and others with presence who remind us what we all may be. People with such presence often have a healing effect on those in their midst for they are not sharing merely their thoughts or talents; they are sharing the energy of their Spirit and Soul.

The good news here is that each of us has the capacity for presence and can be a healing and energizing presence to *ourselves*. We have access to enormous healing resources within ourselves but we may not have known how to connect with, and use, these resources. Learning to access the power of presence is not difficult. It begins with paying attention, being *in* our body, and being aware of our embodied experience.

When we live from the stance of awareness we are in the realm of the Greater Self and the Energy Paradigm, where we simply notice without judgement. When we are a*ware,* we are living from our essence, our BE-ING nature. We are living consciously. If we were *only* aware, however, without experiencing *our human nature* with all its emotions, thoughts and foibles, we would not be living as fully human. On the other hand, if we were living reactively or unconsciously from our humanness (i.e., our feelings and our learned or inherited patterns of behavior) we would not be claiming our capacity for CONSCIOUSNESS which connects us with *our higher nature.*

Mystics may admonish us to stay in the reality above duality. What is preferable to staying in that higher realm is living from both 1) awareness of the realm of unity consciousness and 2) the realm of duality. Shifting from the more energetically spacious AWARENESS of our experience to the more dense energies of the emotional, physical embodied EXPERIENCE leads to enlighten- ment. (It's as easy to remember A&E as 1-2-3 and 4). A for awareness, E for experience.

Consider a wheel with the outer rim of the wheel representing Reality #2, the domain of the more con- crete "stuff" of human EXPERIENCE. Our experience is made up of emotions, senses, thoughts, physical sen- sations, etc. Just like the non-judgmental center that our heart is, the center of the wheel represents the conscious- ness of Reality #1 and the place of AWARENESS from which we simply and gently notice or observe without judgment. The more often we move back and forth be- tween these two paradigms, the more balance and whole- ness we "experience." We could get tricky and talk about the experience of awareness for, it too, is an experience. But we're keeping it simple. Simply put, being aware of the experiences that you are having as you are having them makes for a high degree of consciousness. With practice we can learn to live from both the outer and inner center of the wheel at the same time. The next best thing is to shift back and forth between AWARENESS and EXPERIENCE quickly and often. This leads to mo- ments of enlightenment.

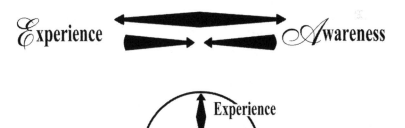

AWARENESS AND THE DIVINE

Some have described God simply as Awareness. Perhaps we could say that "Awareness is as good as it gets." Indeed, virtually all schools of thought in psychology agree that mental health (or "having it together") comes down to the degree to which a person has lost their balance, lost their way ("lost it"). "Loosing it" is a matter of degree, the degree to which emotions or thoughts (and defenses AGAINST emotions and thoughts) have taken over the awareness center. Emotions or the thinking mind will sometimes pull "a coup" and take over, but if one is committed to conscious living or awareness, one's center holds together. We can trust that this place of calmness, harmony, and balance is always there for us to return to."Mindfulness" is what Buddhists call awareness. I prefer the word AWARENESS because the word 'mindfulness'— containing MIND—might be misconstrued as having something to do with THINKING which it clearly does not.

SUBTRACTING TO GET MORE SPACIOUSNESS

Awareness requires a willingness to subtract or release our thoughts and feelings as we experience and then move THROUGH and beyond the clutter of our thoughts and the clanging and tugging of our emotions.

In keeping with this notion of SUBTRACTING to get down to our essential BEING or our awareness center, it may be useful to speak of what awareness is NOT.

AWARENESS IS NOT INTROSPECTION

Awareness is NOT introspection.[32] Introspection comes from our thinking mind and includes the desire to become different than we are, to become better, more perfect. Perfectionism rears its ugly head with introspection. Introspection is evaluative, judgmental. It is rejecting and not accepting like Divine love or spaciousness. Introspection is, therefore, not healing. Introspection makes people self-centered, self- absorbed. The obsessively introspective characters Woody Allen has played in films is a symbol—a tragic symbol—of what little good introspection does. One can become stuck in it. Awareness is quite different a phenomenon from introspection. Unlike introspection, awareness does NOT make us self-centered or self- absorbed. Unlike introspection, awareness does not divide us against ourselves. Awareness enlarges the aspect of ourselves out of which we give and receive love—to one another and to ourselves. Practicing awareness lets us find our center of non-judgmental compassion, our own reflection of divine unconditional ACCEPTANCE.

AN EMPTINESS THAT IS FULL

Awareness is only possible with space, sublime empty space. Awareness is empty, empty of desire, empty of what we think ought to be. Emptiness and the notion of nothingness are not ideas with which our (Reality #2) Western minds are comfortable. In the West we think of empty as meaning hollow, forgetting that Spirit is what fills in the space, making the hollowness hallowed space. It is helpful to develop comfort with the value of NOTHINGNESS which is another word for awareness.

THE SPACE THAT ALLOWS FOR CREATION

The space between a stimulus and a response is a space of profound significance. This is the space that allows Spirit to enter so that creative, clear and constructive communication between two people can occur. In healthy, wholesome, non-defensive relating, we are calm. Calm enough to hear the other and experience the other as a separate being. This calmness and clarity is the energy of awareness. If we REACT to another person's comments without awareness of what we are feeling, we do not allow space for the energy of the Creative Forces to enter. When we take the time to be aware and to gently NOTICE what we are feeling before we respond, we are co-creating with the Spirit. Awareness invites the assistance of Spirit.

AWARENESS COMES FROM THE BODY

Awareness is not of the THINKING mind. Nor does it happen in the head. It is of the heart and body sense. Our mind divides, separates or splits things into dualities (Reality #2). It is comparative and looks for differences; the mind conceives of one thing as being better than the other. Our HEART experiences wholeness and acceptance; the heart holds all things together as One (Reality #1).

BUDDHISTS AND LIGHT BULBS

From our heart space, our awareness center, that place of unity and wholeness within our bodies, we can *notice* (without judgment) the duality of our mental process— a lesson we have learned from Buddhism. Should a Buddhist be asked how many people it takes to change a light bulb they would be likely to say, "It takes two: one to change the light bulb and one NOT to change the light bulb." Our minds are binary and split things into polarities. Practicing Buddhists like to be awake and be aware of these opposites.

OUR SENSES, MEETING PLACES FOR THE REALITIES

The best place to experience the unity behind the duality of our mental process is in our body. Some people engage in out-of-body experiences, an altered state of consciousness, to be sure. However, for WHOLE-NESS we need to be PRESENT in our bodies. We need to come to our senses—our physical senses.

The present moment is the very best place to go for a vacation from anxiety produced by the judgment of our minds. We experience the present through our five physical senses.

The senses seem to be the places where Reality #1 meets Reality #2. For example, the vibrations (Energy Paradigm) of sound waves meet the physical mechanism of our ears (the physical-material domain) giving rise to the sense of hearing. Vibrations of lightwaves of various different hues of color meet the physical apparatus of our eyes and we then have the sense of sight. Vibrations of aroma meet our nose and we have the olfactory sense of smell.

THE SENSE OF LOVE

Coming to our senses means coming into the Here and Now, the Heart's realm. Perhaps we could say that the energies or vibrations of another person which are similar or complementary to our own meet our heart and we have the sense of love.

Being present in the Here and Now, living in the moment, requires that our consciousness be embodied. Our minds are not qualified for the leadership position which calls for the dimensions of wisdom and compassion. "Lead with the heart" is a motto for those who seek greater awareness.

AWARENESS AND CONSCIOUSNESS

Awareness is about being awake to what we are feeling. It is about being conscious rather that asleep or out of touch with what is true for us. Awareness is consciousness. Consciousness has the energy of light about it—

healing light. Light, like fire, transforms energy. The energies of our emotions are transformed as we PAY ATTENTION to what we are feeling. Our conscious awareness transforms those feelings. In giving our attention to our experience we are giving healing love to our human nature.

AWARENESS AND HONESTY

Awareness is about being impeccably honest with ourselves about what we are feeling, honest about what we are experiencing. This is a prerequisite for honesty with others. Indeed we cannot have WHOLENESS without honesty. And when we have this degree of awareness—experiencing without denial of what we are feeling—Grace enters into our lives.

It is interesting to note that Carl Jung, the Swiss psychiatrist who was a Christian and a student of Eastern philosophy, said that when we are simply AWARE, honest with ourselves about what we are experiencing—not thinking but experiencing—then Grace enters our lives. At that point the next thing we need for our growth and development somehow finds its way to us.

Psychoanalyst Heinz Kohut was fond of quoting playwright Eugene O'Neill who wrote these words: "Man is born broken. He lives by mending. The Grace of God is the glue." I would amend those words and say that we are born whole but experience brokenness or separation from our **One**ness realm early in life, to one degree or another. We live by a process of mending. Awareness and the Grace of God is the glue.

BEING AS GROUND, SKY, AND RIVER

Perhaps theologian Paul Tillich who described God as the "ground of our Being" would be comfortable with the notion of God as Awareness, for awareness is our Being, from moment to moment. It is useful as a relaxation technique to meditate on the image of the clear blue sky. We temporarily float across it; only the sky remains constant. We can trust it to be there behind the clouds. Consider the blue sky as a metaphor for our Being, pure awareness. Awareness is what exists when we subtract whatever else might be going on. The content keeps happening and moving on through or across the sky, the background of our pure awareness which is the clear blue sky of our consciousness. We can also think of our Being like a river—constantly flowing water. There is actually no river the Buddhists would say, no self even, only awareness of one moment and then the next, ever changing. Meditation is a practice of letting go of everything and just EXPERIENCING or being AWARE—moment to moment. Awareness—the GROUND of our Being, The Sky of our Being, The River of our Being. Indeed, awareness may be as good as it gets. By practicing awareness, by living consciously, we learn to make living a meditation process.

PROBLEMS AND MYSTERIES

Life presents us with concrete PROBLEMS to be solved and also with MYSTERIES which are never to be solved. Existentialist Gabriel Marcel[33] observed these two different dilemmas and wrote, in an "Essay on the Ontological Mysteries," that the important things in life are mysteries and one cannot solve a mystery; one can only PARTICIPATE in a mystery. The essence of holistic or psycho- spiritual therapy is our willingness to "participate in the mystery" of healing and growth and to feel what a privilege this is.

"YOU MUST BE PRESENT TO WIN"

Doing therapy from our BEING brings therapy to maturity. The wholesome, holistic work of expanding consciousness serves both the therapist and the client. Working from the experience of PRESENCE heals the practitioner doing therapy, while that therapist is also being an example of PRESENCE for the client. As clinicians mature into a holistic perspective they may find that being a teacher of presence is at least as important as being a technician with skills for helping clients create greater degrees of well-being in their lives. Indeed, in the past many years I have felt that simply BEING who I am, sharing my full presence with clients was as significant in their growth as anything I said or did. I am not alone in this observation. Many in the various helping professions have discovered that as they do their own personal work of healing and liberation they discover that who they ARE as a presence is every bit as important as anything they can DO. And therapists must stop their own personal growth work. I believe that when we are actively involved in our own process of evolving to a clearer level of consciousness we give off a quality of energy that invites those who are around us to grow. A sign in my office says, " YOU MUST BE PRESENT TO WIN." Indeed, we are winners, and nothing can be lost once we learn to live from presence, from our soul's BEING. DOING the work of problem solving and creating strategies around relationship issues, while still important, may become secondary to simple PRESENCE, as the culture of consciousness emerges.

GOD, THE GRAND PREPOSITION

A Professor of Religion at Lake Forest College, Dr. Ron Miller,[34] refers to God as "The Great Preposition" or "The Great WITH." This seems to me a wise and mature way to think of the Divine. God as PRESENCE. God as AWARENESS. Children, if taught anything about God, tend to think of God as a noun, concrete like a person, even if they are told God is Spirit. As an adolescent I was delighted by a poster quoting Buckmaster Fuller saying, "For God to me, it seems, is not a noun but a verb." God as love in action, God as a process. And now comes God as preposition. It is transforming to be WITH others when we are fully present in our body while being consciously present to and aware of our own feelings. God is the great CONNECTOR. The energy between us. Within, among, around and through. God is the glue.

The energy we call God is relational. This was the consistent message of Jewish theologian Martin Buber[35]. By being in touch with what is true for us we are in relation to ourselves in a way that brings us wholeness. And by being present to one another, honoring both the humanness and the divinity in one another, we empower the health and well-being of the other.

Our true PRESENCE nurtures others. If our Soul or Spirit has not taken up residence in our body, or if we speak with another while coming only from our head, it is as if nobody is home. If no*body* is involved, no energy of the heart or emotions are shared.

QUIET AND EMPTY

Paradoxically, to empty ourselves of our thoughts and our emotions empowers presence. In order for the energy of spaciousness and peace to heal us we need to transform our busy human nature—with all of its thinking and emotional energies— and become as empty as possible in order that the energy of our Soul can freely flow into our bodies like honey, like nectar, the connector.

Quieting our minds and emotions so that we may embody Spirit is not achieved by pushing away those human energies of thoughts and feelings. In or out of meditation, we must ACCEPT AND EMBRACE our emotions, embrace any thoughts which may arise, embrace any sensations occurring in our body. AND in so doing we transform and heal those energies, bringing ourselves gradually to a place of balance and PRESENCE, the emptiness that is the fullness—for we are then filled with Spirit.

BROTHER LAWRENCE

PRESENCE is the gentle personal power and integrity that one acquires as a result of living with awareness. Nearly 400 years ago Brother Lawrence wrote a book that has become a classic entitled, "The Practice of the Presence of God."[36] The title is actually a redundancy because PRESENCE or awareness IS GOD, at least in the way Brother Lawrence writes of God. The theme which echos through all the writings of Brother Lawrence, the simple and sincere Carmelite monk, is absolute negation of everything that does not include spaciousness or love. This theme is actually very Buddhist: subtraction to get to what is essential. And the book's title may be doubly redundant to a Buddhist practitioner for one Buddhist will say to another, "How is your practice going?" meaning, "How is your 'awareness' these days?". Buddhism does not include the idea of a God. Enlightenment is the goal. But enlightenment and Oneness with All That Is, which IS God, are essentially the same.

TOOLS FOR TEACHING PRESENCE

Teaching clients to be present to their feelings while being fully present ourselves is one of the most gratifying experiences a therapist can have. While the subject of presence may sound abstract, the practice of presence has specifics that are easily grasped, easily experienced and recalled. To gain presence we need only be aware of what we are feeling in our body, noting what we are truly experiencing in the immediate present. The next step is to direct one's attention to the center of whatever the emotional or physical tension may be—to take consciousness, awareness, attention, the power of presence, to the experience in the body. As we stay with this experience for a short time, we might notice that we see or sense a color or a texture to the energy block we are feeling. Imagining that we see a color or texture works as well. Perhaps the energy even has a tone to it. Perhaps some words might want to emerge out of it if we "give it a voice." An image or symbol may emerge out of the energy blockage. These various ways of experiencing the energy brings more consciousness or attention to the particular area. Nearly all the time the tension dissolves within a few minutes or even seconds. Rarely does the tension stay at the same level it was when the experiment began. This quickly demonstrates to ourselves and to our clients the transformative power of consciousness and this is usually NEWS to people, and very empowering news! A very small percentage of the time this exercise is used, a pain or tension will increase. To me this increase seems to say (and I share this with the client) that the feeling that is persisting is saying, "I need a great deal more of your attention, more of your love; don't think you're going to transform me in one little exercise!" I would ask such a client to keep their awareness of the part of their personality that is showing up bodily as an energy blockage *so that* it can receive their attention, their healing PRESENCE. When we take our awareness or our embodied PRESENCE to what we are physically or emotionally experiencing, we are taking the best of us, our goodness or godliness *to* our human nature.

To be as much in balance as the lesser self of our human nature seeks to be, and to experience our Greater Self, connected to our spiritual sources, as Spirit calls us to be, we need to begin to recognize and feel the vibrational difference between our human experiences and our soul's expansiveness. This will be addressed in the chapter entitled, "The Texture of The Two Realities."

LASER LOVE

In this age of laser surgery we can liken our attention to laser love beaming into parts of ourselves, patterns of our experience. Our consciousness is transformative fire, penetrating through density, bringing spaciousness. Consciousness, then, is of both the Yang principle (penetrating) and also the Yin Principle (the bringer of openness and space).

CHAPTER THIRTEEN

THE TEXTURES OF THE TWO REALITIES

Much about life is both wave and particle, like light itself. It is helpful when we consider our life experiences in two different ways: 1) those which require awareness and are of a sixth-sense, or subtle-energy, wave-like in nature and 2) those which are experienced with our five physical senses, less subtle. For example, fear-based experiences are felt as contracted energy within our body, while those experiences rooted in trust feel energetically spacious.

Observing our body's level of tension is the first step of tuning in to these energies. As we become more aware of our body and how its condition varies, depending on where we are coming from (either our Greater Self or from our personality, human nature) we then move into a deepening awareness of more subtle distinctions.

The perspective which I present is not a mere exercise in abstract thinking. These two Realities actually have different textures and can be felt. From the compelling world of "Energy Medicine" (especially from several week-long workshops with Robert Jaffe, M.D.,some training with Alexandria Parness, a number of sessions with Kathryn Nash, R.N. and dozens of attunement sessions with Paul Ditscheit, M.S) I have learned to feel, and teach clients to discern the difference between the spacious energies of soul/wholeness/heart from the energies of the more dense realities of physically based emotions. It is rare that a person is not able to feel these energies during Energy Medicine exercises which direct their attention to their body and its energy blockages.

EXPANDED/CONTRACTED

Fear causes tension. Experiences which are upsetting or stressful cause contractions of energy within our body which can be easily felt and recognized. On the other hand, when we feel safe and content there is a spacious feeling within our body.

FINE/FAST, COARSE/SLOW

The energy of the Soul or Quantum Reality energy is felt as a finer, faster vibration of energy. As more Soul energy is taken into our body we can even acquire a subtle, comfortable electrical buzzing feeling.

In the physical-material Reality, the energies of

the body-mind feel like a coarser, slower vibration. If we ask for a word to come to mind to describe the texture we may be feeling, such a word will often occur to us.

FLOWING LIKE FLUID OR STICKY LIKE MOLASSES

Soul energy is often described as feeling fluid, as if it is flowing. We might refer to it as the River of our Being.

By contrast, the energy blockages or emotions which may be unprocessed and therefore stuck in the body, are described as feeling dense, thicker, slower. We can accurately speak of the molasses of living in our sometimes dense human arena. Perhaps we could speak of these distinctly different realms of Soul and Body mind as *the spacious sky of our being* and contrast it with *the "stuff" of our human experience.*

SELF-ACCEPTANCE GROWS AS SOUL IS FELT

Once we have experienced the physical feeling of the Soul's energy, a newfound feeling of unconditional self-love emerges (which is not the same as the often conditional arena of self-esteem). This experience of love from the Greater Self , which is most easily felt in the heart, allows clients to look at and accept more of the human ways of the small self of personality.

SIDES OF THE BODY FEEL DIFFERENT

An easy way for us to feel the energies in the body is to imagine that a vertical line is dividing the right side of the body from the left side. If we put our attention on one side of our body, examining it for texture, color, a sound like a tone, or the degree of movement of the energies, we will surely notice *something*, unless we are totally stuck in our heads. If all the energy we notice is in and around our head we need to keep our attention on that experience of thinking energy or whatever the head area is showing us. Soon, after doing this, most people are able to move down into their body. Holding attention on one side of the body for a while and getting used to these subtle energies becomes very interesting when, a minute or so later, we move our attention to the other side of our body (the other side of the imaginary vertical line). These two sides always feel different and this is quite a surprise for most people initially. Almost everyone can do this exercise.

DENSE OR SPACIOUS—ALL IS DIVINE ALIVENESS

The energy of the Soul's realm not only holds or contains the learning from the emotions, thoughts, and sensations of the body, it also infuses them with life force, or energy. Both our Soul and our human nature are divinely energized. As quantum physics reports, everything is alive, even surprisingly alive. Mystical poets have long written of a world view much like that of Quantum Physics. Poet and priest Gerard Manly Hopkins wrote, "The world is charged with the grandeur of God. . . ."[37]

Another mystical poet, William Blake, wrote poetry about the whole of life being seen in a part of life, another perspective of The New Sciences, and ancient "right-brain" perspectives of Earth-based wisdom traditions:

> "To see the world in a grain of sand
> And a Heaven in a wild flower;
> To hold Infinity in the palm of your hand
> And Eternity in an hour."[38]

(From Auguries of Innocence)

According to Under and O'Connor, authors of *Poems for Study*, Blake despised Isaac Newton and those who believed in the impersonal, mechanical reality put forth in Newtonian Physics.[39] Later in the unfinished poem, "Auguries of Innocence"[40] Blake wrote:

> We are led to believe a lie
> When we see *with*, not *through*, the eye,
> Which was born in a night, to perish in a night,
> When the soul slept in beams of light.
> God appears, and God is Light
> To those poor souls who dwell in night,
> But does a human form display
> To those who dwell in realms of day.[41]

In Blake's view, those who believed in the reality put forth by Newtonian Physics, lived in ignorance, "in night." Those who could envision human beings involved in the universe could conceive of God as a "human form." Today we could say that when we are living from the realm of the "right-brain" and kinesthetic (body sense) feelings, or are leading with our heart, we are living "in realms of day"or in the light of truth. To Blake and many mystics, dancers, artists and "right-brain" dominant individuals it has been understood that everything is infused with Divine energy. Blake, like most people of his time, thought in the either/or way of believing that Newtonian Physics was either right or wrong. Blake was passionate on his position. From what we now know about "left-brain" ways of perceiving reality and "right-brain," earthy, body sense ways of knowing, we do not need to take a stance of either/or. Both/and is the holistic perspective we can now embrace. There is no longer a need to reject one world view in favor of another; both can be honored. Their differences can be seen as complementary, opposites balancing each other.

Learning to sense, to feel in the body the different qualities of energy of the two realities is not difficult. It has been surprising to me to discover how quickly even clients who seemed to be out of touch with their body sense and living very much from their head, could learn to feel the subtle energies of Spirit and Soul. The more coarse vibrations of emotions are much more easily felt by everyone.

We are humans having a spiritual experience AND spiritual beings having a human experience. BOTH are true, depending on which paradigm we are living from or standing in at a particular moment. To be as complete as the lesser self of our human nature seeks to be, and to experience our Greater Self connected to our spiritual sources as Spirit calls us to be, we need to recognize and feel the vibrational difference between our human experiences and our soul's expansiveness. As with the game of golf, awareness of our stance is important. We need to learn to be aware, paradigm-wise, from whence we are coming. Without much difficulty we can imagine our soul as a container, holding all that we are at the level of our human nature and our accumulated human experience. From this experience we can imagine ourselves, Greater and lesser, to be a microcosm of the macrocosm that holds all of creation.

PANTHEISM AND PANENTHEISM

The philosophy of Pantheism holds that everything in nature is filled with divine life force. This philosophy states that God is in all things, and that everything—even a stone—is as surprisingly alive as Quantum Physics now teaches and as mystics have believed. Everything—vegetable, animal, mineral—is charged with life.

Another philosophy, Panentheism[42] presumes that

Something holds all aspects of nature, forms which are filled with Spirit, charged with aliveness. There is both a Creator, a Force of Creation and there is also That Which Holds All That Is. This philosophy is one which can be comfortably incorporated into the way healers, therapists and coaches view reality; it is a comfortable philosophy, one that kinesthetically, bodily, feels true when we try it on. Some therapists, many healers and life coaches are already working out of the philosophy of Panentheism whether they are aware of this or not.

CHAPTER FOURTEEN

MIXED-UP PARADIGMS

Confusion or foolish-looking behavior can occur when the mindset that is fitting for one reality is applied to the other. New understandings of behaviors emerge as we explore this kind of mix-up.

THE RULES

The rules of Reality # 2 are well known to us in the modern world. From grade school education on we are steeped in the laws of science and any advanced training we receive comes out of this paradigm of conventional science. We've called it, "the REAL world." As a culture we have been encouraged to think in the "left-brain" style, interpreting the world as though Reality #2 was all that existed, its rules of science the only rules with any validity. As individuals we have incorporated this view of reality into our understanding of how life works, whether we know the technicalities of the scientific laws or not. We have unconsciously assumed that this paradigm of reality **is** the only reality. Newton's laws of gravity, indeed all the laws of the physical-material world are obviously relevant to reality as we have generally thought of it in the Western Hemisphere.

A CHANGE IN REALITY

Reality is a-changin,' folk singer Bob Dylan might sing today. Metaphysical laws, the ways of Reality #1, are being incorporated into our lives, into our culture. There has been an increase in recent years of films which lift up the energy paradigm— films such as "Phenomenon," "Powder," "Sixth Sense" and many others. Another example of this is the daily televised segment of the OPRAH show called "Remembering Your Spirit" which honors the workings of Reality # 1 by showing, essentially, what happens when we consciously employ our Spirit and Soul energy. When the power of consciousness (Reality #1) meets the Reality of the physical-material world (Reality #2) individuals can co-create triumph over adversity. Millions now believe that, to a significant degree, we can create what we want to create for ourselves. In the past decade many have been learning that, like it or not, we all participate more profoundly than we had previously thought in co-creating what we have in our life.

CO-MINGLING REALITIES

What we have called "mind over matter" could be stated like this: the energy of consciousness (Reality #1, the Oneness Reality of our Greater Self) infuses the physical material reality (Reality # 2 of our lesser self) at a place where the polarity of the realities meet—the trinity of "left-brain thinking," "right-brain thinking" and the heart's way of knowing.

SURRENDER JUDGMENT

Some people fall into self-judgment for what they have created in their lives— blaming themselves for their physical illness and other difficulties. Unless an individual has adopted the oneness perspective and has felt the empowering self-love that accompanies it, there is a challenge in accepting responsibility for our thoughts and emotions. Judgment is part of the "left-brain" ways of Reality #2; it is not included in the processes of Reality # 1. When these paradigms are entangled with each other, instead of meeting the other in an attitude of mutual respect for their differences, it may be uncomfortable for some to see the effects of their mental and emotional vibrations.

Obviously, the energies of our thoughts and emotions are not the only factors involved in physical health and other areas of our lives. While the energy paradigm—Reality # 1—is a large part of the story, it is balanced by the many physical-material facts of life—Reality # 2. Many forces are at work in the world. The *energetics* of thoughts are powerful but so are the effects of *genetics*, an unhealthy diet, lack of exercise. We need to partake of healthy living in both realities, paying attention to our thoughts *and* our actions.

THOUGHT AND EMOTION TOGETHER

The most basic rule of the energy paradigm is this one: we are attracting into our lives the kind of vibrations which we contain and, consciously or unconsciously, are contributing to our environment. We reap what we sow. Because of the particular quality and quantity of energies we emit, we are creating many of the things that are happening to us. We create through the power of consciousness, the energy of our soul. We create with our thoughts, which are energy patterns. Thought, like prayer, is indeed powerful, depending on how clear and heartfelt the thought patterns might be. We create most powerfully from the place on the reality continuum where the two realities meet, from our heart. Emotions, which come from our body or the physical-material reality, enhance the desired intention. We create with our conscious and unconscious thoughts and emotions.

One of the gifts a therapist receives is the opportunity to see how Life treats people. It becomes very obvious to any even moderately conscious counselor that all people are creating *much* of the fortune and misfortune that occurs in their lives. We cannot "figure out" all the mysteries and discern all the factors involved in the complexities of intermingling energies. Surrendering to the mystery (Reality # 1) while also seeking to master our behavior (Reality # 2) seems to be the wisest stance for us all.

THE "LAW" OF ATTRACTION

Within the Energy Paradigm with its synchronicity or meaningful coincidences, we attract what we wish for. The more of an emotional charge, the stronger the vibration that is given off along with the thought, the sooner the manifestation of that desire will occur. (Note: This seems to be contrary to the Buddha's admonition that we be detached from desire. Comments about this appear in a later chapter, Honoring Heaven and Earth).

Given the energy paradigm's Law of Attraction,[43] why don't more of our wishes come true?

THE NEGATION PROCESS

All too often, self-defeating, negative beliefs about ourselves are emitted along with our consciously felt desires. These negative notions and emotions about ourselves, while unconscious, have toxic effects upon our lives. Just as we get our cars tested for toxic fumes which harm the environment, "Emissions Testing" for human vibrations may be available to us one day. In the meantime, we need to pay close attention to what we are attracting, creating and failing to create in our lives. We undo many of our good intentions for ourselves, energetically. We might call this undoing, or the effects of personality negativity, the law of negation. This feeling of unworthiness and self-doubt can undo the effects of our most sincerely held desires. If consistent energies exist in the unconscious mind such as self-hatred, or repressed hostility toward others, we can create pain, illness and misfortune in our lives. We may block or delay the good fortune and blessings which are trying to find their way to us. We may shudder at the thought of "black magic," but we often engage in such activities within ourselves without realizing it. Negative thoughts, even worry, are the opposite of prayer.

THE LAW OF ALLOWING

Before we can "let the good times roll" we have to *get out of our own way.* This is about letting the density of our human nature become more spacious, as it does when we fill our bodies with our soul energy, letting our heart and soul lead the way. We can more easily let our lives work in accordance with our soul's purposes when we consciously see the polarities of our personality balancing each other. Some have called this phenomenon of the energy paradigm, "The Law of Allowing[44]." It is a Yin process for it is about *receiving*. The law of attraction, on the other hand, is a Yang process for it is about *giving out* energies which are then met by similar energies. (The "Birds of a feather flock together" relationship rule will be discussed in another chapter).

THE RULES OF REALITY # 1

The Reality of One, of spaciousness, requires that we honor the power of consciousness, Spirit, Soul. In this reality we need to recognize the power of thoughts and emotions as energies. We notice, with wonder, the interconnections between our thoughts, feelings and the events which occur in our lives. What the conventional paradigm may call "loose associations" is seen quite differently in the energy paradigm.

In my experience of observing many others and paying attention to my own life, it appears as though the events happening to us at a particular time reflect our internal energies at that time. As it is in our internal experience, so it is outside of us. Synchronicity is a fact of life in the energy paradigm. There is synchronicity in everything; it is everywhere, not just an occasional meaningful coincidence. Therapists who are attuned to the ways of energy often feel that a particular kind of client or a client with a particular type of issue will arrive at a therapy session and seem to reflect something that is going on in the therapist's life. This is very peculiar and mysterious and worth observing, if you are a therapist.

Some days we "get out of the wrong side of the bed" and begin our day from a place of imbalance; these are the days when "one damn thing after another" happens. Our chaotic, inharmonious inner state is reflected in the spilled milk, misplaced car keys, etc. that happen more frequently on such days. Even accidents which are not at all our "fault" seem to occur more often on days when we are out of balance. We can learn much about our own energies and the ways of energy in motion in the world if we ask ourselves how we were feeling just before a mishap or unpleasant encounter occurred. We might notice the positive side of this as well: the world seems kinder and safer when we live from an inner place of harmony, trust, peace. In the paradigm of conventional psychology, we would say that this is simply projection, that we are projecting onto the outer reality what we are feeling and this is coloring our perceptions of what is happening around us. "Beauty is in the eye of the beholder" and the converse is also true: if we are in a negative/pessimistic/chaotic/disorganized frame of mind we will see things in a negative way and notice the unpleasant occurrences rather than seeing the pleasant ones. And, according to the conventional paradigm, our internal chaos will cause us to behave in a disorganized way, causing more mishaps. This is an accurate and valid assessment of human behavior, in terms of the paradigm of science, of psychology. However, the energy paradigm is at work as well.

MAGICAL THINKING

What we have seen as pathology or immaturity may sometimes be an issue of mixing paradigms. Magical thinking is the name given in psychology for the behavior of young children who easily move into fantasy and imagination. Carried into adulthood, this pattern of thinking is called a "thought disorder," a form of pathology—mental illness or immaturity.

There is another way to understand "Magical thinking." It may not always be a sign of mental illness or developmental arrest; this childlike way of comprehending reality is reflective of the energy paradigm, a "right-brain" phenomenon. In the physical-material world, vampires don't really exist and suck blood, but "energy vampires" do exist, sucking subtle energies from others. This can be a dangerous drain to our well-being.

The notion of vampire behavior reflects the energy paradigm but vampires are described as concrete characters of the more dense physical-material reality. Another example of mixing paradigms is this: "Step on a crack, you'll break your mother's back," is merely a simple rhyme of childhood, impossible in the conventional paradigm of reality. Yet, it may reflect a child's affinity for the reality that all things are interconnected and that we affect each other energetically with our thought waves, not only with our actions.

"SUPERSTITIOUS"

When someone is said to be "superstitious" it is generally a derogatory comment. Perhaps someone who is superstitious is someone with an enhanced willingness to see the other dimension. It is often a situation or a matter of mixed paradigms.

LIMITLESSNESS AND ALAS, LIMITS

Limitlessness or boundlessness needs to be looked at in the light of the reality continuum. Limitless abundance is a quality which is of the Soul's capacity, the energy paradigm and spiritual world. Unlimited love exists in the realm of Spirit, Reality # 1. The reality of spaciousness IS love. We ought not limit our experience of living from our heart, from love.

However, in terms of Reality # 2, we need to limit many of our *behaviors* if we are to behave in self-loving, self-caring ways—such as saving money for our later years or limiting our consumption of unhealthy foods. The concept of "limits" applies to the physical-material reality. Boundaries are needed in the psychological realm. They provide us with a sense of safety and security in the more dense material realm of which conventional psychological speaks, Reality # 2. Limit setting is necessary and helpful to people; it may even empower them.

FOOLISH-LOOKING REALITY CONFUSION

Spiritual seekers may sing songs glorifying limit-lessness, which is fitting for the Quantum perspective of Reality # 1. There is a beautiful song which was frequently sung at New Age Conferences in the 80's which ended with the words, "We can all know everything without ever knowing why." This is true for the Oneness consciousness, but such limitlessness does not fit with the mind-set and perspective of the physical-material realm of Reality # 2. Many people throw themselves off-balance or appear foolish by applying the laws of one reality to the other reality or by not living from the place where the two Realities meet on the continuum. We need to have greater awareness of what degree of density of energy we are dealing with, and where on the reality continuum we are standing, to avoid this confusion. The chapter entitled, The Textures of The Two Realities, addresses the density issue.

A "REALISTIC" GOAL?

A woman who had just attended a weekend "transformational" seminar came to my office. She was greatly obese, had not dated in years and had a poor job history. Her transformational weekend had left her convinced that her possibilities were limitless and that by the end of the year she was going to be married and make a million dollars. I suspected that a paradigmatic mix-up might be occurring. A person with "issues" significant enough to have contributed to such a weight problem and a poor job history would probably not be self-loving enough and liberated enough from the prison of personality wounds to quickly create what she wanted. The heart's clarity can present itself to us in any moment, yet manifesting our dreams on the physical material plane seems to require a balanced psychological self as well as a conscious connection with our heart and Soul.

"YOU CAN HAVE IT ALL"

Many members of the New Age Movement believe that, since we create our own reality, we can "have it all." Perhaps we can, if we know and love ourselves profoundly enough to *allow* abundant blessings to continually come our way. People who truly love themselves unconditionally and let their heart be in a position of leadership DO create for themselves what they truly want. Perhaps my favorite thing about being a therapist is getting to see how people attract into their life what they want to the degree that they experience their wholeness. Most of us have to do a lot of work on our healing and growth before we can "get out of our own way" and "let the good times roll." To a large extent we can create good fortune for ourselves by growing in our capacity to trust Life.

There is more to be considered with this notion that "You can have it all." Looking at this from the perspective of mixed paradigms is useful. In the realm of the spaciousness of Reality #1, where everything is One interconnected whole, we each already DO have it all. We are each able to experience having it All whenever we have moments of enlightened awareness, whenever we are "one with everything." A newborn infant arrives into the world BEING it all, being in the Oneness consciousness. Enlightened masters have it all because their consciousness is expanded into the Superconscious Divine Mind of All That Is. Many years ago there were three psychotic patients at Ypsilanti State Hospital in Michigan. They each believed they were Christ. A psychiatrist decided to have them meet each other, no doubt for purposes of "reality testing." In terms of the paradigm of Reality #2, they were without ego functioning, having delusions of grandeur and were right where they should be—in a psychiatric hospital. According to Reality #2, they were wrong and crazy in thinking they were Christ and when they met two other people who also thought they were Christ something interesting would happen.

In terms of Reality #1, these three men who believed they were Christ could be seen as each experiencing the Oneness consciousness, the Christ Consciousness, like a newborn infant without the psychological selfhood, so there was truth in what they were claiming.[45] If we address these three psychiatric patients from the vantage point of Reality #3, the place where the Realities meet on the continuum between the polarities of Realities #1 and #2, we would say, with compassion, that indeed, these people were in need of psychiatric care because their "ego functioning" had broken down (or that they had no sense of psychological selfhood), they were not "in their bodies" and they were in touch with Oneness consciousness and it would be good to listen to what they had to say about being Christ. Such people often have valuable things to tell us about such a boundless, totally spacious state of consciousness. Far better, of course, to have a psychological self that is in balance, to embody much of our soul/Greater Self energy and to be fully human while also experiencing the heart and soul's Oneness Reality. Unified Selfhood is the place that is preferable to the "blissed out" , spacious place of total Oneness Consciousness where there is a feeling of "Being it All."

But is there a possibility that "we can have it all" in terms of physical-material desires, and the emotional-psychological longings?

ENTITLEMENT

To conventionally trained psychoanalytically oriented psychologists and therapists, a client would be seen as emotionally infantile and "narcissistically vulnerable" if the client believed, "You can have it all." A narcissistic attitude of "entitlement" would be noted by a Reality #2 based therapist. In the analytical, evaluative mode of the conventional medical model paradigm in its most extreme or polarized state, "entitlement" is seen as an infantile attitude. An attitude of "entitlement" often comes out of the needy/greedy primitive personality "part" of a person who has not had sufficient nurturing during the formative years of life.

On the other hand, if we are to view this issue from the open-hearted, open- minded posture somewhere on the Reality continuum closer to Reality #1, we might feel that those who are leading with their hearts and identifying with their Greater Selves as their primary identities, and therefore feeling like well-nurtured children of the Earth and the Heavens, would feel *worthy of abundant blessings* from Life. This is entitlement without the "attitude." Instead of a hostile attitude, a person with self love and connection with one's heart feels as deserving of what he or she wants as is every other child of the Universe. Such a person may believe from a place of wholesome emotional balance or wholeness, that he or she can have abundance. Oprah Winfrey has said that, "God can dream bigger dreams for you than you can dream for yourself[46]." If we are made in God's image, we may dream big dreams and feel receptive to good fortune.

In the mind set of thoroughly Reality #2 based therapists, it is impossible to consider that a person could have it all, and those who claimed to believe that they could "have it all" would be judged and evaluated as being demanding and immature.

From the place where the two different paradigms meet, Reality # 3, at the heartful point of balance and contact with our physical material body and world around our body, we realize that, to the extent that we listen to our heart's guidance, we will only "want" what is good for us. We only desire something that is wise and appropriate for us, given the big picture. The greedy-needy energy pattern left over from narcissistic wounds is not a factor when one is coming from the wellspring of one's heart, the place where personality polarities meet in psychological balance. From our heart's energy we can attract abundant blessings into our lives. From the Unified Self where healthy, balanced, emotionally mature "lesser" selfhood meets the Oneness of the soul Self, we can and DO create our heart's desires. Yet the physical material world *does* have it's limitations. Every thing in it is impermanent. From the triple vantage point of Reality #3 we realize this.

THE HEAVENLY WHOLE

We are accurate in terms of the energy paradigm when we say that an infant comes "straight from Heaven." The paradigm of The Whole, The One Interconnectedness of All, is the energy paradigm and the world of "primary process," the unconscious realm. It is the loose, spacious reality. An infant emerges into physical earthly experience already attuned to this One realm, equipped with energy sensitive, intuitive, random, impressionistic, sensual ways of knowing.

LOOSE ASSOCIATIONS

People with a preponderance of "right-brain" processing make associations or connections between things which would never occur to more logical, linear-minded people. The loose, flowing thoughts of the "right-brain" style have gotten a bad name in our Western culture where logic is greatly valued. "Loose associations" are even considered to be a symptom of serious mental illness. This "symptom" might be seen, instead, as an imbalance between the realms of the two brain hemispheres or too little attention to Reality #2, the more dense world of linear thinking.

PRIMARY PROCESS AND SECONDARY PROCESS AS PARTNERS

Modern psychology has taught us that primary process experience is to be replaced by secondary process experience as the ego develops in childhood. Rather than being *replaced by* secondary process, I believe that primary process is to be *balanced with* secondary process as we learn to honor both realities. The form and structure of secondary process makes life more predictable and manageable. We have been taught about the human condition in a developmental, sequential, secondary process way, which is only half the story.

ANIMALS, BIRDS PARTICIPATE IN THE DANCE

In the Reality of **One**ness everything works together. What appear to be accidental occurrences in nature have meaning in the realm of intermingling energies. Many clients have told me about birds and other animals appearing in their lives bringing them messages from the unseen dimension. Often birds will appear and tap on a window with their beak or sit on a window sill until an awareness of something new or loving arises within a person. In Reality #2 of analytical thinking, devoid of the sense of mystery which is the domain of Reality #1, one would say that these occurences which SEEM to have meaning are merely meanings we are attributing to or projecting upon things which occur. Certainly, this is true. But the perspective of the Reality of **One**ness is ALSO true. Animals and especially birds show up in our lives as gifts to us from the compassionate Heart of Heaven, the realm where the energy paradigm of Reality #1 and the physical-material paradigm of Reality #2 meet, and in that Reality #3 a miraculous, synchronistic event occurs. It is a loving universe. Just as God/

Goddess/All that Is can be called The Grand Container
Which Holds the Holy Whole, we could call the Divine
the Arch-Heart.

"HOPE IS THE THING WITH FEATHERS"[47]

Section III includes an amazing story of
synchronicity, a gift of a bird's appearance to a suffering family, a pigeon from the Arch-Heart, God.

CHAPTER FIFTEEN

OF SEPARATENESS AND ONENESS

When we look at our lives holistically, one of the most significant pairs of opposite perspectives to address is our separateness and our connectedness with All That Is. We have a separate individual identity as we also experience membership in the collective energy field.

SEPARATENESS HAPPENS

The experience of ourselves without a separate, individual identity does not for a functional, healthy human make, yet some spiritual teachers would encourage this. Spiritual knowledge and experience alone does not make a person complete; "oneness" without the development of a balanced ("**two**ness") personality is not enough if we are to be whole. As mentioned earlier, some people use spirituality as a defense, abandoning their body to avoid emotions that may be difficult to handle. Some find it helpful to go into an altered state during a crisis, re-creating the peace of "oneness" outside of the body. Yet without a substantial degree of psychological development accomplished, persons have to continually lift themselves out of emotional discomfort into a transcendent state over and over again. This is one way to get through life, but it is better to get to a state of personality selfhood, to trust oneself at the little/ lesser self level, as well as at the level of the Greater Self.

THE STORY OF SEPARATION-INDIVIDUATION

We all need to learn about differentiating ourselves from our families of origin, and we need to find support in doing our developmental work of achieving individual selfhood if we didn't do this sufficiently in our youth. I tell most clients the story of the separation-individuation process and the splitting defense which, ideally, is resolved into healthy psychological selfhood.[48] This linear, sequential developmental process is best put into story form making it something we can actually use in our self-understanding. For some, the story might be told succinctly with only the main steps and stages being mentioned. The shorter version of the story of separation-individuation could be described in this way:

THE SHORT TALE OF SEPARATION INTO SELF

As a newborn we come into the world with only the experience of soul; all our experience, in the beginning, is that of **one**ness. We experience the interconnected energy field of the Oneness Reality. We are not separate entities. Everything is us and we are everything. Baby and mother (or primary caretaker) are one. There is no differentiation between ourselves and other people, other objects. Soon we have the experience of duality as we experience our lives as having both pleasure and pain. Pleasure is freedom from hunger or any physical discomfort and sensual delights. Pain is hunger or any kind of discomfort. We project this experience of **two** onto ourselves/our mother. An infant continues to experience its mother and itself as one, however the newborn also experiences a splitting of experience into good (pleasure) and bad (pain or discomfort). We feel that we have a good self/mother (when our needs are gratified) and a bad self/mother (when our needs are not being met). We experience these opposite states as if we were two different people. This split continues until we begin to walk; it increases dramatically by the time we approach the chronological age of two.

THE STORY CONTINUES: THE TERRIBLE TWO'S

The era of "the terrible two's" gets its name because of the age of the child, not because of the duality of the earlier split in experience. In fact, it is around this chronological age that the good self and bad self come together as a psychologically whole self if we have been developing an emotionally healthy psyche. As a toddler we become a combination of some**one** experiencing **both** experiences which we enjoy and experiences we don't like. The splitting of bad self and good self, which is quite normal in infancy, moves into a sense of being one person with varied experiences. The toddler is then realizing that he/she is not the same entity as his/her mother. This is the birthing of separate selfhood. So energizing, so exhilarating is this experience to the toddler that (s)he demonstrates the sense of separateness from mother by saying, "NO! ME do it MY way!" The Terrible Two's phase of childhood is so named because of the mother's frustrating experience of oppositional behavior of the child. This child is experiencing the surprise of and delight in the newly discovered human experience of being separate from others. This is far more a human experience than a spiritual one.

If a mother has a healthy enough sense of self she can flow through this period, perhaps even enjoy the toddler's experience of discovering its lesser/little self, its separateness. However, if a mother feels threatened or annoyed with a child having a mind and will of its own, the child senses or feels that it is being bad (and fears losing its mother's love) if it moves away from the mother into an exploration of the environment and does things its own way. The discomfort a child has about a mother's response to his/her "individuation" varies greatly in degree.

SIGNIFICANCE OF THIS STAGE OF DEVELOPMENT

Most of the discomfort and dysfunction which bring us to therapy (or bring clients to us, if we are therapists)—behaviors such as addictions, compulsions, depressions, confusion, fear of losing oneself in a relationship, fear of success, fear of failure—have their origins in a compromised separation-individuation process. There are many variations on the theme of unresolved "separation" issues.

THE LONGER VERSION OF THE SEPARATION STORY, WITH PARADIGMATIC EMBELLISHMENTS

We come into the world from the Oneness Reality. We arrive, quite literally, as a "bundle from Heaven." As newborn infants we ARE the energy of Spirit, aliveness, creativity—after all, we've been doing nothing but growing, an intensely creative endeavor, in the womb. As babies we reflect Spirit—God, Goddess, All That Is. There is no cognition as adults know it, no thinking mind with judgment within a newborn baby. A newborn is Spirit, receptivity, the freshly embodied joy of aliveness. Is it any wonder that adults are in awe of a newborn? It isn't only because they are "cute and soft," although that is how we may describe a newborn when we are using the paradigm of concrete form, when we are experiencing life from our physical senses. Beyond the physical-material paradigm, being in the presence of a newborn stimulates our Soul, helps us sense the divine

Oneness as we remember our own connection to **One-**
ness. An infant's experience of reality is similar to our
experience of living life out of the energy paradigm,
consciously or unconsciously.

As a newborn experiencing the reality of **one**ness,
we also feel the excitement of experiencing physical
reality for the first time. It may not be the first time if
reincarnation is a fact of life, but it is always the first
time for this particular body. With the blessing or burden of incarnation or physical reality comes something
new: the o**pposite** conditions of pleasure and pain. Polarities, dualities, dichotomies. Patterns of physical and
emotional experience in partnership with their opposite energies. We very quickly get our first taste of moving from our primary, or most primitive experience—
that of Spirit and Oneness—when we experience the
world of **TWO**'s: we experience pleasure when our needs
are met—tummies full, diapers dry, arms around us—
and we experience pain when we are hungry, wet, wanting to be held.

Because as babies we know only unity consciousness and can't think of "things" which are "separate"
from other "things", we experience ourselves and everything else as **one**. We arrive in the world as a whole
creature with the sense that all is One. We are everything and no "thing." As newborn physical beings we
"know" that we are **one** with everything, but this is not
a fully-human enlightened state because we have not
yet experienced the rigors of Earthy life.

As infants we experience ourselves as being merged with and an appendage to our mother or primary caretaker. But our experience of the physical world is split into the duality of pleasure and pain. We begin to accumulate the human experience of duality. We feel we have two "separate" mothers. We have a good mother who represents pleasure when we are being fed and a bad mother who represents pain when we are hungry, etc. Being merged with our mother, we experience ourselves/our mother as good self or bad self. One or the other, not good and bad. We are split in two, and this "splitting" is a normal psychological experience in infancy. Gradually the world of form and (apparently) separate objects becomes more a part of our life as we begin to walk. Finally, as we approach the age of two, we come to a way of conceiving of ourselves which is quite different from our first experiences as a newborn. From the "all is one" paradigm we begin to move into the paradigm of experiencing a reality of more concrete, separate objects with form leading us to the exhilarating adventure that goes with the discovery of "I am separate!" I am not my mother—I am ME! Is it any wonder that a two-year old feels full of him/herself, oppositional, defiant? Saying, in essence, "No, Mother, I'd rather do it myself " takes more primitive forms in the toddler who simply says "No" many times a day. What he/she is saying, over and over, is "I am not you, Mommy, I am ME! This is really cool, and it is not how I had previously felt or known my world to be."

ADAM AND EVE

This first major "change of life" sounds much like the Biblical story of Adam and Eve eating the forbidden fruit (Chapter 3 of the Book of Genesis). Human beings begin to move away from their oneness with All That Is into the experience of the separateness of their more human condition when they exercise their own willfulness, the experience of a two-year old.

THE STORY CONTINUES

Depending on the reaction of the child's primary caretaker(s) to this feisty, defiant behavior, a child can end up with a nervous system which can stay calm and support him/her through future adventures into more autonomous living OR with a scrambled nervous system with irregularities, faulty wiring. A child with an insecure and anxious mother who may feel abandoned by her child's more independent behavior may "learn" and/or take on the energy of anxiety along with autonomy, adventurousness. Fear of failure, or the other side of that coin—fear of success, have their origins in an early childhood spent with a parent who didn't "find herself" (or himself) before becoming a parent. Very frequently the separation-individuation phase of development occurs in an environment which is less than toddler-friendly, less than ideal for showing a child that life can be a joyful adventure and that the world is reasonably safe for those who trust themselves.

ROOTS OF ADDICTIONS

Addictions have many of their roots in the anxiety a child may have taken on when he/she attempted to act upon his/her sense of separateness. Addictions develop when one unconsciously uses a substance or a compulsive pattern of behavior in an attempt to soothe oneself from anxiety about being/becoming separate.

Relationship fears also relate to this separation-individuation phase of development. These anxieties are twofold: *fear of abandonment* at one end of the polarity and at the other polarity, fear *of merging with another and therefore losing oneself* as a separate entity.

Mothers and caretakers who remember their **Oneness** have greater trust in themselves and the Life Process. From this realm it is easier to support, even enjoy a child's growing autonomy and experience of newfound separateness or the consciousness of the little/lesser (personality) self.

RECAPITULATION OF THE TERRIBLE TWO'S

Most people seem to get stuck, to one degree or another, in their separation- individuation process; age two is only its beginning . Adolescence brings with it an opportunity to re-assert the energy of the urge to emancipate oneself from attachment to parents, yet the sense of belonging or attachment does not disappear—it is transferred to the peer group. Some young people who are stuck in their linear development are very dependent and never able to leave home, or they may leave home but be as dependent on their friends and lovers as they were on their parents. Others go to the opposite end of the dependency continuum and are counter-dependent, rebellious. Neither person is free to be comfortably separate.

Often, an adolescent separating from psychological dependency on parents will become rude and critical of one or both parents. While parents may be hurt by what feels to them like un-loving, disrespectful behavior, parents might choose to rejoice in the individuation process which is occurring within their child. Teenagers who are stuck in their development may stifle their "attitude" and be more cooperative with their parents than is age-appropriate or typical for teenagers. Such teens may sacrifice some of their own energy for growing into themselves and use that energy instead to stifle their urge to emancipate themselves from early-childhood dependency patterns. These adolescents will protect their parents from the discomfort of living with a testy teenager by repressing their normal anger and frustration with parents. When adolescents are disagreeable to their mothers and/or fathers, it may be a reason to rejoice for it often indicates that the adolescent believes the mother and/or father is strong enough in his/her own selfhood to handle the teen's rebelliousness. Wise is the parent who sighs and says to herself, "This, too, is growth."

HEALTHY INTER-DEPENDENCE

Emotional health and maturity brings with it the experience of inter-dependence. When we arrive at a mature enough place in our separation-individuation process we can become aware that we are living in two realities: we are all in this together, each a participant in the **one**ness of intermingling energies. At the same time we also know that we can navigate through our earthly existence as physically separate individuals, leaning on friends and family, as needed. A truly healthy experience of the whole, the Holy **ONE**, comes with a healthy experience of individual, psychological selfhood; it is born out of the journey into and *through* separation- individuation.

CHAPTER SIXTEEN

POLARITIES

Polarities are unities of opposites. Energy in pairs. Paradoxical aspects of personhood, many kinds of polarities including primitive and narcissistic polarities, and "parts" work will be addressed in this chapter.

Every aspect of living in the world can be seen in the context of pairs of opposites. All that nature holds, all behavior falls somewhere along a continuum with opposite energies at each pole. And there are many of these continuums.

Observing our lives and life itself through this filter, this perspective of polarities, enhances balance. In terms of the energy paradigm, to deny or devalue one side will inevitably distort both.

FOR EVERYTHING THERE IS AN OPPOSITE

Polarities are actual energetic realities. Newton's laws say that for every action there is an equal and opposite reaction; what goes up must come down. The

Book of Ecclesiastes, 3: 1-8, tells of fourteen pairs of behavioral opposites (". . . . a time to speak and a time to remain silent," etc.) concluding with the comforting phrase ". . . . and a time for every purpose under Heaven." Acceptance of "all that is" represents wholesome spirituality.

THE SOUL HAS NO OPPOSITE

For everything there is an opposite. But the Soul is no "thing", it is the nothing/everything paradox. Our Soul or the realm of our wholeness has no opposite. The heart's harmony reflects our Soul's inherent balance. The heart is the place where opposite feelings meet in equilibrium and therefore, when we are centered in our heart, we are operating out of the **one**ness reality and there we find no duality or polarity process at work. The place where extreme opposites begin to "see" and accept each other is a place where miraculous transformation is possible. Most of the time, however, our garden variety humanness includes many paradoxes. These feel like contradictory energy patterns until we see them as complementary partners. This *human condition* may become more comfortable as we look at paradoxical behavior from some new angles.

THE HEART'S YIN AND YANG ARE NOT ENERGETICALLY POLARIZED

The heart's realm is both human and heavenly. It is where the best (or most balanced) of human qualities meet the Soul's heavenly connections. We may conceive of the quadrants of this chambered physical organ and spiritual center as being Yin and Yang and YinYang yet each quality of the heart is spacious, or Light-filled, that they are all energetically similar. The masculine and feminine principles of the heart's qualities are so harmonious within the heart that they are not opposites in need of reconciliation, as other polarities in the personality realm may be. Polarities in other aspects of our physical, emotional, mental and social lives are polarities which need to be reconciled in the heart. The heart's OWN energies are already reconciled with each other and so they are not true polarities, simply YinYang togetherness. Reality #3 is the heart's reality. Embodied spaciousness. The heart is the place where opposite patterns of our personhood and Spirit meet in unconditional acceptance and in an energy of balanced and peaceful accord. This is called Heaven.

POLARITIES AND JUDG*MENTAL*NESS

Polarities which we think of as neutral occur in nature. However, our human nature adds an unfortunate or challenging twist to personal polarities. From our judgmental vantage point, polarities can look "good" at one end of the pole and "bad" at the other. The severely wounded (and "borderline clients") may fear that the "bad" will contaminate the "good." Such people have trouble tolerating differences, internally and in their external relationships. These individuals may initially resist having the poles at the opposite ends of an intense polarity come into relationship with one another, until they grow accustomed to remembering that who and what they are, first and foremost, is a whole soul. Wholeness is what is good. Truth is good. Reality, which includes day and night, darkness and Light, is good. To be perfect is to be real, to notice the truth of one's experience, one's thoughts and feelings whatever they might be. Many people of Christian heritage have, in their childhood, heard the verse from the Bible that says, "Be ye perfect even as my Father in Heaven is perfect." To a child this word "perfect" usually means being well-behaved, or exhibiting whatever behavior was seen as good behavior in that child's particular family.

Most people readily enjoy observing polarities within themselves and in the world at large. The capacity for awareness is enhanced in the process of looking for these duos within ourselves. Health and balance can be found and physically felt by an individual when the pairs of poles meet as mutually respectful partners who need each other for a sense of completeness and harmony. It is time for the lion to lie down with the lamb.

PARADOX

Most have experienced the paradoxical experience of trying endlessly to change a behavior pattern, something unacceptable to ourselves. In rejecting this aspect of ourselves we are pushing against it, resisting it. It is an energetic fact of life that whatever we resist persists. What we are resisting and rejecting pushes back.

At the point when we say to ourselves, "I give up," there is a surprising shift into self-acceptance which brings one to a place of neutral balance, a place in the middle of the "Be like this. . . . Don't be like this" continuum. At the point when we give up the polarities of energy, the competing, conflicting forces come into balance and at that place where yes and no find themselves meeting in spaciousness, a liberation happens and one has access to the energy which allows us to shift into the new, moving forward toward our deep desires for ourselves.

Sometimes our minds play tricks with us. (*Often* our minds play tricks!) I recall a time, many years ago, when it was pointed out to me that I had a need to be perfect. Since the observation was shared with me with compassionate acceptance of my personality, I didn't resist this interpretation or description. I remember thinking, "O.K., I'll work on this, clear up this immature, overly-idealistic pattern of wanting to be perfect, and then I'll REALLY be perfect." I couldn't get beyond the need to "fix" myself or be fixed by another. I had not yet become aware of my ONEness perspective, myself as Soul, and I could not step out of my human condition, or turn the dial to a different channel of consciousness.

EMPTY / FULL

It is a paradox that when we *empty* ourselves, or bring extreme energies of our personality into balance or stillness, we feel *full*. Quieting the human condition, emptying ourselves of Reality #2, allows us to feel full, full of our Oneness, Reality #1, the sense of wholeness.

SURRENDER / LIBERATION

When we surrender who we are (as persons both afflicted and blessed with the human condition) to the ONEness of who we REALLY ARE, we are emancipated (in those moments) from our suffering. When we surrender to Spirit, asking to be obedient to our heart's truth and honest with ourselves in the deepest ways, we are liberated from the prison of personality into a freedom to flow with the natural unfolding of our life.

STRONG / WEAK POLARITY EMPOWERS

When we accept and embrace our vulnerability we are actually stronger and more *real* than when we believe we are invincible, feeling totally confident, forgetting that we have been vulnerable at times in the past (when we were insecure little children, at least) and we will be vulnerable at times in the future (as a 90 year old, for instance).

Seeing ourselves as a whole makes us strong because we are complete. Truth makes us strong and it is the truth that we are "a mixed bag" full of pairs of opposites and paradoxes. It is Truth that we are both weak and strong.

Reality supports us. Looking at our human nature through the widest lens possible makes us stronger, en-

ergetically, because we include more of our energies in
the picture. Day and night are Realities. If, during the
day we are not aware that the night is coming we are not
in touch with Reality and vice versa.

CREATIVE / DESTRUCTIVE POLARITY EMPOWERS

It is also the truth that we are both creative and destructive. We have the capacity for both. Owning our
darkness—our fear and the destructive personality patterns which fear gives rise to (or creates)—can actually
strengthen us as individuals. (Not everyone will accept
or need to accept this perspective). When we embrace
the creative-destructive polarity of our human nature
we are empowered. Contrasts serve us. Feeling our capacity to be a predator, for example, makes us feel very
strong. We feel even stronger when we realize that, although we have the capacity to feel rage and really hurt
or use someone, we choose to be kind. Our personal
power and self respect grows greater as we recognize
that we have the capability of being cruel and we choose
to bring that energy into partnership with our capacity
for kindness, choosing to behave with kindness. Those
opposite energies of cruelty and kindness meeting in
the middle do not neutralize each other. Rather than
neutralizing each other, there is a balance that *includes
the energy* of the partner at the opposite end of the pole.
Wholeness is greater than the sum of its parts.

TOO MUCH OF THE HUMAN CONDITION

Splitting or intense polarization of personality patterns need not be seen or experienced as pathology or immaturity. More wisely we can get to know our paradoxes and polarities as energy patterns destined to become partners!

One of the psychological defense mechanisms which conventional therapists speak of is "ego-splitting." It is considered to be a primitive defense because it has its origins in infancy. Ideally, ego-splitting which is considered to be normal in infancy and early childhood, gets resolved in early childhood. The origins of the ego-splitting process and it resolution through the experience of separation-individuation was discussed in an earlier chapter. If the primitive, intense emotions of the first few years of life are not resolved, the beginnings of healthy personality self-hood do not have a chance to develop. People who don't achieve selfhood in childhood or adolescence are in for a difficult and disappointing life experience. Such people are intensely split or ambivalent about many things.(It should be noted that some people may have a poorly functioning part of their actual brain that doesn't allow for easy transformation of ambivalence).

People displaying "ego-splitting" can be viewed as having what I re-frame as *too much of the human condition* and/or not enough awareness of their soul's **ONE**ness reality. Infants have a rich experience of their **one**ness and *also* experience their human condition in the intense experience of splitting. The **one**ness experience of the baby and toddler recedes into the background in later childhood. The intense splitting defense of the first two years of life is supposed to be reasonably resolved during the pre-school years. Rarely does this resolution happen as fully as it could, so most of us are left with noticeable polarity imbalances in our personality which get played out in our lives in many fascinating ways. Becoming conscious of these polarities and playing with their energy can be very enlightening.

FREUDIAN DEFENSE MECHANISMS

Sigmund Freud is the father of psychoanalysis who brought the power of the unconscious mind to the awareness of the world. One set of his discoveries were psychological mechanisms we all use, to some degree, to protect ourselves from psychic pain.

The psychological defense mechanisms as Sigmund Freud[49] labeled and described them are: projection, splitting, reaction formation, denial, undoing, identification and dissociation. Repression is the primary defense mechanism and the others are various forms repression takes. Like all naturally occurring phenomenon, these can be seen in the light of polarities of energy. (Note: The story of splitting is discussed from an "Object Relations" perspective, with the author's embellishments, in Chapter 15, Separateness and Oneness).

All of these defense mechanisms seem to place a person's awareness at only one end of the spectrum, the continuum of consciousness. Defensiveness comes out of the polarized energy of dense human nature without the balancing benefit of spaciousness or Spirit. When we feel psychologically safe and are connected to our Oneness we are unafraid and do not need to defend ourselves.

For example, projection, which is the defense mechanism of attributing to another something you don't accept in yourself, is the polarity of self/other, or "it isn't me, it is them." Consider the television evangelists who passionately preach on the evil of illicit sexual behavior only to succumb to those temptations in their own lives. Projection is also something which we all do, in a less intense way, a great deal of the time. For, how can we not see in another, or attribute to another, what is part of ourselves if we are all One? The degree of judgment or density of energy will show how much a person is using defense mechanisms. The amount of fear and anxiety in our human nature dictates whether we polarize our energy and therefore deny that we also have the characteristic in question. Paranoid people are prisoners of their personality and also of faulty wiring in their nervous system and bio-chemistry. (It may not be necessary to know which came first, the fear or the dysfunctional brain, for they each impact on each other in a feedback loop). People with a well-endowed paranoid "part" (i.e., strongly energized, extremely polarized) are held captive by fear. Many, if not most people, have a paranoid "part" within their personality nature. When this pattern of paranoia is extreme the projection becomes more intense, more noticeable. It is easy to know what a very paranoid person is thinking because they will attribute it to the others outside themselves and deny that it is an aspect of themselves. It is amazing the degree to which frightened people reveal their secrets to others. Those individuals who are most invested in hiding their own truth from themselves will reveal it to others by what they "project"onto others. We are no longer using projection in the clinical sense when what we project onto another is also owned as a characteristic we have within our own human nature (Reality #2) and in our Oneness nature where we are all aspects of the Whole (Reality #1). When we are connected with our Oneness there is so much unconditional love present that fear cannot exist to the degree that paranoia requires for its fuel. People who are operating primarily out of the spaciousness of self-acceptance and compassion for all do not use projection defensively or divisively. They use it in a creative and embracing way; it is love-based projection to say "we are all one, I am you and you are me." Another of Freud's defense mechanisms is "reaction formation." This is a process in which behavior or attitudes emerge that are the opposites of the impulses to which the person is reacting, an obvious energy polarization. Freud taught that behind every fear there is a wish. This is clearly a statement about polarities of energy. When we are conscious or aware that we are doing the opposite of what we want to be doing we are not employing reaction formation as a defense mechanism.

Undoing—doing the opposite of what one has previously done (it is a sort of atonement maneuver)—is another obvious polarity.

Identification, like projection, is related to the self/other polarity, for in this defense of taking on characteristics of someone we admire we are saying to ourselves, "I don't want to be like me, I want to be like you."

Denial (simply feeling something did not occur, like when we first hear shocking news of a loved one's death) is of the "no, it didn't happen/yes, it happened polarity." In modern usage, denial can mean disavowal of thoughts or feelings that we cannot accept in ourselves; this would be of the "it can't be me/it is me polarity." A "little ditty" about denial is as follows:

Denial.
I loathe the liar that you are,
Distorting, bending Truth
Is unacceptable.
Yet, without your style
Of dealing with reality
How would we handle shock,
Unspeakable surprises
Much too harsh for any nervous system?
You are a necessary evil.
Not ONLY dark, dishonest
You're a necessary good
Defense as well;
You get us through
This life.
We do
Need you
At times,
Denial.

Another "defense mechanism" is dissociation. It can be seen as the polarity of being *out of touch* with body/ *in touch* with body.

Repression is a defensive process which is included in all the others. It is simply burying one end of a polarity in the unconscious.

It is tempting to consider much more of Freud's material in the light of polarity theory, but that is not the purpose of this chapter or book.

FREUD AND ENERGY BALANCING

Freud gave us a developmental theory of human energy based on biology. He spoke of opposites balancing each other, compensating energies or urges. For example, he said that a mother's *extreme* overprotectiveness could be a compensation for a wish in the unconscious of the mother that the child did not exist.

Psychoanalytic teachings seem to convey the idea that the primitive feelings in the unconscious are more true or real than the feelings coming from the conscious mind. In other words, the implication is that the mother's wish that her child not exist may be seen as more true or more primary, than the fear that something might happen to the child.

It seems to be more "realistic" to say that both of these energies (fear of losing the child who the mother is very attached to, and the wish to be free of the responsibility of motherhood) are equally real or true in a highly energetically polarized mother.

PSYCHIC MECHANISMS AND ENERGIES SEEKING THEIR PARTNERS

It should be noted here that if a person's life is comfortable, there is no need to go in search of the darker side of a pair of opposite energy patterns. When our lives are working rather well we are probably in rather good balance. Why spend a lot of time looking for polarities? But if and when there is any strong feeling of discomfort or imbalance in our lives, looking for polarities and holding the opposites together can yield benefits.

People who are highly polarized in their internal energies are people who use the splitting mechanism to a large degree. Often these people will notice that shortly after something very "good" happens in their lives, something equally "bad" will happen. Or vice versa. This can be seen in terms of one or several of the above mentioned defense mechanism of the psyche and it can also be seen in terms of energies seeking their opposite partner for balance.

DANIEL LEVINSON'S POLARITIES

Daniel Levinson's (1978) Yale University research[50] on adult development presented four polarities which all adults must face:

```
Dependent ---------------------------------- Independent
Young ------------------------------------------------- Old
Male ------------------------------------------------ Female
Creative ------------------------------------- Destructive
```

CARL G. JUNG, THE MEYERS-BRIGGS TEST AND OPPOSITES

Carl Jung, the inspired Swiss psychiatrist who was a student of Sigmund Freud, taught that for everything that is true the opposite is also true.

The Meyers-Briggs personality inventory which is based on Jungian theory assesses individuals in the light of four polarities. They are:

```
extroversion (feels pulled outward) ----- introversion(feels pushed inward)
sensing (looks at specific pieces and parts) -- intuition (looks at patterns)
thinking (decides with head) ----------------- feeling(decides with heart)
judging(likes structure) ------------------- perceiving(goes with the flow)
```

These are just a few ways for describing this particular typology. It is well worth exploring in greater depth for it encourages tolerance and appreciation of differences.

This system is not a test for pathology, for discovering what is "wrong" with the test taker. The Meyers-

Briggs inventory assesses one's *preferences,* with acceptance. In general, I don't care much for schema which can reduce a person's identity from Oneness consciousness to a category. However, there is a place for systems which help a person know and accept their own innate personality proclivities, preferred tendencies. Sometimes it is a comfort for a person to be able to say to herself something somewhat specific about her human identity, and I could say "I'm an ENFP on the Meyer's Briggs typology and I'm a Gemini and, Numerology-wise, I'm a 7, and I have my very own unique social security number and more passwords than I can begin to remember." These identities help us to keep track of ourselves and our humanness. It is better to identify with these styles and preferences than with our wounds, our symptoms or pathologies. Specific identities are of Reality #2. They are far more concrete and specific than our Reality #1 sense of Soul can sometimes feel for at the spacious level we are only everything/nothing. At the most expanded level of Soul we are wholeness and **ONE** with everything.

HEINZ KOHUT

An entire theory of narcissism was created when psychoanalyst Heinz Kohut[51] focused on one polarity. He addressed simply the "narcissistic" polarity, which he described as having "grandiosity"at one pole and "idealization"on the other (1971). Lionel Corbett M.D., a Jungian Analyst who presented a workshop in Chicago in 1988 comparing Jung and Kohut, spoke of this grandiosity/idealization polarity of narcissistic development as a "Marvelous me!"/"Wonderful you!"[52] polarity. A diagrammatic description of Kohut's theory, as I have depicted it, can be found in Appendix A.

SIMPLY O.K.

Feeling the calmness of centeredness, the balance point of these polarities, was presented in the simply sober title of the immensely useful self-help book of the 70's, *I'M O.K., YOU'RE O.K.* by Thomas A. Harris.[53] This is neither an inflated, grandiose high nor a feeling of being less than another.

PRIMITIVE POLARITIES

Many polarities have their mature and immature forms. I refer to the immature energy patterns as Primitive Polarities. Both sides of the coins of these primitive polarities are equally intense, as is the case with all energies in polarity. With Primitive Polarities, however, both poles are disconnected from awareness of the Greater Self or Soul and so they are both equally dense (contracted energies). Commonly experienced polarities which I have noticed in narcissisticly vulnerable individuals who were deeply hurt or poorly nurtured in the first few years of life are:

Hurt .... Enraged

Wanting to Merge (merger hungry) .... Rejecting, abandoning

Self hating .... Envious (of people with Self-love)

Intensely ambitious .... Self-defeating, shooting self in the foot

Highly creative .... Self-destructive

Intensely self-controlled or inhibited .... Intense affect or emotions

Depressed mood .... Inflated, high mood

Needy .... Very giving (in order to get something; manipulative)

Wants to be invisible (feels ashamed) .... Exhibitionistic, highly visible

Perfectionistic .... Feeling totally worthless

Idealizing another .... Devaluing oneself

Devaluing of another .... Arrogant, grandiose about oneself

All-Powerful, Controlling .... Powerless, fragile

𝒫olarities Sharing a See-Saw

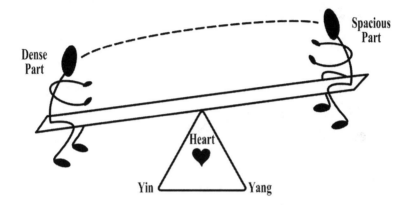

"Parts" of a polarity can sit opposite each other on a see-saw, with great benefit. I have found it useful to take the particular polarities of the deeply wounded or "narcissistically vulnerable" client and have them imagine half of the pair (for example, the enraged child part of the personality) on one end of the pole and the other half of the duo (its partner, the deeply hurt part) on the other end of the see-saw. Reminding the client that these "parts" are **only energy** (which makes them less formidable) I then ask the client to have these "parts " look in each other's eyes, asking them to **exchange a little energy with each other.** I inform them that neither part will disappear; they will both retain their identities. The more aggressive part, which is of the male principle, becomes less intensively aggressive while the opposite energy which is more passive or vulnerable becomes stronger. Meanwhile the neutral awareness of the Greater Self or Soul is lending its profound healing energy to the process.

This exercise can also be done with polarities with only one dense partner. One seat on the see-saw may be occupied by the more expanded, spacious partner and the other may be dense. It is always fascinating to notice that the dense, contracted partner becomes less extreme as it takes in some spaciousness and light from the opposite partner but the spacious partner does not become more dense. This is a mystery.

Imagining that this see-saw is located in a beautiful meadow brings all the energies of nature into play with this balancing process.

Notice that the fulcrum point of the see-saw is the triangle, the trinity with the heart at the center point of the see saw; it is the place where opposites meet and are accepted. A fulcrum point is defined as a support or point of rest. Indeed, the heart is that.

MEETING PLACES

Beyond the comfortable co-existence that the partnered energies achieve through this awareness, something new may be born out of this union of opposites. Another example would be where the energies of infantile-dependency meet rebelliousness (counter-dependency) and healthy assertiveness and interdependence emerges. For example, the energy of optimism may meet its partner named pessimism and, at the point of their encounter, what is born out of the partnership is HOPE, "ultimate reality," peace. The energy of hope may arise. Another example would be where the polarity of excitement and depression meet there will emerge the energy of centered power, gentle joy and peace. Bi-polar clients have the opportunity to balance their energies in this way, as persons with intense affect get used to witnessing their polarities from their awareness center the mood problems becomes less significant.

LIGHT BAR SEE-SAW

I often use a light-bar and ear phones which beep in one ear and then the other, back and forth, as the light moves back and forth on the light bar. This is part of Eye Movement Desensitization and Reprocessing Therapy. Frequently I suggest that a client focus on a disturbing feeling he/she might be having and "process" it until it diminishes. After that regular use of EMDR is done for a while, subduing the feeling, I will have the client put that feeling, or the memory of it, on one end of the light bar and the opposite feeling on the other end of the light bar. The moving light and beeping sound moves those opposite energy patterns back and forth as I suggest that these opposite energies could be partners, balancing each other and that the heart may be the place where those opposites meet in mutual respect.

ON THE OTHER HAND, LITERALLY

An astute mother called me to make an appointment for a family therapy session with her pre-school son who had begun bed-wetting, after having been toilet trained for quite a while. The woman wanted me to do Eye Movement Desensitization and Reprocessing[54] with her son because it had been so helpful to many members of her extended family. The mother felt he might be anxious about something and wasn't sure what the anxiety could be about because her marriage and the careers of both this mother and her husband were going very well and family life in general was good. I knew her as a woman who was extremely aware and honest with herself and others. Shortly before this particular appointment, the 3 ½ year old boy had said to his mother, "You make me nervous." During the mother-son session, the strong-willed, highly expressive little boy was being a bit of a tyrant and seemed to have more power in the family than anyone else. He had tantrums until he eventually got his way. Frequently his parents gave in. He said to me, "I don't like it when my Mom is the boss of me." This was undoubtably true, but I sensed that the opposite was also true and that for this boy to have so much power in his family was actually a cause of stress for him and the rest of the family as well. He wanted to be contained, and yet he didn't want to be contained.

He was very articulate for his young age and we talked about how it felt for him to be the boss of himself at times and how it felt when his parents were in charge, helping him, teaching him things, helping him learn to grow up. Since he did not want to do the EMDR process, I suggested to him that he do this: "When you get upset put one hand out in front of you and say to your-self, 'On the one hand I want to be the boss of myself.' Then put the other hand out and say to yourself, 'On the other hand I want my Mom to take care of me some-times and be the boss.' Then put your hands together like you're saying a prayer and cross your fingers and then put your thumbs out and tap on your heart with your thumbs. Ask your heart to wake up and feel the love inside and ask your heart to help you feel better." This might be something we can all do to bring our vari-ous personality polarities into a partnership.

PARTS WORK

Roberto Assiagoli's "Psychosynthesis"[55] was my first introduction to "parts work" in 1981. The Italian psychoanalyst had been one of Freud's students and, like Jung, believed we have a Soul and a number of "sub-personalities." These are the various identities inside of each of us.

Hal Stone and Sidra Winkleman were influenced by Assiagoli's work as well as Jungian and Gestalt Psychology. They developed a type of therapy called Voice Dialogue which brings personality "parts" into dialogue with each other. Hal Stone speaks from the paradigm of energy and, in a New Directions Video, said he defined God, simply, as energy.[56] Many of my colleagues who were spiritual seekers introduced me to Voice Dialogue because they were finding it so effective in their own personal growth and healing.

Another kind of "parts work" was developed by Sandra Watanabe called "Cast of Characters" work and I was exposed to her work through the Family Institute.

Another family therapist, Richard C. Schwartz, integrated the perspective of sub-personalities or personality "parts" into his vast knowledge and expertise in Family Systems Therapy and created a model called Internal Family Systems Therapy. In 1992, I happened upon a workshop on I.F.S. led by Dick Schwartz at an Alumni Conference of the Family Institute of Chicago where I was also presenting a workshop; mine was about working with The New Age client by teaching them about living in two realities in a balanced way. Much of what I heard in the I.F.S. model rang true for me. I soon became part of a group of therapists led by Dick Schwartz, so we could practice using his Internal Family Systems Therapy.[57] Of great benefit to my clients and to me personally has been the "empty room technique" of the IFS Model (although I prefer to suggest a round, fenced in outdoor area in the sunshine instead of a room with corners). I also appreciate the categorization of "parts" into "exile parts"and "managers." The Self which is described in the IFS model seemed too concrete for me and so were the "parts." I thought of these more as energy. With regard to polarization, I am in agreement with the I.F.S. model where it states that trauma leads to a polarization between "exiled parts" and those other "parts" that are trying to manage the internal system.

"Parts work" is very useful with ourselves and with clients, although it can keep us "in our heads" with analysis and therefore my preference is to work with "parts" as bodily felt "energies." I don't see the personality as a group of "parts" as much as energetic patterns, *always in polarity*, pairs of opposite yet equally intense energies seeking partnership with one another. Many clinicians who do "parts work" put too much attention on the parts of the personality and this may distract clinician and client alike from the essential wholeness, the dimension that needs to be continually highlighted.

Internal Family Systems Therapy (I.F.S). is a wonderfully helpful model but it acknowledges only personality parts and the Self. I feel a personality level self
also exists.

SEEKING THE SELF OF PERSONALITY, AS WELL AS KNOWING SOUL

Perhaps my desire for a very cohesive personality
level self was merely a materialistic desire which became passionate for me in the early 70's. From the time
I studied Object Relations Theory and Kohut's Self-Psychology, I simply wanted to possess a self as described
from those perspectives. I wanted every kind of self.
For many people it may suffice to live from one's Greater
Self/Soul or heart's perspective without giving much
thought to the psychological level of self. That poses
no problem if one's extreme energies of personality
polarities do not occlude the spaciousness of Soul/
Greater Self. If others wish to "work on" developing a
healthy "lesser self" as I desired, the perspective of the
Unified Theory of the Self of this book can lead the
way to wholeness. When one finds the place of balance
of the polarities of the lesser self, The Greater Self simply shows up at the same time.

Seeking and finally finding a healthy degree of co-
herence of my more human, small "s" self has been important to me because I have seen highly spiritual and
expanded people without much of a psychological self.
Many individuals have easy access to the "at one with

everything" experience of the Soul; actually our Greater Self is never apart from us: it is who we ARE. Yet, if cohesion of lesser self level through partnership of all of our "parts" has not been achieved, a person's presence is neither powerful nor effective in the world.

STORY OF NOAH'S ARK ANEW

Stimulated by the Internal Family Systems group of therapists, I discovered a new "take" on an old story inside my head during a church service when the minister was preaching about Noah. Perhaps I could have paid attention, but the energies of my imagination were more compelling; I went within. This is, more or less, what I found:

Noah was directed/guided by God/Goddess, The Great Spirit, The SuperSelf, to build an ark. Without allowing the resistant "part" or pattern of his personality to interfere, he decided to *just do it*, by calling into service the energies of his assertive, managerial "part" or pattern of energy which allowed him to get the job done. Earlier, Noah had been sensible enough to choose to surrender to the leadership of the SuperSelf, God/Goddess/All That Is. Goodness only knows what he had gone through earlier in life for Noah to have finally made that decision, yield to the urge to surrender and allow The Spirit to run the show. He'd probably spent a fortune on therapy, sessions with his shaman, buying herbs, etc.

The Ark was constructed and Noah decided to call it his Self, honoring and reflecting the SuperArk. He welcomed all the other "parts" or energies of his personality on board. Their polar opposite parts were included, nobody was exiled; this kept everything in balance. It was years later that Issac Newton noticed that every action had an equal and opposite reaction, which made polarities, i.e., parts and their opposites, official—indeed, even respectable. Every energy has an equal and opposite, complementary energy; Chinese medicine, the YinYang perspective, shows us this for sure.

I've heard that Noah prayed for a wife and God sent him Grace. She surely must have been on board as well.

The animals (sometimes appearing in our dreams as symbols of our instinctual, emotional energies) were safe within the Ark, called Greater Self. It contained them, held the many partners, energy patterns two by two, in harmony. Thank Goodness, for soon it rained excessively. Flooding was all around—unparalleled stress. But the Ark warmly embraced and contained Noah and all his personality polarities and held them together. Nobody even got seasick.

SuperArk presented a rainbow overhead and said, "NOW HEAR THIS: YOU ARE PROMISE when you REALIZE you have a Self which holds and keeps all of your pairs of personality energies cozy and afloat on whatever the high seas of life may bring." The many and varied pairs of male and female personality patterns, as we become more aware and let them become known to us—welcoming them on board, counting and naming them—all are kept safe and protected no matter what the high seas of life may bring. Unless, of course, a mutiny occurs. At times like that an extreme personality part which is out of relationship with the Greater Self can create great chaos.

IMAGINE ENCOUNTERS OF INNER MALE AND FEMALE PATTERNS

From Energy Medicine training I have learned to have clients bring the image of their inner male energies into an encounter with their inner female energies. This may bring to light aspects of their parent's relationship with each other, for we internalize our mother and father's relationship within our own psyche. For those who enjoy visualization exercises or active imagination, it can be revealing and even fun to have the image of our inner male dancing to music, and then "see" or sense the inner female dancing the dance of the feminine energies and then have them dance together.

Looking at the inner male-female polarity may also reveal one's own degree of the splitting defense in need of resolution.

POLARITIES IN DREAM WORK

Once we begin to think in terms of polarities of energy, we notice that our dreams are full of these pairs of energy patterns seeking to come into our conscious awareness. A whole book could be written with examples of my client's dreams, the male and female aspects of themselves moving toward partnership with one another. Many variations on this theme emerge in dreams. It is often easier to see these polarities seeking their partner in the dreams of someone we know well, than it is to see them in our own dreams. As we honor these polarities more in our daily living we will be able to notice them more easily in our dreams, and it is very heartening to see how deeply our psyche wants us to experience the balance of our energies.

ZIPPER IMAGE

A client went through a period of time when she was continually dreaming of zippers. This recurring image came from the psyche of a client who was hard at work (and softly, too) on bringing her inner male and inner female (which are called "animas and anima," respectively in Jungian psychology) into a healthy, balanced relationship with each other. (My apologies to Freud who might have had another interpretation of the image!) A zipper is an excellent symbol of two separate sides dove-tailing into one another, each retaining its own yin and yang zipper teeth qualities yet coming together into a cooperative partnership which is stronger than the sum of its parts.

A DREAM OF COINS

A client in her late 50's had persevered through a very painful life. She brought great courage to a life of bleakness. Her childhood contained little nurturing, abuse and tragedy including the discovery that her father had hung himself. As an adult she had always wanted children and, tragically, her only pregnancy had ended with a still-born baby. She was twice divorced and single, working in a job which was not very gratifying and struggling with low grade depression (and unfortunately she resisted the option of taking anti-depressants). She wanted to overcome her need to please others, for this need was out of balance with her own self-care. And she wanted to let go of her training to be "nice" without becoming the polar opposite, " a bitch." (Our culture has presented women with only these two polarized options with little in-between). Essentially, her psyche was longing for a marriage of her inner feminine, Yin (cooperative, yielding) side with her inner male, Yang (competitive, forceful) side which could bring her to a place of healthy assertiveness with kindness and caring for others. Most of her life experience had been painful. It had left her inner feminine side wounded and frightened, and she adapted to this by developing a strong energy pattern of "nice girl" and "pleaser." Her inner male side had become distorted during her woundings so that when it emerged, it could be belligerent.

A blessing had recently occurred in her life. Her niece had just had a baby and my client was asked to be the Godmother. With this blessing from Heaven, new energy flowed into my client, energy for her deepening integration. She had a dream about foreign coins. She was simply counting many foreign coins. This dream image suggested a coming together of male and female energies, the two sided coins integrating. Foreign people appearing in dreams generally represent disowned parts of oneself, aspects of one's personality that are ready to come into awareness. Foreign coins would represent, for this woman, the integration of two masculine and feminine sides of herself, and seeing clearly these sides which had been unknown to her. This client was on the verge of "owning" her inner male energies. And she had a sense of a whole new era of her life about to begin. She sensed, intuitively, that a good mate was "out there for me somewhere, we just have to meet." (And as it is internally, so it will be externally). She was beginning to feel emotional and spiritual wealth in her life and was moving into the experience of her wholeness.

SUGGESTING POLAR OPPOSITE QUALITIES

When I hypnotize clients I help them deepen their trance state by having them imagine that they are going down a staircase, each step taking themselves into a deeper level of relaxation. I suggest that they imagine the sensation of a *smooth*, sturdy banister beneath one hand and *rough* wool carpet under bare feet and between the toes during the descent on the stairs. As I do this, I mention that these opposite textures are balancing each other. In "right brain" states such as hypnosis and dreams, symbols of opposite textures can serve to enhance balance.

SO WHAT?

Here is a fun paradox: What's So?/ So What?[58] For several months I saw a client who had experienced many hardships in her life including widowhood at a fairly young age followed by breast cancer. Her oncologist referred her to me because she was depressed. When she got to a place of reasonably consistent well-being we decided to wrap up our work together. I had used many different treatment modalities with her and was feeling good about my various "skills" which I felt had helped her. In the last session I asked, of all the things we had done in therapy what had she found most helpful. To my surprise she said, "The time you taught me to say, 'So what?'"

The other side of the coin of what is so, or what is true in your life, is simply, "So what?" We can say this to ourselves when what is so is uncomfortable. It can help us remember to let go of unpleasant feelings once we have felt and acknowledged the feelings. Most of us hang on to many things that happen for too long a time when we could choose to simply let them go and feel better.

THE SIMPLE PRAYER OF SAINT FRANCIS

A great and Earth loving saint left us with a prayer which is about polarities. It admonishes us to balancing energies in the world and to make dense energy more expanded, more spacious by choosing to let the energy of our hearts flow freely. This is shared in Chapter 20, "Honoring Heaven and Earth."

POLARITIES—FROM DENSE TO EXPANSIVE

Looking at pairs of opposites simply as energy makes it easier to be non- judgmental. Many years ago a gifted Hana Kane Bodyworker, Joseph Mina,[59] with whom I had several healing sessions, shared with me his practice of looking at opposites moving from the most dense energy pattern to the most expansive. Here they are:

Guilt --- Gratitude

Fear -- Love

Worry -- Wonder

Revenge ------------------------------------- Revelation

Impatience --------------------------------- Being Present

Powerless --- Powerful

Procrastination --------------------------- Determination

Lack of support -------------------------- Total support

Abuse --- Nurturing

Blame --- Blessing

Shame --- Sharing

Sabotage ------------------------------------- Fulfillment

Pain -- Pleasure

Frustration -- Fun

Reluctance ---------------------------------- Movement

Bitterness ------------------------------------- Sweetness

Trying --- Being

Need --- Want

By simply noticing, or bringing the transformative power of awareness to any of the energies on the left one moves toward the more expansive polar opposite energy on the right hand column.

This is an another enlightening way to look at polarities. It is a perspective that can help us balance the two paradigms, the continuum of energy along the Reality polarity between Reality #1 and #2. By observing the degree of spaciousness in our experience we may move more easily into fullness of heart, a gracious, spacious condition.

SOCIO-ECONOMIC POLARITIES

As more people experience the benefit of getting to know and accept the polarities of their inner world and have their polarities meet in the middle for greatest health, there may one day be a desire for the family of our outer world to have the extremely wealthy and extremely impoverished sisters and brothers come together and share their resources, balancing the energies of material resources with each other. A sociological study done a few years ago by Phillip M. Harter, M.D. at Stanford University School of Medicine showed that 6% of the world's people possess 59% of the entire world's wealth, and 50% of the human race suffers from malnutrition. The shock of these statistics may awaken a desire for, and vision of, balance and justice among the Earth's family members. This vision may be the delusion of a social worker, but it is a one in which we might all engage thereby creating a stronger energetic thought field out of which the physical reality can emerge.

PITHY POLARITIES

Harry Truman said, "A pessimist is one who makes difficulties of his opportunities, and an optimist is one who makes opportunities of his difficulties."

A "double-negative" polarity in a poem by William Butler Yeats: "The best lack all conviction, while the worst are full of passionate intensity."[60]

On the other hand, Mother Ann of the Shaker Community said these words: "Do all of your work as though you were going to die tomorrow and yet as through you were going to live 100 years."

ONLY AN IDEAL

Balancing the polarities in our lives by honoring internal and external opposites is only an ideal. Yet, it is an ideal which can move us closer to our heart's realm as we play with it. Simply observing ourselves for imbalances, such as too much work and not enough play or too much inner life and not enough outer life lived in connection with others, is something which is "common sense." However commonsensical they may be, we serve ourselves and others well when we remember to observe our lives for these imbalances. Common sense refers to the deeper inner knowing, the "sense" or realization that something is true for ourselves and others.

Just as *quieting the thinking* mind with meditation is something that enhances physical health, *quieting our personality* by balancing the opposites within us can bring us greater harmony.

We are all unique creatures and each of us moves in and out of balance in a variety of ways continually. We need each other's energy to balance our own at times. My son has told me that I "need a techno-slave," a mate who could free me of technological angst so I could use my energy to write poetry. Perhaps my creative energies would contribute to the balance within such a mate. Yet it is good for my personal balance to gain at least small amount of mastery of things mechanical, and it would serve someone opposite in his inclinations to open to his "right-brain" domain. Honoring the opposites and balancing the polarities within and without is a perspective that may eventually bring greater equilibrium and peace to the planet; for as we find it within ourselves, our heart feels the desire for peace and justice for all others as well. When we are in love, we want others to be in love as well. So it is with bringing our own polarities into our heart.

CHAPTER SEVENTEEN

FAMILY ENERGY SYSTEMS

Family Systems Therapy has seemed to me to be a far more enlightened type of therapy than many forms of psychotherapy.

VIRGINIA SATIR, SPIRITED MOTHER OF FAMILY THERAPY

One of the founders of this field, indeed the "mother" of Family Systems Therapy, is Virginia Satir[61]. This warm, playful and sensitive social worker was the first teacher of Family Systems Therapy who seemed to have a feel for the energetics of relationships, before the new Energy Paradigm had begun to emerge. She had brilliant insights into family dynamics and made a significant contribution to the helping professions as a whole. Insights with heart. Spirituality seemed obvious in her work. I spoke with her at a workshop she was leading and mentioned that she seemed to have a sense of mystery and Spirit included her work. She replied with a wonderful image. She said:

BE LIKE A TREE

"We need to be like a tree." Virginia Satir, an earthy individual, added essentially that we need to: 1) be rooted in the Earth; 2) expand our consciousness, reaching toward the Light of the Heavens like the tree's leaves; and 3) reach out to others for connection, like the branches of a tree. We may remember Dr. Satir's image as a tree trinity.

FAMILY CONNECTION

Family Systems Therapy comes closer to a partnering of paradigms than most therapeutic models because it looks at the interconnectedness of family members and points to the fact that when one member of a family system changes, the whole system changes and everyone is effected in some way. However, these dynamics are most often spoken of in the concrete behavioral terms of the conventional scientific paradigm of Reality #2.

The field of Family Systems has not yet actually embraced the Energy Paradigm. I propose that a new field of study emerge that we could call Family Energy Systems and a new model of marriage and family counseling be born out of this Family Energy Systems Theory.

Having been trained in Family Systems Therapy and also in Energy Medicine, I have found myself looking at couples and families with one eye on the dynamics of the behavior and another eye attuned to the ways of energy. A sense of the whole system of family energies seems to come very quickly when we look for this energetic dance. This is a most fascinating and enlivening way to understand and help couples and families. It is also a very comfortable, even fun way for couples and families to think about their interactions. People seem to get much less defensive (i.e., energetically contracted) when we speak in terms of the energy each person may be carrying.

LIKE ATTRACTS LIKE *AND* OPPOSITES ATTRACT

An aspect of the previously mysterious ways of energy in relationships is the issue of attractions among people. *Like attracts like* is a principle and a processes which occurs in the reality of the Energy Paradigm. Indeed, "Birds of a feather flock together" and other phrases like "It takes one to know one," show that on intuitive level we already have known this rule of the system of subtle energies.

The mental and emotional vibrations we emit will attract from our environment similar vibrations of energy; a metaphysical law of attraction is at work, a matching of inner and outer energies. Parents have good reason to be alarmed when their children want to hang out with friends who are miserable little people. The people who we consciously or unconsciously pick to play with say a great deal about how we are feeling about ourselves at a particular time.

PARENTS DILEMMA

Many parents who try to steer their child away from what they feel is "a negative influence" will notice that another miserable child will take his or her place. The tendency for an unhappy or angry child to attract a playmate with negativity and internal chaos is likely to continue until the child begins to feel better about him/herself and moves into a different chapter of life where he/she carries a more loving vibration of energy. We can assess what state a person is in, energetically, by who that person is magnetizing to him/herself.

EQUAL IN INTENSITY AND WOUNDEDNESS

In my observations of many clients, it appears that persons emitting energies of equal *intensity* and *woundedness* (usually unconscious) are magnetized to each other. We can learn a great deal about ourselves by noticing who has come into our life. Often people become a part of our life, for a long or short while, who reflect aspects of ourselves of which we are unaware. We are mirrors to one another. Therapists working from only the conventional paradigm may suggest to a client that he/she "needs to make better choices," or needs to *do* something differently, if their client is getting into destructive relationships. On another level, the vibrational level, we are always attracting people into our orbit which reflect aspects of ourselves. In general, and in terms of synchronicity of energy, the people who come into our lives can show us something about ourselves. Of course, we don't always have to marry those people!

When we are in a relationship with someone who is our energetic opposite we take on the other's energy (especially if our "lesser self" is not available to us) and the other takes on our energy. If there is love present in the relationship the two people each become a bit more like the other over time. If there is an absense of love the two opposite people become more opposite in their energies, more polarized.

DOVE-TAILING NEUROSES

Marriage counselors have noticed how superbly matched most couples are in terms of their degree of well-being, mental health or emotional disturbance— at least at the time of their original mating dance. Couple therapists speak of "a dove-tailing of neuroses" that brings people together as mates. We have been some-what mystified about how a person finds a partner who is equally complicated or disturbed, or equally self-actualized, self-accepting. The behavior and style of the two people may be very different, but at one level *like has attracted like*. Each energy pattern is like a coin with two sides. Sometimes we attract the flip side of a particular coin of energy and so we can rightfully say that "opposites attract." We often attract someone who is our opposite to bring us balance yet that opposite person has the same degree of complexity, woundedness, mental and emotional well-being or the lack of it. In my observations, energies seem to have partners hence "opposites attract" but these energetic partners are alike in their degree of intensity. Sometimes couples show a polarity described by counselors as, "over-adequate—under-adequate." One spouse will be an "over-functioning" person and the mate "under-functioning." Each spouse is equally extreme in distance from the place of balance. Being an over-achiever (or doing over-achievement) in our culture is far more acceptable than underachievement. Each person is "extreme" to the same degree, an equal degree of distance from the place of balance. As a couple, however, they balance each other. This makes them each a half of the whole that the duo represents. In the 21st Century this is no longer what couples want for themselves. There seems to be an urge to experience one's own wholeness, which enhances the health of the marriage and family system, which, in turn, raises the vibrations of the collective energy field of human consciousness.

POLARITY OF INTIMACY FEARS

Numerous relationship experts have written about the polar opposite fears an individual may have around intimacy and committment. On one hand is the fear of abandonment. On the other hand is the fear of being smothered, engulfed and therefore ceasing to exists as a sparate individual. One individual may go back and forth between these two polarities. Sometimes one person in the partnership will stay in one of those fears most of the time and the other person will carry the energy of the opposite polarity.

RELATIONSHIP AS A STRUCTURE, AND AS ENERGY

We can look at relationships themselves in two ways. Through the filter of our more concrete human nature of Reality #2, we speak in terms of "**a** relationship," *a thing* with a history, with structure; looking at "it" in this way means that **the** relationship has a past (which may be still hurting us in some way) and a future (something that we might worry about it actually having). From the experience of Reality #1, there is no actual relationship, no actual "thing." All we have with another are moments. Experiences of the present moment, the eternal now. Here there is no fear about the future or pain about the past. This is the place of spaciousness, freedom and love in relationship to another.

MUCH MORE TO NOTICE AND DISCOVER

Athough Family Systems Theory and Practice has uncovered many of the dynamics of couples and families already, there is much more which we can discover as we bring the Energy Paradigm more significantly into the process.

EQUALLY ENERGIZED ORDEALS

Author Jay Haley of the Family Therapy Institute in Washington, D.C. may have been integrating the Energy Paradigm into Family Systems work when he spoke about creating "Ordeal Therapy."[62] He said that when a couple has experienced some very painful times and can't seem to let go of the hurt and anger that accompanied the ordeal(s), they have to create or participate in *an ordeal that is commensurate with the original ordeal*(s). He shared an example of a couple who loved each other and wanted to stay together but they continued to hurt each other deeply: the wife kept having affairs and her husband kept beating her up in response to the affairs— or perhaps the wife was having the affairs to punish her husband for beating her up (it is not necessary in family systems work to debate whether the chicken came before the egg). Haley had them commit to a ritual he would devise, without their knowing ahead of time what it would be. He told them that their participation in the ritual would bring an end to this primitive behavior. He then had them shave off their hair, bury it in a box in the ground in a park; that would signify for them the completion of the mutually felt pain in the marriage. Neither of them were to engage in or speak of these behaviors to the other except when, once a year, they would visit the park where the box was buried and then and there they could bring up the ordeal, if desired.

This seems to be an energy balancing process.

THE SAME, ONLY DIFFERENT

An example of the paradoxical pair of energetic truths "like attracts like" and "opposites attract" would be a pair of people with an equal degree of early childhood woundedness (and none of us get through our formative early years without at least *some* disappointments, if not abominable traumas); this twosome would be *alike* in the intensity of vibrations, subtle energy, each bodymind carries. And the dynamic that "opposites attract" could be true at the same time. For example, if both these individuals had experienced a fairly large amount of the chaotic energy called anxiety during their childhood they might have adapted to it to the same degree but in opposite ways, giving them symptoms in their adulthood which are opposite in "style" but equal in intensity.

CHILDREN AND "IDENTIFICATION"

Children identify with or "take on," the behavior of their parents. In the conventional paradigm of psychology we call this a defense mechanism and label this particular mechanism "identification." By becoming like or identifying with a parent a child unconsciously keeps a parent close, thereby reducing the child's stress. This is especially noticeable if a parent dies when a child is in his/her early years; the child may take on the deceased parent's behavior to keep the parent alive.

In terms of Reality #2, we report that children learn from parents by observing them, imitating their behavior. We are perceiving from the Energy Paradigm of Reality #1 when we say that children learn by "osmosis," a word which conveys the absorption of vibrations of energy.

Without my having shared with my son the ideas I had been teaching for a number of years, he created for himself in 1995 a business card with the following design. It is striking how much the design reflects my perspectives.

By Kevin Ging
Copyright 1995

PICKING UP PRIMITIVE PATTERNS

It is a common observation among family therapists that children often "pick up" and act out the feelings that are repressed or buried in parents. Why might children unconsciously take on the disowned or "shadow" parts of the parent's personalities? The younger a child is, the more this energetic absorption of patterns of thought and emotions occurs. It seems to me that the repressed energies within the parents may be particularly compelling for children because the parents' repressed emotions are as intense as the primal energies a young child feels. The child is attracted to this kinship of intensity, this similarity. The repressed emotions, buried memories of the parents, are *primitive*. (There is no need to repress a feeling that is NOT intense; such a "lite feeling" is simply felt and released). Children are attracted to and identify with intense, primal, unadulterated energies which were driven underground in the parent, often when the parent was young. We generally need help from another with the "processing" of emotions. Human beings need to have their feelings heard by another. When we do not have the opportunity to have someone be present to us and listen to our feelings, our particularly extreme feelings get buried in the unconscious. We know from the field of metaphysics that "like attracts like." Babies and young children are, by their very nature, also primitive with regard to their emotions; everything is felt in its primal, purest form. Frustration rather quickly becomes rage in an infant or toddler. And pleasure in the young human creatures looks like boundless orgasmic bliss, pure joy.

When the cognitive ability or mind of a child matures, it becomes complex enough to unconsciously "manufacture" the less primitive psychological defense mechanisms which enable the young child to modify and modulate his/her intense emotions. This makes the world a safer place, for certain primitive energies in adult bodies (as in people having psychotic episodes) can spell disaster. This degree of unbalanced behavior could not be what is intended by the compassionate Creative Forces, The Heavenly Whole, The Heart of Heaven, the Superconscious energy of the Divine Mind. What this Divine intention seems to prefer is balance, harmony, a marriage or partnership between primitive, instinctual emotions WITH the controls that defense mechanisms or psychological structures contribute to the partnership. The primal energy of "Primary Process"[63] is to be balanced by and partnered with the psychological structures of "Secondary Process."

POLARIZED SIBLINGS

I have often noticed that in families with a great deal of marital disharmony, the children in the family are more polarized than in families at peace a large part of the time. The energetics of this is easiest to see in families with only two children. Examples of this family dynamic abound once we are awakened to this dynamic.

Children are all unique and come into the world different from one another, different from other members in the same family. Ideally, given healthy nurturing and psychological safety in early childhood, each child becomes more who he or she is meant to be, a unique individual. In families with intense marital conflict or stress, I've noticed that children have less of a chance to become the balanced whole persons who they are meant to be and more of their energy goes into turning themselves into the polar opposite of their sibling.

I recall a couple who had a marriage that appeared on the surface to be a comfortable union. Underneath, however, there was intense anger within both the husband and wife. They had two attractive daughters. One became an academic who was a philosophically minded theologian with much insecurity about social behavior and doubts about her attractiveness to men. She allowed herself to become somewhat overweight and had little sense of how to dress with style, nor did this especially matter to her. She was deeply interested in spiritual matters and was an impassioned and sometimes angry social activist who worked hard for world peace and justice. Politically, she was a Democrat, if not a Socialist. The other daughter became a very social person(but was far from being a Socialist politically), was apparently confident, concerned about her popularity and her sex appeal, and with staying trim. She focused on her physical attractiveness, her clothing, money and materialism in general. She was not interesting in learning, was not a good student, nor was she concerned with spiritual matters or with politics. She voted Republican. What she valued was having fun and being social, which was her contribution.

Another example comes to mind of two children who grew up with much marital tension in the household (even though their parents loved each other). The daughter became a corporate litigation attorney who was very much into planning ahead, a concrete thinker, and very hard working and determined. The son became an artist who did not plan ahead, was abstract in his thinking and put a higher value on playing and enjoying life than on working and becoming established. He was more into allowing things to happen than into making things happen. He carried the Yin side of things, while his sister embodied the Yang. Fortunately, there has always been a natural attraction between these polar opposites siblings who happen to be my own children.

MULTIPLE CAUSATIONS AND NO CAUSES

There are various ways of assessing and/or understanding how children turn out the way they do. One can make a case for the position that there is a particular "reason" that "causes" people to turn out as they do. It could be inherited genetic tendencies. It could be parenting styles. It could be any number of things and a combination of nature and nurture.

Depending on the paradigm in operation within one's psyche at a particular time, the *reason for things* varies. And the concept of "a reason" may have different connotations. There appears to me to be no *one* "cause" behind things that occur. Nor are there even multiple causes with one primary "cause" for things being as they are. Our "left-brain" ways like to think up reasons why things happen and find "causes." The Reality #2 paradigm comes up with some excellent information and intelligent, sensible ways of explaining things. Some of these may actually have much validity, certainly from the point of view of Reality # 2. On the other hand, from the perspective of the Energy Paradigm of Reality #1 it feels as though there is a convergence of many, many factors relating to how a child "turns out." All these factors seems to "reflect" each other, and no "cause" can be pointed to as most significant. In terms of astrology and planetary influences, the energy of various planets do not cause a person to be a particular way; the planets "reflect" the way that person is while many other aspects of a person's life and environment also reflect upon behavior. The Reality # 2 paradigm of concrete information and understanding wants to know how and why our children turn out as they do. The Reality #1 of the Energy Paradigm is about the interconnection of all things, and one could say that everything is involved and/or there is no "causes" (a-causal). It is also true that in metaphysical teachings there is a "law of cause and effect" that says every thought, every feeling we emit has an energetic effect upon everything else. And we reap what we sow, as Jesus taught. "What goes around comes around." The law of Karma. We reap what we sow, therefore we'd be wise to treat others as we'd like others to treat us, as The Golden Rule recommends. This is both a (Reality #1) reflection about the way of energy and it is also a (Reality #2) moral rule of concrete, practical advice about behavior.

Bridging the paradigms, where the two polar opposite Realities meet, there is compassionate acceptance and intelligent discernment. The spacious "interconnectedness of all things" of Reality #1 meets the focused, critical judgment of "left-brain" Reality # 2 thinking, and the partnership of these paradigms meeting in the heart's miraculous energy of reconciliation give us *wise evaluations.*

"STAR CROSSED FAMILIES"

Intensity attracts intensity. When we look at family systems in the light of the energy paradigm we might notice that certain families, certain systems of energy, seem to have more than their share of intense, dramatic things happen to them. These occurances might not all be tragic. There could be remarkable good fortune as well as remarkable misfortune. There is a correspondance of energy that exists with a family's collective vibrations and the events of their lives.

In terms of Reality #2 which is based on observable or analyzable behavior, we speak of multi-problem families. Such families seem to need to have up-roar and drama. Chaos may be the organizing principle with certain families. As with hysterical personalities who use their hysteria and drama to distract them from deeper internal pain or uncomfortable feelings of emptiness, some families like to keep things in a wild, confused state. It is understandable, in terms of Reality #2 how certain families continually re-create more of the same pattern—the pattern of chaos.

In terms of Reality #1, energy attracts similar energy. Intense or primitive energies in the conscious or unconscious minds of individual family members attract intense events. And the collective energy field of a family system may attract dramatic events as well. These can occur even with families who would not be described as multi-problem, chaotic families. There are many reasonably functional families who have more extreme things occur than one would expect. This may be understood in time as "an energy thing."

An intense polarity within a family's energy field may take several generations to be brought into a place of "relative" peace. Yet, an individual within a family system can emancipate him/herself from the family patterns and be less affected by the energy that seems to "possess" others in the family. It is never too soon or too late to begin to awaken, become more conscious and aware of one's own energies and choose to bring them into the balancing, harmonious place of the heart.

IF ONE CHANGES ANOTHER CHANGES

In a system, if one component of the system changes the other aspects of the system adjust to the change and therefore, change also. This appears to be true energetically, even when one family member does not know about the changes that have occurred with another family member. Dr. Kenneth McCall, M.D.[64] a British surgeon who became a psychiatrist, discovered that when a family member changed and became more emotionally healthy, another family member residing in the back ward of a mental hospital, had a spontaneous remission of the mental illness.

PARENTING IN A PAIR OF PARADIGMS

The best thing a mother can do for her children is to love and honor herself. And the best thing a father can do for his children is to love and honor himself. And the next most important thing that parents can do for their children is for the husband and wife to love each other; this is more likely if they first love themselves. In response to this energy of love that is present in the household, children *grow* into healthier human selfhood and stay better connected to the Greater Self which was all they knew at the time they were born. And, as the children observe the constructive and caring behavior between parents, the children *learn* loving behavior.

PARENTS, BE WARNED

Children "pick up" and embody the emotions of the parents when the parents are experiencing intense and painful conflict in their marriage. This is especially true of the very sensitive child, or "energy sensitive" individuals. It is often the case that a child will absorb the intensely chaotic energy in a disharmonious household and come up with a serious disease. This is certainly not always the reason an unexpected serious illness afflicts a child. Many of those reasons remain a mystery. However, the onset of a serious health problem in a child is a sad situation which family therapists often notice and wonder about. The story of my own three-year old son being afflicted with leukemia and another life-threatening blood disease at a very tense and trying time in his parents marriage is a story I share in Section III, as an example of this dynamic.

HIGH-ENERGY MOTHERS

Mothers with a great deal of Soul power, a strong connection to Heaven and Earth, are high-energy mothers. I have noticed a number of situations in which their energy made the mothers *seem* to be overly involved with their children when it was their energy that was the factor, not the *behavior* of the mothers. (Sometimes both are true). The presence of a high-energy mother may be such a powerful force that the mother may have too strong an influence in the child's life; the mother, then, might be thought of as being intrusive or simply "too much" for the child. Children may believe that such a mother is too involved in their lives but it is the mother's energy that the child is feeling. In terms of actual behavior, the mothers *may* not be doing anything that could be seen and described as "too much." Some mothers are simply high-energy mothers. Mothers unfortunately too often get judged or assessed by family counselors as being intrusive or too entangled in their maturing children's lives. (Certainly, many mothers actually ARE overpowering in their behavior and intensity of emotions). Thinking of these relationships in terms of energy can be a kinder way.

CHAPTER EIGHTEEN

THERAPISTS, COACHES AND HEALERS

Confusion abounds for people seeking help or support in this era of conventional, alternative, and complementary therapies. Shall we choose a therapist or a healer? Perhaps a coach can serve us best. Possibly we are wanting to create a career of helping others but don't know which angle on the helping professions or the healing arts is the one that would be best for us to pursue. This chapter explores some of the ways that the previously described paradigms operate in the helping professions and healing arts. It may help seekers of wholeness to make more informed decisions.

A PARTNERSHIP OF PARADIGMS IS POSSIBLE

The linear, sequential, developmental, male mode, "left-brain" perspective is the domain of developmental psychology. It is important to be aware of its process and its pitfalls. Many spiritually oriented therapists who focus on supporting a client's spiritual evolution may

abdicate their responsibility to support the linear process of differentiation or separation-individuation. It is
my belief that clients are best served when they are informed about the reality of separateness; we all have
the psychological need to experience separate selfhood.
It is also important for us to learn together the language
of the energy paradigm. We begin by recognizing that
we are all one unity of intermingling waves of energies.

ART AND SCIENCE

Holistic techniques of the energy paradigm are often an art, a healing art. The therapies which deal with
behaviors which can be quantified or problems which
can be observed, even solved, are more of a science.
Many techniques of therapy have components of both.
I see therapy modalities as on a continuum, some being
closer to the concrete realm of form which strengthen
boundaries and improves functioning while other
therapy modalities are closer to the wave-like world of
the creative unconscious, where everything is connected to everything else. A good clinician needs to
bring balance. At least therapists can help clients discover where they are coming from at a particular time,
in terms of the continuum of the **TWO** *realities* of life,
and the various *polarities* of human experience (discussed in another chapter).

DIFFERENT STROKES FOR DIFFERENT FOLKS

Many hyper-spiritual or "triple P" (Primary Process People) with a preponderance of energy-sensitivity, use spirituality as a defense, an escape from their human condition, a condition which may be rejected as too painful when the personality polarities have not yet been addressed. Meeting such clients in their preferred realm of the vibrational milieu, or energy paradigm, may be suitable for some—with dream work, trance work, energy healing, art and music therapy and the new (and ancient potions and notions of vibrational medicine which are now becoming plentiful as more of the population discovers alternative medicine. However, with highly sensitive people who are already able to actually feel subtle energies, I'd consider *balancing* their paradigms by taking a more linear, cognitive approach. A client who has very loose boundaries, or is dissociated and "spaced-out"(found in abundance among those who are very much identified with the New Age, who could be called "New Age Fundamentalists"[65] may not benefit from dipping further into the unconscious world of energy. An open-eyed, more structured and grounded approach would serve to bring balance and strengthen their personality (little/lesser self). Conversely, a less creative, tightly organized, over-functioning client could benefit from therapies reflecting the energy paradigm which would expand their consciousness and their sense of the Greater Self.

CLINICIANS CAN FLOW

If clinicians can flow back and forth between BOTH realms—(Reality 1): creative, healing, vibrational, mysterious and also (Reality 2): evaluative, linear, developmental, problem solving—they will get excellent guidance about their work from their own intuition, which has been well-informed by a background in psychological development and other linear forms of psychology. The duo or **TWO**ness of *informed intuition* is what holistic therapists can acquire, with practice. And anyone, therapist or not, can learn which reality they need more focus upon to achieve greater balance in their lives. *Life is a balancing act* and for this balance to be found the **two** realities need to be honored.

HELP IS ON A CONTINUUM

Conventional ("medical model") clinicians work out of the Newtonian Paradigm or Reality #2. At the other end of the continuum, healers and clinicians doing "energy work" are operating out of the perspective of The Energy Paradigm, the **One**ness Reality, Reality #1. Healers and therapists of all kinds can do both, demonstrating to clients how to dance between and respect these two realities. Eventually we may see these two Realities as opposite polarities of ONE reality continuum which meet each other to create a new synthesis, Reality #3 Therapy. It should be noted that most people doing psychological counseling fall somewhere on the continuum and not at polar opposite ends. For purposes of getting better acquainted with the realm of each Reality out of which human service professionals and various other people who feel called to be therapeutic, it may be helpful to get to know them in their pure forms first.

CONTRASTING THE POLARITIES ON THE CONTINUUM

* Boundaries are honored and highlighted in the work conventional therapists do; boundaries and their development are encouraged. This is one of the biggest differences between the polar opposite ends of the paradigm/Reality continuum. At the other pole (the Energy Paradigm end) boundaries blur or temporarily merge during healing work for in the realm of the Reality #1 everything is energy intermingling. This area is one that needs to be understood and addressed in both spheres of the helping fields.

* Conventional "medical model" therapists work on the PERSONALITY. Energy workers/healers elevate the SOUL.

* Conventional therapists honor developmental psychology, sequential stages of development, and base their work on the Newtonian model of reality or Reality #2. Energy workers, transpersonal or psychospiritual therapists serve people out of the Energy Paradigm, Reality # 1.

* In the Reality #2 based therapy of conventional clinicians, the process of healing, growth, and personal-

ity development is seen as linear, sequential; it is acquired gradually. With the Energy Workers of the Paradigm of Oneness, Reality #1, healing and wholeness *is possible* in any moment for we all already have it and need only awaken to this wholeness.

* Conventional counselors and therapists may focus on the PAST or FUTURE. Healers and Energy Paradigm therapists keep the focus on the NOW.

* Conventional therapist use an EVALUATIVE mode; assessments and diagnoses are made in the medical model of psychology; judgments may be included in this work. Healers and energy sensitive counselors give help from the CREATIVE mode; it is non-judgmental and diagnoses are not central to the work.

* With Reality #2 based conventional therapists, *integrity* is seen as integration of a client's personality fragmentation; there is a goal of cohesiveness of the personality (or recognition and understanding of the client's "personality parts"). With healers and Energy Paradigm practitioners, *integrity* is seen as awareness of one's experience in the moment, awareness of one's Greater Self or wholeness.

* Self-ESTEEM is often a goal conventional psychotherapists have in their work with their clients; self-esteem is conditional and, unfortunately, is occasionally acquired at the expense of another person. With healers and Energy Paradigm, Reality #1 therapists,

Self-LOVE is the goal rather than self-esteem; unconditional self-LOVE[66] is intended and this love
serves the collective of humanity. It is never acquired at the expense of another.

* In the conventional realm of Reality #2 therapists, self-
esteem is often nurtured through "ego-supportive"
psychology, supporting the ego's defense mechanisms. With healers and people doing energy work,
self-love is nurtured through Soul awareness.

* Therapy may focus on *changing behavior* with conventional psychotherapists. In the healing model of
psycho-therapy a client is helped to love and accept
who he/she is, "as is."

* *Solving problems* or teaching problem solving is often an aspect of conventional therapy. In the opposite paradigm of Reality #1 the healer or
transpersonal therapist teaches presence and encourages *participation in The Mystery.*

* A conventional therapist is *a therapeutic resource.* A
healer is *a healing presence.*

* Reality #2 therapy work may be merely mental and
include much thinking *about* issues. With the other
paradigm the work is always experiential.

*With the conventional paradigm, working to move the
personality to a more mature level of development

is often a goal. On the other end of the continuum AWARENESS and bringing Soul consciousness or Greater Self into the lead is the aim.

Introspection (a mental process) may occur and even be encouraged in conventional therapy; this is a dualistic/judgmental/evaluative endeavor. Psycho-spiritual therapists, transpersonal counselors and healers have an intention for embodied awareness without judgment.

COMPARISONS AT A GLANCE:

ENERGY WORKERS/HEALERS:	CONVENTIONAL THERAPISTS:
Elevates SOUL	Works on PERSONALITY
Healers and transpersonal or Psycho-spiritual therapists serve people out of the energy paradigm	Clinicians who honor developmental psychology, sequential stages of development, base their work on Newtonian model of reality
Healing/wholeness is possible in any moment; we already have it and need only awaken to our wholeness	Healing, growth, development is linear, sequential, acquired gradually
Focus on the NOW	Focus may be on PAST or FUTURE
Help given from CREATIVE mode Non-judgmental	Therapist uses EVALUATIVE mode Judgments, assessments are made
Integrity as awareness of one's experience in the moment Awareness of one's wholeness, Larger Self, High Self	Integrity as integration of one's personality parts or patterns, cohesiveness and balance of the personality self, small self
Self-LOVE is goal;	Self-ESTEEM is often a goal;

It is unconditional love; Serves self and the collective	It is conditional and may be at another's expense
Self-love nurtured through soul awareness	Self-esteem nurtured through "ego-supportive" psychology
Healing model accept "as is"	Therapy may focus on changing behavior
Teaches "Presence" and "Participation in The Mystery"	Solves problems or often teaches problem solving
Healer is a healing presence	Therapist is a therapeutic resource
The work is always experiential, processing feelings	The work may be merely mental, thinking *about* issues
Boundaries blur or temporarily merge in energy/spiritual healing	Boundaries are honored and highlighted, their development encouraged
Awareness and bringing Soul Consciousness or Greater/Higher Self into the lead is the aim	Moving personality to a more mature level of development is often a goal
Intention for embodied *awareness* With NO JUDGMENT	*Introspection* (mental) may occur; this is dualistic/judgmental/evaluative

SUSPENDING JUDGMENT

As we step more deeply into the new Millennium, we may be noticing that many spiritual and metaphysical teachers are encouraging their students to suspend judgments. This would be a reality of where the norm would be compassionate acceptance, a world without mental judgments, a world where the *vast majority* of people would be living, primarily, from their hearts. It would be a reality where darkness would be accepted as a necessary balance for light, a reality where both sides of every coin would be simply accepted. The Life process would be recognized as energies balancing opposite energies. It would be a world at peace because its people would be living from the place of peace within themselves. It would be a world in balance in all ways because balance and peace is the way of the heart. Imagine being able to observe the unfolding of our lives and the lives of others with total unconditional love and acceptance, from the heart's vantage point—seeing the big picture so that people's motivations were understood and therefore accepted with compassion.

FULL-SPECTRUM REALITY THERAPY

Ideally, therapists can become eclectic enough and conscious enough to do therapy from many places on the continuum from Reality #1 to Reality #2. The place of miracles is the realm of Reality #3. There are moments when a therapist, healer and/or coach may find themselves empowering clients from this place. The rest of the time we can learn to move along the spectrum of reality as we do therapy or coaching. And healers may wish to learn more of the ways of developmental, linear psychology to balance their favored paradigm. Full-spectrum lighting is good for us. Full-spectrum Reality offers a wealth of therapeutic diversity and richness.

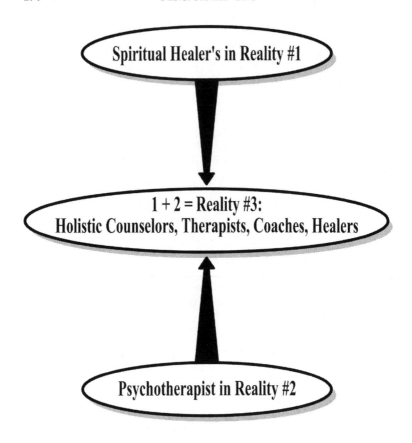

TEN STRATEGIES

"Ten Strategies For Doing Holistic (Bio-Psycho-Spiritual) Therapy" is found in Appendix B.

come kindness,
softness,
gentle flowing ripples
of a heart's vibration,
replace the harshness
of mind calculations,
comments,
mental traps
so cold with judgment,
more evaluations;
come instead with kindness, heart
soft as a baby's blanket
now's the time
and here's the place
for grace and loving kindness;
do descend on me,
impart the peace
your ever warm and tender love can bring
and share again the wealth of your
wellspring.

JUDGMENTS ARE HUMAN, "ONLY" HUMAN

As long as we have the very rational, analytical, left-brain phenomenon which splits things into dualities and is inclined to judge and compare, we will make judgments.

Spiritual seekers wanting to live *entirely* from their hearts sometimes attempt to suspend all judgment, and, ironically, fall into the mental trap of judging judgment as being bad! Even those most motivated to live in the spiritual realm of profound acceptance of All That Is cannot escape from their human condition which includes the judging capacity of the "left-brain" style. In a moment of frustration after seeing on television an extremist of some variety, I recall having had the thought, "I think all narrow-minded, bigoted, rigid, intolerant people should be taken out and shot!" How often and how easily we can recognize ourselves as card-carrying members of the human race, capable of all manner of feelings and thoughts. Living without judgment is impossible as long as we carry from the human condition. As long as we are in a body with a "left brain" we will make judgments. Judgments in their most benign form are assessments, evaluations. Obviously we need this mental capacity for survival in the physical world. We were given a left brain and we need it. A left-brain tamed by the heart's energy would serve us best.

WHAT HAS ULTIMACY?

A question that helps us bring paradigms to a meeting place is this one: "What has ultimacy for you?" This suggestion was given to me by a very special teacher, Harmon Bro.[67] What is your "ultimate concern"? Theologian Paul Tillich used this phrase to bring seekers to an experience of their goodness. It is a questions for all of us to ask ourselves frequently and it is an appropriate question for counselors to ask their clients, if they wish to bring spirituality into their work.

SPIRITUALITY IS NOT MERELY AN *ASPECT* OF THERAPY

Some therapists think of spirituality as a *part* of life, an aspect of peoples lives, something like a person's cultural influences. Spirituality is not merely a part of one's life—it is aliveness itself. It is that which holds the whole of life. It is the most primal, the most primitive of all dimensions, all experiences. It is the energy of our essence, the energy that infuses everything, giving it life. When colleagues in the psychotherapy professions ask me how they can incorporate spirituality into their practice, my reply is that they have always been doing so, but may have been doing it without awareness. We are living, breathing, working from Spirit. It is Spirit that moves individuals and the collective energy of humankind forward. Spirit is the Creative Force, that which brings healing. It is Soul which moves us into greater depths of our being and holds us together. Often it has seemed to me that we grow in spite of ourselves, in spite of our lesser selves. To love someone is to invite them to grow. It is our Spirit which urges *us* to grow. We are loved by our soul, invited to grow by Spirit.

LIFE COACHING

People participating in the new field of "Life Coaching" are many and varied. Many who call themselves coaches have been conventional therapists prior to becoming coaches. Some therapists simply change the name of what they do without having changed to any great degree the way they work. Others have made a shift, incorporating new paradigm thinking into their work before putting on the coach's hat. There are therapists who have not begun to call themselves coaches who are already working from a world-view akin to a coach's stance.

Coaches vary tremendously in their experience and skill. Most people who are coaches have done a substantial amount of work on themselves, having participated in transformational seminars and having used the help of therapists, healers and their own coaches in their psychological growth and spiritual awakenings. The world-view of coaches is much like that of healers in terms of their faith in what is possible and their focus on the present. Coaches believe that people are not limited by their past experiences, that **what we want** we **can** manifest; this is the metaphysical and spiritual perspective of Reality # 1. Yet most coaches also help their clients move forward in a step-by-step linear way toward a goal, keeping an eye on concrete behavior that is interfering with the achievement of dreams; this linear progress reflects Reality # 2. Coaching, depending on how it is done and the energy out of which it is accomplished, can marry together both paradigms.

"COACHING FOR CONSCIOUS LIVING"

"Coaching for Conscious Living" is the name I've given to the coaching dimension of my therapeutic, healing work. The name appeals to me because it lifts up the realm of consciousness (Reality # 1) while the word "coaching" implies helping clients take action, moving forward (Reality # 2) and manifesting their desires. Actualizing our dreams requires a partnership of the **two** primary paradigms of Yin and Yang. Out of these two paradigms therapist/healers can work/love. With a balance of these two realities all people can learn, grow and live fully and abundantly.

CREATING YOUR OWN REALITY AND SURRENDERING

We will notice, at times, a pair of polarities, or a paradox of living, in which both polarities are of the same paradigm. In other words, there can be polarities within a polarity of either Reality #1 or Reality #2.

Consider the ability to create your own reality, to create what you want for yourself with your intention, your heart's desire, your passion. Thoughts are things;

they are vibrations of energy which are not as dense as a material object and not as spacious as the heart's gentleness. If we focus our attention on what we are wanting, and if we have no reservations or resistance to receiving what we want, it seems that sooner or later it will manifest in our life. This process is something more than the power of positive thinking. When we're admonished to think positively the admonition may be coming from a place a bit closer to Reality #2 on the continuum of paradigms. For with "positive thinking" from the conventional paradigm, we are operating with the idea that positive thoughts will make us feel happier and more confident and therefore we'll more likely be successful at having things turn out more closely to the way we want them to. This seems understandable, a Reality #2 modality.

We are tremendously powerful beings with the capacity to create what we want for ourselves. This intention to create something for ourselves has a Yang quality to it. Creating in the more spacious and metaphysical paradigm has some mystery and almost magic to it. It is something that people of the new consciousness or the consciousness culture speak of a lot and celebrate. Some New Age zealots believe they can create absolutely anything they want and they may have such faith that who can doubt them? The dilemma here, for me, is this: if we are coming from this place of focusing our attention on what we want we aren't letting The Great Mystery flow in our lives. The opposite polarity from that powerful, assertive Yang energy of creating, is the Yin energy of the process of surrender. Surrendering our willfulness, releasing our desire to be in complete control, yielding to The Great Spirit seems to be often times the wisest thing we can do for ourselves. It is a fallacy to believe we are ever in complete control. The longer we live the more we seem to believe this. So here we have a paradox or a Yang/Yin, Create/Surrender polarity.

Fortunately, we do not have to make an either/or choice. As we bring these two energies together into a partnership we create with wisdom. We set our intention (Yang) and then we let go, surrender (Yin) turning our control over to the Co-Creator we may call God/Goddess/All That Is. From this place of YinYang balance we surely can make many things happen for ourselves.

I have heard a great many stories of healing and have often heard of a situation when a mother was praying fervently for God to bring her dying child out of a coma and heal the child. Perhaps the mother is begging, pleading and coming from a controlling energy of too much density. Because, as these stories often go, when the mother moves into a place of acceptance of "whatever" and surrenders, the child will come out of the coma and get well. Not always, of course, but moving into the spaciousness of acceptance makes whatever the outcome might be more manageable. We get in the way of the process of "flow" when we are TRYING to CONTROL the outcome.

It is one of life's most amazing paradoxes that MASTERY (Yang) of our lives goes hand in hand with SURRENDER(YIN).

Sooner.
Wise are those who do it sooner.
Surrender to The One.
We do this when the day is done,
When deathbed gives no other choice.
So why must "I" not have a voice
About my life while I am young?
 Why should I turn it over,
Give control away
By saying, "Take me, Spirit,
Make me what you see
That I could be."
By giving not ourselves to God
When we are young
We get to see, eventually
The errors we make,
So many woes
Which aren't undone
Without the Grace which comes
Replacing our remorse
At having not surrendered
Sooner.

CHAPTER NINETEEN

SEX AND THE UNIFIED SELF

The sex lives of people are ever-changing and fascinating. As a marriage and relationship counselor, I'm
often struck by the large quantity of lost opportunity
for sensual and sexual pleasure in the couples I see.
This is a grievous waste of earthiness! Certainly a trusting and harmonious emotional connection is a prerequisite for a gratifying sexual partnership. Sometimes
even couples who have such a healthy bond on the emotional and physical planes may be missing some other
dimensions during their sexual encounters. Additional
levels of connection and communion are possible providing pleasures which extend beyond the physical levels into ecstasy touching the spiritual realms. The grand-
est sexual communication requires a Unified Self. This
is experienced when the integrated, cohesive and balanced (i.e., emotionally mature) personality self meets
the Greater Self or Soul. The Unified Self is felt at the
heart of awakened individuals. When both members of
the partnership share this level of awareness and aliveness, a divine connection can occur.

ENJOY THE EARTH AND ITS WONDERS

Just as the Earth has its natural wonders, so do our bodies have their varied terrain, textures, superb processes and abilities for experiencing and giving pleasure. To live in the United States and never see the Rocky Mountains or play in the ocean surf would be a great loss in pleasure for anyone with a car or the means to get to the mountains or ocean.

Neglecting to share one's sexuality, at least with oneself, is to miss out on beautiful processes of energy for anyone with a body that is able to enjoy itself or another. Some people do not have a way to get to the mountains or ocean, and a small percentage of people are physically disabled to such an extreme degree that they may not be able to engage in actual physical sexual activity. For these people life holds other pleasures. The majority of individuals are able-bodied and therefore, for most, sexuality is a wondrous gift to be enjoyed throughout their lives.

ESTRANGED FROM EARTH

Perhaps one reason why so many people in our culture have an unbalanced preoccupation with sex is because they are unconsciously longing for an experience of nature.[68] Intimacy with our planet has not been taught by those cultures who took our country over from the Native Americans. Most Americans have become estranged from nature, preferring an amusement park loaded with stimulation to a national park abundant in natural beauty and connection to Spirit.

The Earth herself has been seen by our Reality #2 dominated culture as a "thing" rather than as a living entity. Our planet is the usually hospitable home to which we, the Earth's children, are related and with whom we are enjoying intermingling our energies (a Reality # 1 perspective). However, our dominant culture has encouraged people to think of their bodies and the bodies of others as "things." When we "thing-ify" or objectify a person or planet or any other aspect of nature we are less intimately related to it. We are no longer a part of "it" and "it" is no longer part of us.

SOME SEPARATENESS NEEDED FOR ORGASM

However, if we are *totally* one with everything and have not yet experienced or achieved cohesion in our lesser self, the psychological self, we may have difficulty achieving orgasm.

We need a substantial degree of separation-individuation before we can feel truly safe in merging with another as thoroughly as we do in physical, emotional and spiritual communion. At a deep unconscious level there is, in many people, a fear of losing oneself completely and not being able to find one's way back to one's self if one risks having an orgasm. This may be particularly true as a relationship moves into deeper levels of commitment. This may seem backwards, but for many people who have not achieved sufficient separation-individuation, a superficial relationship of casual sex may work better, in terms of orgasmic potential, than a relationship that has developed over time and carries with it much commitment.

"THE LITTLE DEATH"

The French word for orgasm is, "le petite mort." Translated literally this means "the little death." Indeed, at the moment of orgasm all boundaries of the psychological self (the "lesser self") are blown asunder and we lose a sense of who we are as an individual in the ecstasy of pleasurable merging. Without a sense of a cohesive psychological (lesser) self, orgasm is often inhibited in both men and women.

We need to have tested our boundaries of psychological, lesser self before we can test that those tried and true boundaries will support us as we surrender this sense of psychological self for a few seconds or moments and merge with the other. When we have also experienced our **one**ness dimension, truly ecstatic and sacred sexual union is possible.

ORGASMICALLY CHALLENGED

It should be noted that other medical or medication-related factors may also be a significant consideration for those who are orgasmically challenged. The boundaries of self or degree of individuation is of great importance but other issues may also be involved in the "natural," yet sometimes challenging experience of orgasm.

HEALTH ENHANCING, LOVE ENLIVENING

Sex may be used for regeneration, rejuvenation, renewal of oneself physically, mentally, and certainly the health of the relationship of the partnership can be greatly enhanced by love-making. As spiritual aspects of a sexual union develop over time this deep energetic union can make one more accepting of any loss of the physically vigorous sex of one's younger years.

AN ADMONITION ABOUT ENERGY EXCHANGE

Energy sensitive individuals in particular will notice the price they pay by engaging in sexual intercourse with a person of "lower vibrations." Just as in the physical-material paradigm of Reality # 2 people pick up sexually transmitted diseases, in the energy paradigm of Reality # 1 people transmit their energies to each other. This may be a good thing for the partner with an over-all lower vibration of energy, but it is not a win-win situation; the person with the higher, finer frequency of energy will sacrifice something energetically.

My rubber stamp collection contains a gem which says: "Never Sleep With Anyone Crazier Than Yourself." This admonition is fitting for both paradigms.

A RESOURCE FOR REGENERATION AND RELAXATION

Sexual stimulation and orgasm is, for most people, vital for physical health, regeneration and balance. The brain works better when libido flows fluidly, unencumbered by mental, emotional or physical blocks. These are practical and physical reasons why individuals would be wise to nurture their own sexuality. And for the health of the relationship with one's mate, sex is a healing balm and joy that bonds these two individuals together and nurtures the soul of the relationship, renewing the feelings of love.

REQUIREMENTS FOR ROBUST SEX

Robust and wholesome sex requires a commitment to self, both "the lesser self" of our personality and the "Greater Self" of our Soul's wholeness. Joyous and gratifying sexual expression calls us to first find the place of love and wholeness where our earthiness meets our expanded **one**ness dimensions for full-bodied, "inspirited" connection. A Unified self/Self carries with it great pleasures of aliveness which take many forms.

HEARTY SEX

When clients are given the suggestion that they might not be "in their body," they initially will disagree based on the fact that they enjoy sex. Often people will shift between the state of being "in the head" and then, at other times, experience pleasurable sexual activity. It is not uncommon for a person to bounce back and forth between the arena of thinking and the arena of sexual sensations, bi-passing the heart and emotions. Wholesome sexual behavior is about the integration of all aspects of our humanity with spirit and soul. For this, the heart must be engaged.

ORGASM AND COMMITMENT TO SELF

Commitment to our own wholeness is a necessary ingredient to connecting with our own sensuality and sexuality. Trust in both our Greater and lesser selves is necessary for the best of sexual expression. We need to trust ourselves to contain the powerful sexual urges so we can consciously *choose* a partner with discernment and use our sexuality wisely when we are single. We need to trust that we can manage and contain our possibly strong feelings of hurt and anger if a relationship runs its course and we are alone again. And if we are half of a committed partnership, we need to be able to trust that we will not lose ourselves in the merger which sexual intercourse represents (especially with orgasm).

With our own inner connection and cohesion we can connect with another in a psychologically safe and loving way. Until we experience our own wholeness we are somewhat divided against ourselves, making commitment to our own well-being unlikely. Without commitment to our own happiness we are unlikely to attract a suitable partner, and even less likely to sustain feelings of love for that partner. Commitment to the experience of our own wholeness is a prerequisite for the capacity to commit to another, and to remain connected to the desire to stay committed.

BEING SMITTEN AND SUSTAINING LOVE

It becomes obvious to people who have been "in love" a number of times that the capacity to "fall in love," to be smitten with attraction for and from another, is not the same capacity as the capacity to sustain the heart connection, remain in love, enjoy enduring feelings of deep love once the initial "high" of romance in a new relationship has changed into another phase of that relationship. Allowing love to endure, sustaining the heart connection once the wonderfully delusional "high" of the first phase of love has subsided is a challenge for those who have not committed themselves to the partnership of their own internal polarities and live from a place of their own wholeness.

ONE WOMAN'S SURRENDER INTO SUSTAINED, COMMITTED LOVING

A client with a rather active romantic life had learned much about herself and others through relationships with various men. She could not, however sustain love in a relationship for long before she would either run away from the relationship or get bored with it, losing her sexual ardor and ability to orgasm as the weeks and months of a relationship were accrued. This had happened so many times that she realized she had an internal problem. She was ready to release her pattern of finding fault with the boyfriend, devaluing him within her own mind to justify her loss of love-feelings, or say, "I just haven't met the right man for me." She realized that had not yet met herself, but she was finally ready to do so.

SIMPLIFYING THE ROAD TO COMMITMENT

By choosing to identify *first* with her **One**ness dimension, then honoring her **two**ness by bringing the polarities of her personality into partnership with each other as she became aware of the various dichotomies within herself brought her to a place of trusting both her Greater Self and her lesser self. She noticed that at the same time that she was able to truly commit to a man she was dating (who she had run away from twice before, in earlier chapters of their lives) she was also able to allow herself to succeed with her career dreams. Prior to this experience of moving into her wholeness she would sabotage her success in achieving goals. She honored her **three**ness or internal trinity by becoming aware of how her body was speaking to her as well as her mind and spirit. And she developed a rich awareness of the **four** chambers of her heart and all of her many heart qualities. If her deep feelings of love ever waned or fear of losing herself in the commitment arose, she simply moved her attention to her heart and asked it for its truth.

THE ENERGIES OF LOVE

When we are enjoying our senses we are, to a great degree, in a state of love. We are loving our own earthiness and the Earth herself. Sensuality and sexuality can be experienced in relation to the beauty of flowers, trees, mountains, all aspects of nature. Beauty created or brought into manifestation through people can stir sensual and sexual feelings within us; music and even language written so well that it is an art form can stimulate erotic feelings. Libido is an energy which can be felt throughout one's body in relation to life itself, even without a romantic partner. It is a feeling of total aliveness. The more one experiences one's spirituality or connection with The **One,** the more electric the energy becomes.

When the young dancer, Billy Elliott in the film (2001) by the same title was asked how he felt when he was dancing—inspired dancing with passion and total presence—he said, "I don't know," then after a moment's hesitation added, "I feel electric." When we are living in alignment with our soul's purpose we feel charged with electricity. We feel joy. When we are connected to our heart's loving and aware of being plugged into our Spiritual sources of energy while making love we feel electric, as well.

Another film favorite illustrates the marriage of bodysense with Spirit. "Michael"[69] is a film (1996) about the Archangel Michael embodied (and acted) by John Travolta. In this charming film the archangel, visiting the Earth in physical form, is a character who is both totally spiritual and throughly sensual. He is tuned into All That Is so completely that he is able to "know" everything. When asked by another character who was surprised by his awareness of something in her past, "How did you know that," he responds with a smile and tells her, "I pay attention." This is a succinct and delightful illustration that awareness or presence in the Oneness dimension leads to the awakening of the heart's intuition. "All you need is love," was Michael's refrain throughout the film. Unconditional acceptance, caring for another from his heart and soul, and *thoroughly enjoying the Earth and all his earthy physical senses* was part of that loving. He knew he only had a little more time to exist in physical form so he was going to enjoy the beauty of the planet and his physical senses as fully as was possible, while being respectful of others. He even had a one-night romantic interlude with a waitress he had met hours earlier. Because he lived out of unconditional love, the brief encounter was a clean and open-hearten experience, leaving both with only good feelings in the morning.

Wholeness requires that we live in two paradigms concurrently, that we bring our earthy, sensual nature into partnership with our busy, productive, thinking ways of living.

DEGREES OF SEXUAL CONNECTION

A continuum of sexual activity can be envisioned with **communion of bodies and soul (Greater Self)** at one end and, at the other end of this continuum, **mere titillation of sexual feelings** without cohesion or integration of the personality self. Examples of immature and unwholesome sexual behaviors at the darker or more energetically contracted end of this polarity of sexual expression would be sexual addiction acted out with others but without emotional connection with the partner, or with oneself as in addiction to masturbation and/or pornography. Preoccupation with sex, to the exclusion of having balance in one's life, often occurs when people sexualize their anxiety or any other uncomfortable emotion, turning emotions or troubling thoughts into sexual sensations. This provides a distraction from anxiety, as various addictions do, but the underlying extreme personality energies go unchanged.

DEGREES OF EXPANSION

Much lies in between the polarities of energetically expanded and contracted sexual experiences. Sexually expanded experiences occur more often when people know and have unconditional acceptance for themselves. Simply put, unconditional love equals spaciousness, expansiveness. On the other side of the coin is fear. Fear equals contracted energies so the more fear a person carries, consciously or unconsciously, the more often a person will have energetically contracted experiences, less love, less aliveness, less flow. (Note: In the discussion of this continuum of sexual behavior, sexually deviant, abusive behavior is not included because issues and energies other than sexual desire are involved).

FROM "HAVING SEX" TO "MAKING LOVE"

As people become more conscious and heart-centered they can move from the more emotionally detached places on the a continuum which would include recreational sex without love with a consenting adult, to the more energetically expanded experience of recreational sex *with* a loving connection to our partner and on to even more expanded sexual moments of profoundly loving connection. Even peak experiences of deeply loving sex as a spiritual experience can occur in these most spacious realms.

LOVE AND THE HERE AND NOW

There is no more potent place from which to make love than from true presence. Being fully present in our body, living from our essence in the Here and Now places us in the realm of the heart. It is a place that is entirely open to the energy of aliveness where thinking takes a back seat—a distant back seat. When we are centered in the spaciousness of the heart with the intention of feeling an emotional connection with another and giving and receiving sensual pleasure a shared experience of the **One**ness, a spiritual connection may occur as well. Time and pleasure can be expanded in the timelessness of the heart's space; the no time/all time of Eternal Now is the optimal locale out of which to enjoy sexual pleasures. We've heard that " Love is eternal."This applies to compassionate love of the heart's connection with another. This kind of love is not generally thought of as sexual in nature. However, when deep caring, emotional, physical/sensual/sexual and spiritual connection are all present at once, the experience can be so great as to make such moments feel as though they will live in eternity.

We can expand our sexual pleasure when we begin to appreciate and even honor the power of the Here and Now more fully.

WE ARE TRANSMITTERS OF LIFE

Poet D.H. Lawrence bridged the paradigm of spacious, vibrational experience with the paradigm of the physical world of matter more solid in his poem, "We Are Transmitters,"[70] which began,

"As we, live we are transmitters of life
And as we fail to transmit life, life fails to flow through us.
That is part of the mystery of sex, it is a flow onwards.
Sexless people transmit nothing."

Lawrence also wrote of the depth of sensual experience that our sense of justice includes.[71] He wrote, "the. . . . deepest sensual experience is the sense of justice."

SEXUALITY, SPIRITUALITY AND CREATIVITY

The sex act can be merely a physical act, a physical function in which all creatures of the earth engage. Sex with emotional, heart-felt and spiritual connection is an act in which the creative forces are involved. We call it *making* love. Something is created during love making at the more energetically expanded places on the continuum of sexuality. More love is created. Any act of creation involves Spirit.

Sexuality and spirituality are sometimes referred to as kissing cousins.[72] A great deal of energy in one realm can mean an abundance of energy in the other for mature individuals. And often much activity in one arena can stimulate energy in the other. A sexual experience of union can be a spiritual communion moving the individuals into an experience of the **One**ness Reality. Reality #1, the spiritual reality, can meet Reality #2 of the physical/material realm bringing individuals to a true marriage of their human earthiness and their spirituality. Making love is an ideal way for the two paradigms of reality to meet and, momentarily, merge.

Robust
Those lusty ways
So primal
While we have these bodies
Let us get from them
The mileage that we may
Connecting to divine aliveness
Merging with the great beyond
Communing with The One
Through union with another
Lover
Spirits flowing
Arms enfolding
Hearts of gold
No withholding
Share this Earth
Give birth to making
Fertile now
At any age
And any stage of life
A time for pleasure-making
No mistake in waking
To a time to savor
Bodies which have brought
Us through and on beyond
Our suffering to now enjoy the bonds
Of blissful union,
Sweet communion.

CHAPTER TWENTY

TO HONOR HEAVEN AND EARTH

Spiritual teachers, Medicine Men and Medicine Women, mystics and gurus have taught about the ways of Spirit from a place on the Reality continuum that is more spacious (Reality #1) than concrete (Reality #2).

Mainstream Protestant seminary education is far more factual which means it leans toward the realm of concrete information, Reality #2. It is not surprising, then, that Protestant clergy are frequently accused (especially by New Agers) of being " too much *in their heads"* and *"not 'spiritual' enough"*. The word "religion" connotes more form than "spirituality" which infuses every aspect of life, not only religions.

Spirituality (Reality #1 of spaciousness, Energy Paradigm) and Religion (Reality #2 of form, more concrete) are both meant to bring us to wholeness. As seekers of the wholeness which we already ARE but may not realize that we ARE, we are best served by naming and honoring each of the two realities in which we operate, the material world as well as the realm of spaciousness. (Such a statement is a refrain found in every chapter; becoming comfortable with new ways of thinking about Reality requires repetition of the concepts)! As the culture of consciousness grows there will be greater desire for more members of the evolving species to claim and balance their human nature and their holy nature, Greater Self, Soul. It is time to marry our physical Earth nature with our Spirit, for all is infused with aliveness described by one paradigm or another!

ANCIENT, EARTHY PERSPECTIVES

Centuries ago, in pre-Christian or pagan times, the matriarchal, earth-respecting cultures honored the human body, sensuality and sexuality in ways quite different than the way we now think of our physicalness. Everything in nature was seen as alive with Spirit (or spirits, divas), infused with divine energy and therefore sacred. It is ironic that the paradigm of modern science defined what is real as that which is known through the senses, yet the loving, spaciousness of the energy paradigm has not been integrated into that perspective of the Western World. The sense of the sacredness of everything was lost long ago. The conventional paradigm of the Western World has made concrete, or "thing-a-fied", the human body and the Earth, seeing them as material things, objects. This is simply how "left brain thinking" conceives of the Earth and human bodies—as objects. Some are quick to judge our Western, left-brained culture as bad. It is only missing its paradigmatic mate which can bring to the marriage the reality of energy, spaciousness, flow and a sense of the divine feminine.

SPIRITUAL-MATERIAL TEACHINGS

The teachings and historical contributions of all great spiritual leaders are valuable to study. One's own particular religious or spiritual tradition may be more deeply understood, even enhanced, when we learn how various spiritual teachers from other traditions have spoken about reality, about the way the life process works. Some great teachers have been especially wise in a particular area of life.

THE BUDDHA

The Buddha's teachings, for example, are especially helpful for taming our busy minds. Simply watching our thoughts, without judgment of these thoughts or the fact that we are *thinking* again, can bring us peace.

Regardless of how enlightened spiritual teachers may be, their own lives on the physical material plane must have an influence on the kinds of revelations these teachers may receive about reality. (Intuitives or psychic "readers" invariably get their own personal experience mixed into their "readings" about others. This must also be so about all those who teach about the life process, at least to some degree). A central focus of the teachings of Siddhartha Gautama, who became The

Buddha, is the attachment and detachment polarity. He taught that life is suffering and that suffering is caused by too much attachment, by clinging to our desire or the objects of our desire. He taught that living from a place of mindfulness or awareness of our experience is the way out of suffering. He stressed the impermanence of all things. Much wisdom and truth is found within the teaching of The Buddha.

It is interesting to note that Siddhartha Gautama experienced the *impermanence* of the physical bond with his mother at a crucial time for developing trust. He was separated from her when she died shortly after his birth in 563 B.C.E. We can assume that his experience of physical, emotional reality (Reality # 2) included significant psychological pain. Supporting this idea is the fact that when the Buddha was a young man of 29 he caused history to repeat itself when he left his wife and infant son. In addition to great wisdom and guidance, it is interesting to notice that his teachings reflect "issues" around separation, loss and how to avoid the suffering that generally accompanies these experiences. He stressed *detachment* as a way to avoid emotional pain. He taught that desire was something from which we should disengage if we want to lessen the suffering that accompanies the human experience.

In the light of contemporary metaphysical teachings, it may be important for us to strongly desire something, and feel our emotions in a potent way, in order to manifest what we want. By no means do I wish to discount the teachings of The Buddha. His teachings have great value and have stood the test of time. They have been helpful to me, personally. My intention, here, is to show that Reality # 2 may have an impact on the thoughts of every human being, even influencing how great spiritual teachers interpret the high truths that have been revealed to them.

Since all that is "truth" eventually converges, many spiritual teachers have said the same things in slightly different words.

YIN MEETS YANG IN JESUS' TEACHINGS

Jesus of Nazareth was a teacher who addressed both paradigms—spacious/spiritual *and* dense/material. He was a great metaphysical teacher, demonstrating much about healing with Divine Energy. He was also concerned about the material needs of people. His words "Feed my sheep"[73] did not only apply to spiritual feeding. The physical care and feeding of human beings was a significant aspect of Jesus' teachings as well. Perhaps Jesus knew that a person's physical needs must be met before wholesome spirituality could be achieved. And this was long before Abraham Maslow's "Hierarchy of Needs"[74] was presented!

AN EARTHY BIRTH

The story of the birth of Jesus—in a barn with animals and hay—is symbolically valuable in showing earthiness, the material reality (Reality #2) intimately meeting one who has represented for many the Divine Light of Reality # 1. As a spiritual teacher, the speciality of Jesus was love from the heart. While many spiritual teachers have spoken of compassion, the love of which Jesus taught was healing love from the human heart. In the treasure chest within the physical chest of the human body the Light of Spirit is ever- ready to pour forth its human-divine love.

HEART AWAKENING FOR CHRISTMAS— AN IMAGERY EXERCISE

At Christmas time and other times, here is an imagery exercise: Gently take your attention to your physical heart and imagine that it is a stable, a humble and earthy barn where a birth is taking place. Imagine that an infant is just now being born and now is being placed in a manger. Allow yourself to feel your awe about new life, awe about a newborn baby. Stay with this feeling awhile, stay with the feeling of the way you behold a newborn. Allow yourself to really FEEL the wonder of it all. Breathe deeply into this feeling. This new baby is bringing a spark of pure white Light into your heart, Light so bright that it is dispelling darkness within your body and mind. Allow that spark of holy Light to become a candle flame within your heart and consider your heart to be an amazing candle holding the flame, the transformative energy of your heart's fire, and stay conscious of the sacred fire there, in your chest, recalling its power, looking to that flame often. Let the story of the birth of Jesus also be about birthing the capacity for compassion within yourself, reawakening your heart's ways, the best qualities of your personhood. Honor the spark of divine light within the four-chambered pump which brings you to your wholeness—human and divine. Keep your attention in your heart and love yourself 'til the cows come home, and love the cows and all the human animals as well as you go about your business of the day.

"I AM" IS THE WAY

Both Jesus and The Buddha and lesser known spiritual teachers are reported to have made statements that have led their followers, their students, to believe that there is only one true way, only one true spiritual teacher. While Jesus' spirit and teachings are central to my own personal life, I do not believe that other spiritual teachers need to be dismissed. He is my personal guide for many reasons but I believe that other teachers and other religions have brought truth and truth's Light to the world, have taught us how to meet the Divine and re-create ourselves. When Jesus said, "I AM the way, the truth and the Light,"[75] it is my heartfelt belief that he was saying that "I AM," or the energy of BEING is the way to truth, Light, wholeness. Experiencing the energy of **"I AM" is the way** for each of us to find our true self and our connection with Spirit. In those moments we join with the Divine and in those moments we could say, as Jesus said, "I and my Father (i.e., The Creative Forces), are **ONE**."[76] Jesus is one who has represented for many the energy of "I AM," the energy of Holy Wholeness. I do not believe he is the only representative of the spirit of the " I AM" pattern of energy, a very, very fast and fine vibration of energy. We all have the capacity for union with the Divine, for **ONE**ness. We can aspire to actualize this capacity more and more frequently. A few years ago a magazine called "Enlightenment" emerged[77] because enough people are beginning to believe that, at least to some degree, we can all experience this state.

Moses reported that he heard God speak to him through a burning bush; the voice of God said "I AM that I AM."[78] I believe that we access the energy of "I AM" in our Unified Self when the Soul or Greater Self of Reality # 1 meets the balanced personality "lesser self" of Reality # 2 in the heart.

HINDUISM

The Hindu religion teaches a world view very much like the numbers 1-2-3 that are used in the "formula for wholeness" presented this book. Hinduism teaches that the *atman*, which is the individual soul, is identical with the *brahman* or the universal soul. (Just as "He's Got The Whole World in His Hands," our soul embraces our whole array of personality parts in its arms.) Atman and brahman pertain to the "Oneness." The "**two**ness" appears in the multiplicity of deities, male and female gods and goddesses, demons and demonesses—many pairs of opposite energies. They remind me of our personality parts who can cause us trouble if we have no knowledge of them. In the Hindu religion, the many deities demand to be acknowledged, respected, feared or honored in some way. And there is a trinity or **three** major deities: (1) the god that creates (Brahma), (2) the god that preserves (Vishnu), and (3) the god that destroys in order to transform (Shiva).

THE TRINITY IN CHRISTIANITY

The Christian tradition honors "The Trinity" as "The Creator, The Son and the Holy Spirit" (sometimes still spoken of as "Father, Son and the Holy Ghost"). Parallels with the triangle, the grand trine or trinity within our body, are described in a number of ways in Chapter Six entitled "We Are A Trinity." Comparing the Christian Trinity to the human trinity of energy we can see ourselves in this way:

* 1) the "left-brain," Yang energy of the male principle that takes action could be compared to The Creator;

* 2) the "right-brain"/body sense, Yin energy of the feminine principle could be a parallel with the incarnate Jesus Christ;

* 3) the Heart's energy is reflective of the Holy Spirit.

SAINT FRANCIS AND ENERGY BALANCING

"A Simple Prayer," was written approximately 800 years ago by Saint Francis of Assisi (1182-1226). This highly sensitive man was deeply attuned to nature and his prayer suggests that he realized the need for *simply balancing* the dense energies of (polarized aspects of) human nature with the spacious aspects of our heart's ways. His often quoted prayer is this:

Lord, make me an instrument of your peace
Where there is hatred .... let me sow love
Where there is injury .... pardon
Where there is doubt .... faith
Where there is despair .... hope
Where there is darkness .... light
Where there is sadness .... joy.

O, Divine Master, grant that I may not so much seek
to be consoled .... as to console,
to be understood .... as to understand,
to be loved .... as to love,
FOR
It is in giving .... that we receive,
It is in pardoning, that we are pardoned,
It is in dying .... that we are born to eternal life.

WHAT MUST DIE?

Eternal life is the life we experience within our heart's realm, the eternal NOW. What is it that must die? Separation must die. As often defined by Christian theologians, *sin is separation*. Perhaps the polarizations or extreme separation of opposite energy patterns within our human nature must be buried in the heart where they meet. Separation from our Greater Self can be seen as living in sin.

SURVIVAL AND "THRIVAL" OF ALL

The awakening people of the culture of consciousness can bury in the heart of the collective consciousness of humankind the separation that exists between different races, nations, religions, cultures and classes of people. Diversity is part of nature and will endure. But survival of the fittest, destruction of one form in favor of another, is an idea based on the paradigm of Reality #2 alone. Survival of the fittest is fitting for Reality #2 of the physical-material realm. It is not fitting for the emerging culture of consciousness. In the Energy Paradigm, to raise your own vibrations is to raise the vibrations of the collective human species.

EAST MEETS WEST

The polarity of Eastern and Western points of view are meeting in the middle of open-minded people and there miracles can happen. On the other hand, there is an intense polarization of religious people with fundamentalists of most every religion populating the contracted end of the polarity and openhearted people who seek harmony among a diversity of religious forms at the other end. Perhaps when the "lion lies down with the lamb" in the Middle East a partnership, will be born. Working to promote respect for diversity of religious traditions is a worthy endeavor. I choose to envision harmony of a diverse array of religious forms, rather than a unity for all religions into one. ONEness is the Reality of the Energy Paradigm (Reality #1). We can be one in the Spirit realm, but religions, like people, have physical form and there will always be a multiplicity of forms; that is an aspect of the concrete, material world of Reality #2. Interfaith spirituality is one of the brightest sparks in the world today. Hans Kuhn, the Dutch Catholic Theologian, said at the 1992 Parliament of the World's Religions, that when the world's religions are at peace with one another, we will have world peace. It is a hopeful sign and symbol that The Pope, in 2001, apologized for the Spanish Inquisition and apologized to the Jews for the Vatican's erroneous behavior during World War II.

THE WHEEL OF CONVERGENCE

Consider each of the world religious traditions (and even ancient wisdom traditions prior to "religion") as spokes on a wheel.[79] On the outer rim of the wheel is the exoteric level of each tradition with its form and structure. At this outer level these traditions all look very different. They each have their own sacred book, their own ceremonies, celebrations, costumes, and leaders. This is the paradigm of concrete, observable behavior, Reality # 2. At the exoteric level religions look like they have very little in common with each other. Wars have been fought because of differences at this level of Reality of religions.

At the hub, the center of the wheel, is the esoteric level of religions. There is a convergence of spiritual experience at this level regardless the particular tradition one has known and is part of. All that is spacious and of the heart's energy meets and "gets along well with others" at this level. At this level there actually are no OTHERS. We are all one in the realm of Spirit. At this esoteric level all religions meet in Reality #1, where we sense that "we are all in this together." This is a place of honoring the mystery. It is a place of peace, acceptance and wonder.

Within every religion there can be found people who are more concrete and identified with their particular way of thinking about spiritual and religious matters. And within every religion there can be found the mystics, those boundless thinkers who are less concerned with the formal aspects of their religion and more involved in the spiritual and mystical life.

SPIRITUALITY AND SOCIAL ACTION

Spiritual practices for inner peace, such as meditation, are on one end of a continuum with social action toward peace and justice and service to others at the other end. Mature spirituality includes service in the world, and wholesome social action with spirituality of some sort is more effective. (Actions for justice, when performed by a person with inner rage, will not serve the collective energy field of consciousness—speaking in terms of Reality # 1; the energy paradigm). The

Dali Lama is a symbol of the marriage of paradigms as he actively works for peace and justice with a peaceful and loving heart, in spite of the cruelty inflicted upon his Tibetan people.

A MIXED-BOUQUET

It was Rev. Dr. Martin Luther King, Jr. who inspired me to go into social work when I was a teenager. I desired to work for social justice as much as I wanted to help people with their inner and outer relationships (and learn more about my own). Prior to that time I had wanted to be a Child Psychologist, even though I had never met one (perhaps I wanted to). In 1964, while living in Boston, I heard Dr. King speak of how much "God loves variety! Humanity is like a bouquet of mixed flowers." It is difficult for anyone who considers him/herself to be a part of nature, with all of its variety, to think that there is one master race or only one true religion.

FOR WHAT DO WE WANT TO BECOME WHOLE?

Wholeness may be sought as an end in itself, an achievement, a goal. Yet there may be something missing in simply seeking wholeness for its own sake. It is my feeling that the reason WHY we seek wholeness will make itself known to us when we arrive at the place in our hearts, where balanced, healthy human personality self meets the Greater Self of Soul.

For what purpose do we seek wholeness? Seek first, and surrender to, the reign of the heart and there, in that realm all questions will be answered.

CHAPTER TWENTY-ONE

THE "SHADOW" OF THE NEW AGE MOVEMENT

The following is a paper I shared at a 1990 workshop at the Mid-West Conference for Association of Humanistic Psychology.

If every person, every organization, every movement has its "shadow," that is, those unconscious parts of ourselves that we would rather not see, what does the shadow of the New Age Movement and the Human Potential Movement look like? I ask this as one who is very much a part of the New Age Movement. So far, it has served me well and can continue to serve humanity well. It has a better chance of doing this if it is willing to take a gentle, loving look at itself. Carl Jung (and I believe The Buddha) said that everything contains its opposite. Whether or not you buy into that perspective, it is useful to at least try it on for size. Certainly there are two sides to every coin. Checking over our behaviors and our motivations as though they were coins with two sides can only yield greater awareness, wholeness, integrity. This exploration has to be done with acceptance, not with judgment. A willingness to take a look at oneself is a sign of healthy mysticism. Saints do it. Shouldn't the New Age Movement be willing to have a look at its own undertow?

Acceptance of "all that is"is a New Age value. Yet, is there not a great deal of rejection of what one could call the Western way within "The Movement"? Is there not a great deal of rejection of the masculine in favor of the feminine? Is there not a rejection of traditional establishment medicine in favor of Eastern and other alternative forms of medicine? I say this as one who has benefited greatly from alternative health care. I am a sincere advocate of Chinese medicine—herbal medicine, acupuncture for everything from endogenous depression to an aching back. I have been a victim of Western Medicine which is frequently iatrogenic medicine; its cures often cause more harm than good. When I was three weeks young I was given radiation to my thymus gland—a measure which was supposed to shrink my thymus gland so that I would not become a victim of SIDS, sudden infant death syndrome, by choking in my sleep on my thymus gland. Three decades later I was one of millions so treated in infancy to develop thyroid cancer. Certainly Western medicine does a lot of harm with its technology. Its treatments are frequently gross rather than subtle and gentle as in the East. But to write Western, establishment medicine off as "bad" and see Eastern medicine as "good" (when it may be at times too subtle, too slow) seems like foolishness. Foolishness that many New Agers get caught in. This "all or nothing thinking" is a danger to which many people are prone—not only New Agers.

For all its emphasis on acceptance of all that is part of the whole, many New Agers fall into a trap of splitting things into bad and good. Many make the New Age style the "right" style and anything else "bad" or inferior. This is contrary to acceptance of the whole.

Do many New Agers fall into the trap of emphasizing the world of spirit, energy and vibration to such an extent that they forget that, while we are here on the Earth plane, we have to make our lives work on the earthly, material plane as well. When caught in a storm while at sea we have to pray to God AND row toward shore. In the Middle East one is admonished to "Pray to Allah AND tether (tie) your camel." As Ram Dass, one of The New Age's wiser teachers puts it, "You have to remember your zip code even when you're in the middle of intergalactic bliss." The motto of the Green Political Movement captures the idea of the balance we need: "Think Globally, Act Locally."

The tendency to split the whole of life into "bad" and "good" can create problems for New Agers who sometimes devalue the cognitive-physical-material realm in favor of the spiritual levels where meditation, prayer and imagery surely do their wonderous works. Both Realities need to be honored. While balance is a word often used in the New Age Movement, it is sometimes missing among New Agers who would rather be "out there" in the ethereal realms than operating in both planes at once.

For all our tendencies to neglect our groundedness and our fullness of functioning on the material plane, many a new ager loves his/her "stuff" of the New Age. Crystals, Bach Flower Remedies, Birkenstock sandles. Every movement has its "things"—but things do not make a movement. Sometimes the essense, the vision, the values of the movement seem to get lost in the material tokens of the very movement that is, in part, about transcending the material.

Much of what "The Movement" is about is Love and Brotherhood/Sisterhood. Do we not, however, have more than our share of difficulty with intimacy? Dealing with our relationship with the Divine is infinitely more comfortable than moving through our fears of intimacy.

Those of us who are drawn to the realm of spirit, dreams and vision are frequently involved in what the good doctor Freud named "primary process." This realm of the visionaries and the psychics has its pitfalls. We would all do well to be aware of them.

A DOZEN YEARS LATER

In the years since the comments above were delivered, the change in the consciousness movement that is most noticable to me is the degree to which spiritual seekers have moved into their bodies. Various kinds of body work and body-focused psychotherapy therapies have been serving seekers well.

CHAPTER TWENTY-TWO

HELP FOR EXCESSIVELY SPIRITUAL, PRIMARY PROCESS PEOPLE

In the 1970's, I found myself fascinated with "left-brain" linear, developmental psychology of all kinds. In 1973, I read a book by psychoanalyst Heinz Kohut which struck me as a very profound (but not very readable) understanding of people with early childhood wounds, traumas or deficiencies (or excesses) in nurturing which leave people with what therapists call "narcissistic injuries."

In the early '70's, I also had serious medical problems which motivated me to explore the new field of Holistic Health. And that led me to the Human Potential Movement. This Movement seemed to me to be something like the polar opposite of the linear psychoanalytic thinkers I was reading. For the first 15 years of my adventuring, I felt like I was leading a double life as a secret agent. The cultures of these two different movements were so divergent that I choose not to tell people in one "camp" that I also spent a great deal of time in the other. I spent many weekends going to Human Potential Movement workshops until I would find myself thinking, "There are a lot of flaky, needy people here and I'd like a little more STRUCTURE in these workshops." Then I would bounce over to the other side and attend a good many dignified classes and workshops of the conventional schools of psychology, until I would find myself thinking, "These people are so stiff, so uncreative, so stuck in their heads—I better get back to the other folks who are more loosey-goosey and fun!"

Back in those days I knew I would look foolish if I mentioned to a (Reality #2) psychoanalytic, academic type of person that I was thinking about going to a psychic healer or an astrologer. On the other hand, I could talk about all manner of far-out things with people involved in the consciousness seekers of the Association of Humanistic Psychology. The people I met and studied with during the 70's and early 80's were very polarized, only comfortable and interested in one mode and not the other. I found it exciting to be traversing this continuum from the "Far Out" to the "Far IN" (i.e., "in" the establishment).

There were many New Age seekers involved in the Human Potential Movement. Over the years I began to see a continuum of people within this open-minded (Reality #1) Consciousness Movement itself. At one end of *this* continuum I noticed many emotionally vulnerable, wounded people who seemed to believe everything they heard. (They made me miss my more mentally critical but sometimes rather formal acquaintances at the other end of the OTHER continuum!) At the other end of this continuum of people with expanding consciousness were many clear thinkers who seemed quite well put together, in terms of their personality cohesiveness and mental discernment. The more fragile and needy people sometimes had only the beginnings of a cohesive psychological self and I sometimes feared for them because of their vulnerability. So many of these people were tuned in to higher consciousness and were well-intentioned wonderful people, but they made themselves look foolish by not becoming better integrated on the personality level. The establishment did not take many of these New Agers seriously for this reason and I was frustrated that these high Truth tellers were not presenting their experiences to the world from a place of better personal balance and Unified Self/selfhood. These were the people who had the job of ushering in the New Heaven and New Earth, The Aquarian Age, and I wanted to see this job done by people who had their own lives in better working order. While doing my own work of getting to know and trust my own wholeness, I wanted everyone else to be doing the same!

After many years of study and observation I began to present workshops on "Therapy With the New Age Client," where I first talked about two different paradigms, two qualitatively different Realities and the need for a bridge between them. The descriptions of my workshops given in academic settings (The Family Institute of Chicago) were more formal in style. For the more "informal" Association of Humanistic Psychology Conference in 1990 my workshop description said this:

> Increasingly, we are seeing clients who are metaphysically hip—tuned into Higher Reality and healing energies—but whose loose boundaries, idealism and tendency to use spirituality as a defense may be complicating their lives and diminishing success in relationships and work. We'll explore ways to help these clients set goals, get better grounded and use new age concepts and tools constructively.

TWENTY QUESTIONS

I began my workshops by sharing the following list of 20 questions I had been asking myself after more than 15 years in the Human Potential Movement (with a secret life in the other arena).

1. Do some people make the very open-minded and "loose" New Age perspective into a closed system and therefore an unhealthy system? Do these people make the New Age vision into a set of behaviors which are the "RIGHT" way, and do some people use tools of the New Age compulsively?

2. Are we seeing a misuse or over use, an abuse, of some excellent tools and an exaggeration and distortion of some basically sound principles and techniques?

3. In other words: Are there such folk as "New Age Fundamentalists?" (Jim Kinney's phrase).

4. What is a fundamentalist? Are Fundamentalists of any ilk more like each other than they are different from each other?

5. How does one guard against becoming a New Age Fundamentalist?

6. How do we help clients and colleagues out of that trap?

7. What will Adult Children of New Agers be like? (ACONA groups, anyone?)

8. Who are the people who could be most easily thrown off balance and hurt by New Age abuses? And wouldn't these same people be abusing something else if it weren't spirituality and metaphysics?

9. Can spirituality be used in counter-productive or defensive ways? Do people sometimes keep themselves stuck or stunt their growth or even flirt with psychosis with some modes of spirituality?

10. What are some healthy ways of employing New Age perspectives and paraphernalia?

11. Do a significant percentage of the people with visionary, prophetic and intuitive gifts and inclinations also tend to have specific personality deficits, cognitive distortions and relationship problems?

12. Do visionary people who are truly in touch with higher reality need to pay more attention to their own growth needs at the lower, human, PERSONALITY level in order to be more effective in their lives or, as New Agers like to say, in the healing or "transformation" of the planet?

13. Is the Primary Process experience of infancy and early childhood which Freud identified—that primitive, "right-brainish," holistic, non-linear, intuitive, dream-like, vision-like mode—something that can be BALANCED WITH rather than REPLACED BY the development of Secondary Process (i.e. reasoning and ego development)?

14. Can the Self-Psychology of Heinz Kohut give us a useful framework for working with New Agers and understanding ourselves (Humanistic, Transpersonal therapists)? (And why are followers of Kohut called Ka-HOO-Shuns rather than Ko-HUT-ians?)

15. Is it time for Humanistic and Transpersonal psychology to be IN PARTNERSHIP WITH the more evolved aspects of the psychoanalytic tradition? And wouldn't that synthesis have more structure and substance?

16. Should therapists be aware of the wisdom and balance of Matthew Fox's Creation-Centered Spirituality?

17. Do we need to know the difference between healthy mysticism and unhealthy mysticism?

18. "Should" (a word which certified New Agers are never supposed to use) therapists of every variety be informed about chakras, healing energies and planteary energies and other facts of life?

19. If every person, every organization and every movement has its SHADOW (those unconscious parts of ourselves that we would rather not see) what does the shadow of the New Age Movement contain? (And The Human Potential Movement?)

20. Are the established, main-stream churches missing the boat and losing members by not embracing what is real and true in The New Age Movement?

VULNERABLE PRIMARY PROCESS PEOPLE IN HOLISTIC CIRCLES

People who are emotionally vulnerable are easy pray to the spiritual leaders, teachers and gurus who are grandiose and need a following of people to idealize them. (This comment reflects Reality #2, the analytical paradigm of the science of psychology). There are, of course, many wholesome and respectable and respectful spiritual teachers and gurus. They are the leaders who are humble rather than grandiose and who do not have a need to control people or be worshiped/idealized. (Notice that the polarity which Heinz Kohut described had grandiosity on one end of the pole and idealization on the other end). It has been said that gurus and their disciples deserve each other. This is, speaking from the Reality #1 paradigm and its metaphysical Law of Attraction, an example of how people of similar vibrations find each other, and also how opposites attract (Bad gurus with grandiosity who feel "one up" in relation to their followers need followers who idealize the guru and feel "one down" in relation to the guru). Good gurus are not controlling and do not **need** deciples. They seem to attract people who are in better balance than the gurus who are operating out of their own personality imbalances.

A very good "guru" named Ram Dass, one of the most helpful and appealing spiritual teachers among the gurus I have encountered (who was a psychology professor at Harvard University before his life-changing visit to meet *his* guru in India) told a group of us at a meditation retreat that guru was spelled, "Gee, you ARE you!" Truth and wisdom is within each person, not only within someone deemed a guru.

DIVINE OR DEMONIC

Rev. Morton Kelsey[80], an Episcopalian clergyman and Jungian Analyst who taught at Notre Dame and whose workshops and lectures I have enjoyed, had this pithy comment which I have found useful to share with my clients: "The difference between the demonic and the divine is that the demonic wants to control and the divine only wants to encounter and transform."

THE PSYCHE OF THE PSYCHIC PERSON

A number of my clients have been professional psychics, intuitives, and healers. I have become acquainted with the proclivities of people with these gifts as they have come to me for counseling. And I have been the client to many other people with such "right-brain" talents, benefiting (usually) from their input.

The majority of the many, many psychic people I know have been traumatized or deeply hurt as children, causing them to split off from their bodies and "dissociate." There are exceptions, of course. Psychic ability seems to also run in families so many people are simply born with these gifts. However, a large percentage of the psychic people I have known as clients or as people I have gone to for input for myself, have been driven out of their bodies by trauma as children. Once out of their body they became very aware, observing from a higher vantage point. Fear can make a child hyper-vigilant and this is often the beginning of extreme psychic perceptiveness. It is not uncommon, then, for people of great sensitivity and intuition to also be deeply wounded psychologically. When such Primary Process People with psychic abilities move their consciousness into their physical bodies and do the work of getting to know their personality polarities they can then experience their own wholeness, have intimate relationships which work and still retain their psychic gifts which can be of great help to others. Without this integration of self and Self psychics often get their own issues mixed into their "readings" about others and this can cause much confusion and sometimes even harm.

Some psychic individuals who were born with these gifts were so misunderstood as children that this caused their hurt, which in turn led them to disconnect from their feelings/body.

There is also intuition which comes to people gradually and gently as a result of many years of doing spiritual practices which opens the heart and visionary capacities. These people are inclined to be less psychologically vulnerable, unless they began their spiritual disciplines from a deeply wounded place.

VULNERABILITY IN A NUTSHELL

Some characteristics of people who might be vulnerable to unwholesome spiritual leaders or unethical holistic healers are (these are from Reality #2, the judgmental paradigm):

* 1. loose boundaries
* 2 impulsivity
* 3. flooding with feelings
* 4. grandiosity
* 5. demanding attitude, entitlement ("you can have it all")

* 6. self-centeredness (oneness, center of the universe)
* 7. tendency to split into bad and good

It is interesting to notice that in a list of characteristics of vulnerablity from the conventional paradigm of Reality #2, self-centeredness had "oneness, center of the universe" parenthetically added to it. This would imply that people who honor the oneness Reality might be fragile or immature. It also implies that "oneness" is the SAME as being the center of the universe, a mindset of a very young child, a toddler. This is an exellent example of a paradigm mix-up! For conventional and academic clinicians, at least a dozen years ago when these workshop notes were made, a "oneness" perspective was synonomous with personality fragility and emotional immaturity. An interest in the unity of all things, or in harmony among diversity, is not a symptom! This Reality #2 paradigm of psychology has taught that Primary Process was immature, erroneous, unrealistic thinking and needed to be outgrown, and replaced by Secondary Process which moves a person from the perceptions of Reality # 1 to those of Reality #2. It is my belief that Primary Process and Secondary Process are to be *partners* who complement and balance each other. The Reality at the center of the continuum where Primary Process and Secondary Process honor and respect each other as different but both of them very "real" halves of the whole, is the Unified Reality of a Unified Self/self.

COGNITIVE STYLES

Cognitive Therapists look for distortions in thinking which emotionally vulnerable people are prone to exhibit. These have been attributed to depression-prone people by Aaron Beck and David Burns[81] and the Cognitive Therapists but I think they fit for people who are immature in general or not well individuated.

COGNITIVE DISTORTIONS DESCRIBED IN COGNITIVE THERAPY

David Burns, M.D. described "10 FORMS OF TWISTED THINKING" in his book, *Feeling Good, The New Mood Therapy*:

1. All or nothing thinking;

2. Over-generalization ("always" and "never");

3. Mental Filter: pick out a single negative detail and dwell on it exclusively so that your vision of reality becomes darkened, like the drop of ink that discolors a beaker of water;

4. Disqualifying the Positive: You reject positive experiences by insisting they "don't count" for some reason or another, or think "he's just saying that to be nice," or "I've fooled him;"

5. Jumping to conclusions: (Interpreting things negatively when there are no definite facts to support your conclusion). Contributing to this are: a) Mind Reading and b) Fortune Telling;

6. Magnification (catastrophizing) or minimization;

7. Emotional Reasoning (You assume that your negative emotions necessarily reflect the way things really are ("I'm terrified about going on airplanes. This means its very dangerous to fly."or "I feel angry; this means I'm being treated unfairly.");

8. Should statements;

9. Labeling (Instead of saying, "I made a mistake," it's: "I'm a jerk).";

10. Personalization: You blame yourself for an event you were not completely responsible for. If a child is having trouble in school, the mother tells herself, "This shows what a bad mother I am."[82]

THE MANNER IN WHICH THESE ARE OBSERVED

These mental distortions are useful in self-understanding and are very helpful for therapists in their practices. One of the many very positive things about Cognitive Therapy, I feel, is the awareness that develops when a person begins to examine his or her cognitive styles. Awareness, in and of itself, is healing and trans-formative. It is important that this examination of men-tal habit patterns be done with an open heart full of com-passion.

PARADIGM BIGOTRY

Obviously, the above description of cognitive pat-terns comes out of the conventional, "medical model" paradigm of psychology and psychiatry of Reality #2. Instead of speaking of "Cognitive Distortions" which pathologizes certain ways of thinking, I would speak of cognitive styles, proclivities of thought.

People with a great deal of Primary Process energy ought not to be pathologized, or devalued as our "left-brain" dominant culture has done. Psychics, artists and mystics are entitled to their little peculiarities, as is ev-eryone else.

The opposite paradigm, the energy paradigm of Re-ality #1, holds that thoughts are vibrations of energy which can be sensed and experienced by persons other than the person who seemed to have originated the thought. Therefore, "mind reading" can be an actual occurance, in Reality #1 perspectives.

WHAT DO PRIMARY PROCESS PEOPLE ("PPP") NEED?

Triple P's—those "right-brain," intuitive, mystical, often creative, imaginative people who may have imbalances in their personal energies or have a shortage of structure in their psyche (in terms of Reality #2) may need any one or more of the following:

1. Triple Ps need to be IN THEIR BODIES. Body work and massage is to be encouraged concurrently with other types of therapy.

Parents must be IN THEIR BODIES to be agents of growth for their children or to channel growth producing love. And therapists have to have their Consciousness in their body to empower their clients. If someone is not in their body and is too much in their head, those people who encounter that person do not feel nourished by the conversation. It is as if "nobody is home." Without presence there is no empowerment.

2. Triple Ps need to strengthen boundaries. They (we) need to learn to be aware to value differences among people. Triple P's need to learn to differentiate self from other. They (we) need to learn to be aware that loose boundaries could be a factor in their make-up. Triple P's need to know the peril and pleasures of having loose boundaries. Therapist may need to "sell" a New Ager on the value of boundaries and the value of being separate, differentiated. Too much of the ONEness paradigm makes for dysfunction.

Boundaries are essential to good parenting and healthy intimate relationships.

3. Triple P's need to spend more time with non-New Age people for balance and to learn to grow into greater tolerance of differences.

4. Triple P's need grounding experiences. Anything that puts a person in touch with the Earth, and also details of living in the world, helps "ground" a person, bring them down to earth. Money management brings "airy-fairy" people down to Earth. Planning a budget and other such mundane activities help bring triple P's into better balance.

Balancing metaphysical pursuits with physical work for the Earth's welfare is wise, as is any activity which honors nature.

5. Triple P's need to understand limitations and "limitlessness." Narcissistically vulnerable people often hate limits. The "You Can Have it All" idea is hardest on the most vulnerable people because of the pain of disappointments in their past if their dreams are not manifested. An understanding of the two different Realities, two different paradigms can help.

6. Triple P's need to know that people with loose boundaries have trouble with intimacy because of an unconscious fear of engulfment, fear of losing themselves in a committed relationship. Vulnerable people often have trouble being content in a relationship.

7. Triple P's need to focus on awareness of FEELINGS as a way to help create boundaries. Some vulnerable New Agers avoid their FEELINGS by focusing on their "Spirituality." This is using Spirituality as a defense. One can temporarily transcend one's pain and perhaps bring some equilibrium to a personality self that is fragmenting through the use of spiritual practices, affirmations, etc.

8. Triple P's need to be aware of potential cognitive distortions they might have, particularly "all or nothing" thinking which is very damaging to people's lives.

9. Triple P's need to be aware that "WORKING THROUGH" feelings has lasting healing value whereas TRANSCENDING a feeling has to be redone constantly.

Permanent growth/healing is most often GRADUAL, something that happens in incremental doses. Instantaneous healings do actually occur, but most often, it is a process that occurs over time. There are NO QUICK FIXES. (A Whole Life Expo has been referred to as:"Quick Fix Gulch"). The notions, lotions and potions in the field of Alternative Medicine have some validity but the vulnerable New Ager has to be aware of his/her tendency to be disappointed. Instantaneous healings do happen. Miracles happen and they come by surprise and as a gift. Some of the techniques and items found at holistic expositions may open our energy field to Grace.

10. Triple P's need to be given permission to use CONVENTIONAL medical and psychiatric help and encouraged to not idealize all things "alternative."

11. Triple P's need to know that loose boundary people may have a hypochondriacal "part" of their personality. This doubt about one's health represents fear of fragmentation of the psychological self. It is projected onto the physical body. Instead of worrying about the state of the psyche, psychologically vulnerable people will often worry about their physical health. It is important that people who are very worried about their health do not let themselves be taken advantage of by the less wholesome "alternative health care people."

12. Triple P's need to give some attention to the development of balance in their personality, their psychological self. Often too much time and energy is spent by New Agers in seeking Spirituality and Higher Consciousness. This is all well and good but to very little avail in the final analysis when getting one's life to work over-all is what is important for wholeness.

13. Triple P's need to consider this formula: K + P + F = D[83]. This stands for Knowledge + Practice + Feedback = Development (or growth). Note that a circular loop happens between practice and feedback. Many New

Agers, especially those who are particularly narcissistically vulnerable, want to go right from Knowledge (workshops, self-help books, etc.) to Development. They may not put into Practice what they have taken in and they may not be open to Feedback.

14. Triple P's need to recognize a tendency to get taken over by grandiosity. Vulnerable New Agers may get flooded with grandiosity and then act impulsively; they need to know about these tendencies and learn to stop themselves and take 10 deep breaths. They're "into" breathing.

15. Triple P's need to hear about "Creation-Centered Spirituality". New Agers need to know about some forms of Christianity that are compatable with their New Age perspective. Why? Because throwing out one's past, loosing connection with one's religious roots can be costly. For some a total divorce from one's religion may be a good thing. It is not necessary for all New Agers to throw the baby out with the bathwater.

An alternative Christianity, quite comfortable for New Agers is the form of Christianity brought forth in the 1980's by Matthew Fox[84]. Creation-Centered Spirituality brought forth by Fox "combines medieval mysticism with contemporary psychotechnologies aimed at self-actualization. He (Fox) rejects flatly the classical Christian distinction between God and the world, as depicted in the doctrines of fall and redemption. He replaces these with the pursuit of a diaphanous consciousness through which we can see all things as divine."[85]

Matthew Fox makes comparisions of healthy mysticism and pseudomysticism, a comparison which is useful for New Agers to explore lest they fall into less than wholesome mysticisim which denies the dark side of the psyche.

16. Triple P's need STUCTURE however it is given. Anything with factual matter or a system of knowledge has structure. Astrology is an exmple. "Over-using" astrology—may be an attempt at getting structure—so don't try to take it away from a vulnerable New Ager. Even taking vitamins daily is structure building as well as self-nurturing.

Carrying or wearing a favorite crystal or healing stone is looked at differently, depending where on the continuum of paradigms one stands. At polar opposite ends, such an object carried with a person might be seen as a "transitional object" (like a toddler's blanket, or thumb-in-mouth) to the most polarized Reality #2 psychotherapist. In terms of the Energy Paradigm of Reality #1, these crystals and stones actually can balance a person's energies, if the right stone is used.

17. Triple P's need to know their vulnerability to disappointment and need to be careful who they pick to idealize. Because of their deprivation, people who were neglected in childhood are looking for good parents; they'll often look up to workshop leaders.

18. Triple P's need to know how to deal with advice from psychics so as to not enhance fantasies and possibly give rise to disappointment. The impressions a psychic receives about a client is symbolic input, just as with dreams. New Agers and others need to know that most of what an intuitive may say is SYMBOLIC. Paradigm mix-ups may occur on the part of the psychic and/or the client and vulnerable New Agers take this input from psychics too literally.

19. Triple P's need to recognize when they are getting into oracle abuse or the excessive, compulsive use of tools for divination such as Tarot Cards, Rune Stones, the I Ching or dowsing with a pendalum. While they may provide structure in some ways, their use can also become addictive.

20. Triple P's need to use Inner Advisor Imagery work. This can help to bring together split affect of emotions polarized into good and bad. When a New Ager starts flooding with emotion or needs to relax they can pause and flash on their inner advisor.

21. Triple P's need to re-parent themselves with nature (Mother Earth and Father Sky)by self-nurturing through connection with nature and images of a nature connection.

22. Triple P's need to consider the best kind of meditation for themselves. The more common forms of meditation may not be wise for people who are not in their bodies. Prayer is to be encouraged rather than meditation, unless it is body-focused meditation which keeps the meditating person in the body. Prayer has more structure and keeps vulnerable people more anchored in Reality #2, physical-material reality. It is a good form of prayer for vulnerable people (and others) to write a letter to God or their Greater Self.

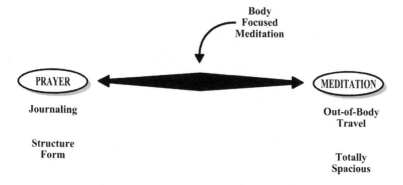

Body Focused Meditation

PRAYER

Journaling

Structure Form

MEDITATION

Out-of-Body Travel

Totally Spacious

23. Triple P's need to learn that "ego" is not a dirty word. There has been a tendency for extreme New Agers to polarize the words ego and Soul and make the ego "bad" and the Soul "good." Perhaps the word "ego," which is a theoretical construct given to us by Freud, has to be retired now because of the confusion about it in the minds of New Agers. Or, the original understanding of the word needs to be presented anew. The ego is not a bad thing, in fact, without a functional ego we do not have the ability to regulate our lives. There are, however, ways of understanding ourselves without using the word ego which has become distored in its meaning and confuses excessively spiritual people. The Unified Self concept presented in this book may be a way out of this confusion.

24. Triple P's must be wary of a new genre of Energy Paradigm pick-up lines such as, "Boy, you really know how to hold your Light." Or, "You've got a GREAT aura." Or, "Wow, I've never met anyone who can shift back and forth between their right and left brain hemispheres the way you do."

FOR A THERAPIST'S EXPANSION AND MIND BROADENING

If you should happen to be a very linear, "left-brain" Reality #2 psychotherapist, I would recommend that all such therapists and counselors bring more spaciousness (Reality #1) into your cosmology to prepare yourself in working with members of the Consciousness Culture.

To have a better appreciation of what your New Age clients are exploring, I recommend these things:

1. Get your own astrology chart done (with your MINUTE, date and LOCATION OF BIRTH) and have it read by an actual astrologer;

2. Have a "reading" by a numerologist;

3. Have at least one psychic reading so you are exposed to the fact that minds CAN be "read." (Note: Do not go to a psychic with a big sign in the window; that often means the reader is a gypsy psychic who tries to get people to turn control of their lives over to them and become dependent on their "advice");

4. Be respectful of alternative health care and try, at least, an acupuncture treatment and/or experience Reiki healing or some form of Energy Medicine;

5. Learn SOMETHING about The Course in Miracles, Synchronicity, Astrology, Numerology, Tarot Cards, The I Ching and Rune Stones.

It would be wise for any therapist to read something by some of the wise Spiritual Teachers or gurus such as Ram Dass, Krishnamurti (very Jungian-like), Muktananda, Yogananda or Choagum Trungpa Rimpoche.

CHAPTER TWENTY-THREE

PAVING THE ROAD TO WHOLENESS

In the realm of Spirit, Reality #1, we are already whole and free. In the physical-material world we have had to fight for freedom and many have died so that we can enjoy freedom.

A client of mine with a high degree of consciousness commented to me about a film she had also just seen, Steven Speilberg's *Saving Private Ryan*. "Is it worth it? The cost of lives lost and lives tragically altered from war; has it been worth it?" she asked.

With his final breath a dying American soldier who had sacrificed his life whispered, "Earn this," to the young Private Ryan.

What have we done, as a people, with the freedom that has been hard won? We've become a nation of people out-of balance, a people numbing ourselves with excessive amounts of food, drugs, alcohol, sex, work and shopping. We've become a nation of excessive consumption. Ecologically irresponsible, we're a people who directly or indirectly rape the land, dishonor the Earth. We've become a people driven by our most base or immature needs of greed, willing to knife each other in the back in the race up the competitive ladders of corporate America. We've become a people who have been willing to put the health of ourselves and our most precious relationships on the back burner while pursuing financial wealth and power over others. Rather than attending to our psychological health and spiritual wealth we've become masters of distraction and denial—pulling our attention away from the love and support we could be giving and receiving—putting our energy and attention, instead, on addictive numbing behaviors when we could be experiencing what is most real—love, and the true joy of experiencing our connection with one another and the pleasure of our senses in relation to the Earth and our own personal earthiness, our bodies. Instead of putting our attention and time into balancing our psychological nature which can open us to loving and *remembering who we REALLY ARE* and flowing with our creativity, we have denied these barriers and numbed ourselves to LIFE. So much blood has been shed in wars. What have we done with the hard won freedom, the sacrifices that have been made in the name of freedom?

Many have physically fought for freedom on the battleground, on the geographical levels. Those of us who have not been sacrificed in war must use our political freedom to free ourselves on the psychological levels, freeing ourselves to become all that we can be psycho-spiritually. And REMEMBERING our *essence*.

When we remember to feel our wholeness, the gratitude present will make us want to use our life in ways that will make meaningful the sacrifices others have made for freedom in the material world. In this hard won freedom we can know wholeness, live with full aliveness in both Realities, live playfully and in love with ourselves and others.

The experience of **wholeness** is our greatest longing. It is a more primary topic, bigger and more compelling than the fields of Holistic Health or Alternative Therapy. But the many new (and also ancient but recently rediscovered) techniques of Holistic Healing, Alternative and Complementary Medicine and Therapies can pave the road to wholeness for us.

ENERGY WORK HELPS

The healing experiences provided with body-focused energy medicine can lessen suffering. This kind of healing help allows us to release painful memories and tensions which are often stored in the body. Much help can be found through various techniques which consciously, intentionally use energy.

It may be useful to put these many modalities into four general categories:

1) Body-focused psychotherapy in which the therapist does not usually physically touch the client but directs the client's attention to places in the body where they may have energy blockages, releasing them in the process. Shamanic Counseling is another type of therapeutic work with energy ("non-ordinary reality"[86]).

2) Hands-on energy work such as Reiki Healing, Therapeutic Touch, Healing Touch, MariEl, and many other techniques where the healer or holistic practitioner actually touches the client or nearly touches them by scanning their energy field. This is usually considered to be Spiritual Healing and/or Energy Balancing.

3) Energy work where the therapist teaches the client to touch his/her own body in a healing, energy balancing way, such as Touch for Health, Thought Field Therapy, etc.

4) Vibrational Medicine[87] includes many techniques that effect the energy field of the body, move energy and release energy blockages. Just a few examples of this type of energy work are sound and light therapy[88], aromatherapy and flower essences.

ENERGY BLOCKAGES

Energy from intense emotions which have much density can accumulate in the body and eventually lead to physical illnesses. Our "shadow" or unconsious emotions take up residence in our body and cause problems for us. Energy blockages interfere with our experience of joy; there is no reason to hold onto them and good reasons to release them.

Help from therapists, coaches and healers using body-focused techniques creates more spaciousness into which we can welcome more of the energy of consciousness which had been blocked out by dense pockets of energy and tensions.

Hands-on healers are also employed to release energy blockages, as are the techniques which people can use on themselves. With energy medicine and body-focused work we have new paths on the wide road to wholeness.

ALTERNATIVE FANATICS

There exist some individuals who are extremely grateful for the help they have received through alternative medicine—treatments of various kinds which fall outside of conventional medicine. Some of these people are so grateful that their loyalty to the culture of "alternative" help makes them closed minded to the mainstream medical practices of the establishment. I call these people, alternative fundamentalists. Their loyalty to alternative medicine can sometimes be hazardous to their health.

A few years ago, a client of this ilk was putting her physical health in jeopardy by refusing to take drugs.

She honored herbs with a religious fervor. This "New Age Fundamentalist" found identity and emotional security in the structures and forms of the New Age movement. The thought of including established medical treatment in her life was genuinely frightening for her. Care had to be taken to not pull apart, too abruptly, this client's cherished dogma. To her it was simple: drugs were BAD, herbs were GOOD. She could not see the continuum, only the polarities on the end of it. As she had a highly polarized set of personality parts, a serious split in her psyche, it was a big step for this woman to allow the "good" to cavort with the "bad". She was quite surprised that a therapist such as I, reputed to be a friend to and teacher of alternative therapy, would recommend that drugs might even be considered. Her idealization of me as a person coupled with my approval of conventional medicine when alternative therapies would not suffice, helped bring her internal split into a closer partnership.

OPENING MINDS

A holistic perspective helps those people whose minds have snapped shut learn when to open to the other side's offerings, and to not feel that they are being a traitor to their cause if they do so. Some people may need to consider the wise use of drugs, synthetic chemicals which can right a wrong in the body. Some people with the opposite mind-set who may blindly follow the advice of their conventional M.D. may need to be given permission to explore alternative medicine in all its amazing manifestations.

Adorning my wall is a paper sculpture in the form of a circle. The artist has written these words around the circle: "The Earth is the center of the Universe. The Sun and the Moon and the stars and the planets revolve around it. The Earth is flat. This is the truth. All else is magic and nonsense and the work of the devil and as so heresy." It is entitled 15th Century Thought.[89]

A CONSUMER DRIVEN COMPLEMENTARY APPROACH

Complementary medicine is coming into the main stream in the new millennium. This bringing together of ancient, conventional, and very new treatments is what holistic medicine is about. Likewise, holistic psychotherapy needs to be complementary psychotherapy, keeping the best of the old, adding the brightest of the new treatments. Alternative medicine has been a consumer driven movement; the public has demanded that drug stores sell herbs, aroma therapy and alternative help previously only found in the health food stores of the "granola people." Consumers of counseling and therapy must now encourage therapists and doctors to become knowledgeable about the energy paradigm, vibrational medicine and learn to integrate its modalities into their practices in a way which encourages the balancing of Realities.

PARADIGM SURFING

Whether we are mainly concerned about our physical or our mental/emotional health, we may be helped by shifting our paradigm or by surfing back and forth along the continuum of Reality. If we are clinicians or academics teaching in one of the helping professions, expanding our knowledge and awareness of these complementary opposite paradigms can empower our effectiveness and enhance our heartfulness in delivering services to our patients and clients.

A REVIEW OF 36 CONCEPTS IN THIS BOOK

1. The fields of psychology and psychiatry have accumulated many theories and techniques causing distractions from the most essential aspects of *who we really are.*

2. We are each *primarily* a Soul, a ONEness, a wholeness, a reflection of The One.

3. To simplifiy living it is helpful to think of ourselves as living in two Realities

4. Our "right-brain" realm interprets Reality as Quantum Physics understands it (as waves of energy).

5. Our "left-brain" realm interprets Reality as Newtonian Physics understands it (as particles).

6. We can think of these Realities as the Oneness Reality (Reality #1), which is our primary and Eternal Reality, and the time-limited physical-material Reality (Reality #2) which is our secondary reality of mortal existance.

7. Usually one Reality is in the foreground, the other in the background; the more often we let these Realities change places (foreground to background, background to foreground) the more balance and wholeness we experience.

8. People with Attention Deficit Disorder are often disorganized and unable to prioritize because they are unconsciously living in both Realities more or less simultaneously.

9.The two qualitatively different Realities are reflected in and understood by two different paradigms which are the conventional paradigm of modern science (more concrete or dense, energetically) and what I call The Energy Paradigm (more spacious, energetically).

10. Reality #1 and Reality #2 are polarities which exist ON A CONTIUUM.

11. Different "laws" or rules apply to the two polar opposite Realities at the ends of the continuum or spectrum of Reality.

12. The place where the two Realities consciously meet (Reality # 3) is a powerful and Holy place of New Creation where a sacred synthesis of opposites occurs; it is a place where love rules and love is "the rule."

13. The senses are found at the meeting place of the the two Realities (i.e., where the paradigm of vibrations of energy meet the more dense and identifiable "things" of concrete, physical-material reality).

14. Our body is our own personal portable plot of Mother Earth.

15. The major wonders of our physical nature—physical brain and heart—can be thought of as our inner-friends which, like National Parks, can be better known and loved (with scans, and bio-feedback devices) and therefore, better cared for.

16. Love can be described as a sense, like the sense of sound, smell, taste, touch and sight.

17. Lack of understanding of the two paradigms/two Realities can lead to Paradigm Mix-ups resembling either narrow-mindedness or lunacy.

18. Our human personality consists of many pairs of complementary opposite energy patterns, destined to be partners; like the two Realities, they also exist on a continium with extremes at each end.

19. An understanding of behavior can be found in terms of Genetics and Energetics, both.

20. Understanding our emotions in terms of "energy" leads to more self-acceptance and balanced behavior.

21. Our personality energies meet at a place of balance in the human heart.

22. Each human heart, like the Soul, has access to the energetic resources of the heart of Heaven AND the heart of the Earth.

23. Our Soul is a container/not a container. It can be thought of as the container which holds all our life experience and, paradoxically, the soul cannot be contained and has no boundaries, eventually becoming part of the Wholesoul or Universe.

24. When our whole bodysense (Yin) and mental reasoning faculties (Yang) meet within our heart/soul a powerful trinity is formed.

25. Our heart has four cloistered chambers which can be considered as Yin and Yang chambers, the places from which we receive and emit only spacious energies.

26. Simply remembering numbers 1, 2, 3 and 4 is a way to experience more flow, more fluidity, less rigidity.

27. The experience of balanced personality polarities along with an awareness of our ONEness brings us into Unified Selfhood.

28. Unified Selfhood moves us toward experiences of enlightenment.

29. Wholeness means that we are both human and Holy.

30. Spirituality is awareness of our aliveness and the energetic wave-like interconnection of every*thing*. We are each human beings having spiritual experiences AND spiritual beings having human experiences. Spirit is the most primitive and primal of energies.

31. Like the small circles in the YinYang symbol, our humanness contains some Divinity and our Divinity contains some humanness. We are made in the image of the Creator and the Creator is much like the best of us, only more so.

32. Therapist's clinical perspectives and techniques fall along a continuum between the polarities of Reality #1 (The Energy Paradigm) and Reality #2 (The Medical Model Paradigm); full-spectrum Reality therapy only is an ideal for the open-minded, open-hearted therapist, healer and coach but an ideal worth keeping in mind.

33. Paradigm surfing is safe and can be fun for everyone.

34. Family Systems Theory and Metaphysical Laws (of the Energy Paradigm) expand our understanding of relationships; this can be called Family Energy Systems Theory.

35. Sexual behavior can be considered in the light of the spectrum of Reality, leading to more wholesome experiences.

36. Excessively "spacious" (Reality #1) people, Primary Process People, are prevelant in metaphysical and New Age circles and often have psychological vulnerablity which has caused people in scientific (Reality #2) circles to fail to take them seriously until NOW!

OF WHAT USE IS ALL THIS?

These ideas may be merely interesting for those curious people concerned about cosmology and the integration of paradigms. Practically speaking, they may be useful for some people looking for a way to make life more manageable. We can use our awareness of 1, 2, 3 and 4, these four different points of view, to become more comfortable. Having our personality energies in balance *feels better* than being out of balance. Such balance also leads to greater physical health.

Being in Reality #3, where Reality # 1 and #2 meet as partners, feels better than anything else. We are usually in either Reality #1 or Reality #2, one being temporarily in the background, the other temporarily in the foreground.

A TRIO OF REASONS

1.When we are feeling an extreme energy that is uncomfortable, we can take our attention to a memory of a time when we felt wonderful[90]; this simple "remembering" will bring our energies into balance. When our body is remembering or imagining something it experiences that memory or image as "real."

2. When we are feeling discouraged about behavior (our own behavior, our partner's behavior, our family's behavior or the recurring uncomfotable processes into which our relationships may fall) we can"remember" that *everything is energy in motion*. This gives us more hope for creative change. Hope, a place of balance within the heart (as long as it is not extremely future oriented) is spacious; its energy allows the Creative Forces to be at work and at play in our midst.

3. Awareness may be its own reward for ultimately it brings enlightenment. Keeping the meaning of these four numbers in our mind/heart partnership, which is all this simple formula for living involves, leads to far greater awareness of one's personality self ("lesser self"), one's Soul ("Greater Self") and to a physically sensed connection with The One.

WHAT'S IT ALL ABOUT?

Is physical and emotional well-being, wholeness, an end in itself? For WHAT do we seek well-being? Our attunement, or at**one**ment, to the Reality of **ONE** will bring us to an answer to the question.

1, 2, 3 and 4

Keeping in mind that life is a balancing act, the four square numbers of this formula may help any of us keep our human equilibrium and align us with the harmony of the Heavens and even move the collective human family toward a place of peace and justice. The challenge is to remember these numbers and what they now may mean to us. They are sequential and familiar. *There is nothing to* **DO** *with these numbers other than to* **BE** *what they represent.*

May the simplicity of the Formula for Wholeness, 1-2-3-4, make the sea of life more smooth. Life on earth has never been easy. Four easily recalled numbers may make the course less rough and rigorous as we remember them in this way:

One is for our *oneness*; may we know the wholeness which we already ARE and **o**pen to that energy of spaciousness.

Two is for the coming *together* of (non-identical) **t**wins within, and the **two** Realities, the pairs of polar opposite energies, the lion and the lamb lying down to-gether.

Three is for our inner-*trinity*, the powerful *trio* of Head, Heart, Hara connected as a *triangle.*

Four is for the *fountain* of compassion and wisdom, the ever-flowing effervescent wellspring of inner re-sources from the four-chambered heart, our core, our greatest human treasure.

SECTION III

INTRODUCTION TO SECTION III

The *stories* of our lives, for certain, tell the tale of how life works—more than any theory. Stories and anecdotes are not of much use to Western science and its research methods. However, anecdotal evidence of the way life works is very valuable in the paradigm of Reality # 1. Since "all is one" in Reality # 1, we each ARE one another's stories and all of our stories add to our understanding of the collective story of the evolving consciousness of humankind/Divinekind. In hearing stories, we're heartened by an anecdote of healing. Conversely, we're collectively shamed by news from across the globe of torture or depraved behavior by another brother/sister in our human family. Just as "hard science" of Reality # 2 is useful in its research of many things, so are the anecdotes—the tales which show the mystery and the power we have to create our lives with our thoughts, our intentions and our heart's desires.

How the dual realities balance, bringing life to wholeneses, peace and self-love, shows up in every story of a life. Unbalanced realities bring angst, much suffering of many kinds and unfulfillment. When we listen to our heart and feel our soul's surges through our life, we notice what it is that we are called to do. In doing this, we find ourselves both Great and smaller (personality level)

This section is about my own story, particular pieces of my life which may be useful in helping you examine and simply notice the flow and/or times of stagnation in your own.

CHAPTER TWENTY-FOUR

PLACES ALONG THE ROAD

This woman's health has been hard won;
Enormous work at growing has been done.
It's never finished, more's to come.
Just how another's life is going
Ends up showing much about creation
And the living ways of life mysterious;
Thus in hearing of these truths
We may create less strife, less serious
Pain within our own unfolding.
We learn from stories of another's life;
We gain from teachings, tales of others,
Each one our sister or our brother;
The happenings which clearly flowed
From seeds of energy they've sown
Will show the power of our hearts,
Our thoughts, our kinds of minds,
Both human and divine.
At the place these paradigms can meet
We see the making of a life complete.

BEGINNING THE STORY IN THE MIDDLE

In l989, a thought occurred to me which felt like a joyful "mindgasm." My "Ah HA!" experience was this: what is referred to metaphorically as "right-brain thinking," or the feminine (yin) principle, seems to interpret reality in the way that Quantum Physics describes Reality; "left-brain thinking," the male (yang) principle, has been interpreting reality in accord with the scientific paradigm of Newtonian Physics which emerged as the dominant paradigm of Western civilization in the seventeenth century.

My particularly pleasurable intuitive flash, which I fondly recall as a mental orgasm, came after many years of questioning, studying, and becoming reasonably informed about a number of fields which fascinated me. Intuition seems to work best for everyone when it is "informed intuition",—when we have accrued some information or knowledge about the areas into which we are asking our Soul to dip into and bring answers to our conscious, questioning minds. This questioning began for me 40+ years ago. As I have reviewed my life, those moments in which I felt the most aliveness, joy and passion, were those times when I felt I was participating in the creation of a bridge between science and spirituality. For each of us, whenever we are experiencing something that resonates with our Soul's purpose, whatever that purpose might be, we feel a particular quality of joy, a kind of electricity, a feeling that "this is right, this is my heart's desire, what my true work is." Furthermore, our creations are autobiographical in the sense that they are manifestations of our own particular patterns of energy whether we are creating a painting, a song, a psychological theory, or even making a scientific discovery. Our creations reflect the story of who we are as individuals; however we are more than individuals. We are individuals who are also participating in a larger reality.

A SURPLUS OF THE HUMAN CONDITION

Because of serious trouble in my parents' marriage when I was in the womb and during my formative years (all my years, actually), I quite naturally acquired internal unfriendliness between my inner male and inner female, or between my "left-brain" and "right-brain" functioning. And I developed a bit of a split between my mind and my emotions/body sense. Putting this in terms of planetary energies, my astrological "chart" (based on the exact time, date and location of birth) reveals that my Sun and Moon are "squared," meaning that these planetary forces were in opposition to each other at the time I was born; this is another way of saying the same thing that I have mentioned about my parents' intense conflict. And the fact that I am loaded with Gemini energy (my Sun Sign) and with Scorpio energy as well (my "rising" sign, or ascendent) reflects my diversity of interests, my desire to communicate these interests, the pleasure I feel in playing with words (writing poetry) and the depth and intensity of my quest for the natural polarities of human nature to find their resolutions. In short, I've had a surplus of the human condition. And, perhaps not by coincidence, I've had plenty of Soul as well. A great deal of humanness—personality energy (sometimes depression, sometimes vitality, sometimes doubt, sometimes trust) and highly polarized personality patterns creating a dynamic tension internally—caused me to sometimes lose touch with my Soul's wholeness as its joy got buried underneath the abundance of personality "stuff." All is calm, all is quite bright and in balance now, finally. It has been, as we say, "a process."

There may be many ways to look at factors related to the lack of internal harmony and peace I experienced, intermittently, for approximately half a century. The themes about life which have attracted me throughout my life show that my Soul—the depths of my unconscious—has been moving me, through several decades, to the experience of wholeness. This is true, fortunately, for all of us. There is something in our Soul which longs to have its wholeness known and experienced by our humanness.

The insights and interests which we have noticed in our lives relate very intimately to the purpose that the Soul of each of us has. To me, thinking up theories (such as the Unified Theory of The Self) and synthesizing several fields of interest seems to be my purpose which has run parallel to the urge to fully experience personal integration, unification of my former complexity. Playing with ideas, inventing and receiving new ones has been a source of great joy for me.

BUILDING BLOCKS FOR THE MISSION, MINE AND YOURS

Several steps and stages over many years were building blocks for my juicy Gemini curiosity, preparing me to be receptive to new insights later on. The first such moment came in 1960 when, as an adolescent, I heard O.Hobart Mowrer speak about his book *The Crisis in Psychiatry and Religion*.[91] This topic stimulated my Soul to such a degree that I felt as if a jolt of electricity had gone through me. I felt "a calling" deep within my body sense, a passion to build a bridge or manufacture within my mind a harmonious relationship between science and spirituality; this dilema confounded me in 1960 (as had my parents' marriage, earlier).

It seems as though whenever we are living our heart's desire, doing those things which give us joy—those things which turn up the volume of our aliveness—in those joy filled moments we are probably most aligned with our Soul's purpose. The enlivening and " inspiriting" we experience around a particular activity or subject matter may be our clue that we are doing that which God and our Soul, in partnership, have in mind as our mission, this time around. Perhaps you, the reader, could honor yourself by taking some time to review your life from childhood to the present time, asking what things have made your heart sing. This assignment is being offered more to your heart than to your brain.

MARRIAGE AND MARIJUANA

Marriage and children, joyfully, were my entire focus from the mid-60's until I fell into "the dark night of
the soul" in the Spring of 1971. My first experience
with marijuana brought with it a substantial shift in my
psychological structure. I had justified my decision to
"experiment" with this recreational drug because I had
been quite well-behaved as a wholesome adolescent,
college girl and young adult. It was time for some mis-
chief. Living with my high-achieving attorney husband
in a conservative suburb of Chicago, I didn't want to
think of myself as someone who was living the life of
total conventionality; it appeared as though I had joined
the establishment as a young adult and was continuing
to live the life of respectable, responsible behavior
which I had always lived. I secretly admired many of
the perspectives of the flower children; while idealistic, their psychedelically induced visions of the possibility of world peace, justice and harmony held great
appeal. I was not interested in taking the risks that psy-
chedelic drugs presented, but I did smoke, and inhaled,
my first marijuana "joint" with my hippie sister-in-law.
While under its influence I had an insight: palms of
hands held together in the posture of prayer brought
right and left brain hemispheres together. This was interesting, because it was before news had emerged about
right brain and left brain differences, and I knew nothing of Eastern perspectives relating to YinYang at the
time (1970 or '71).

After altering my consciousness, I plummeted into depression but did not seek professional help. Instead, I read books by Karen Horney, a psychiatrist, and I consumed and was soothed by the theology of Paul Tillich. I was struck by Tillich's words: "If one is asked how nonbeing is related to being-itself, one can only answer metaphorically: being embraces itself and nonbeing. Being has nonbeing within itself as that which is eternally present and eternally overcome in the process of the divine light."[92]

I translated Tillich's "nonbeing" as darkness, the depression which continued to intermittently annoy me.

TRAGIC BLOOD DISEASE

In November of 1971, seven months after I had experienced an enormous psychological crisis for which I chose not to seek treatment, I had a dream which terrified me. I "saw" in my dream my 3 ½ year old son running out into the middle of our quiet suburban street and witnessed a huge truck running into him. I saw him lying face down on the street, presumably dead. The dream was of a quality I had not known before in my dreams. It felt so real that I was afraid to tell my husband about it when I woke up screaming. I simply reported that I had experienced a bad dream. I didn't want to make it more real by speaking of it. The next night my husband had a dream in which our son died, and he didn't tell me about it at the time. The day after that our son developed a life-threatening blood disease which was idiopathic, meaning *cause unknown.* Apparently, out of the blue, this youngest of my two children, developed a bruise that looked like a blood-blister in the center of his forehead. The next day our pediatrician, Frank Tracy M.D., ordered blood tests which confirmed his worst fear; the diagnosis was Acute Idiopathic Thrombocytopenia Purpura and possibly Leukemia. Kevin had less than 10% of the normal number of platelet or thrombocytes and could hemorrhage to death if he bumped into anything or even sneezed; the disease was like an internal hemophilia. By the next day there were bruises all over his body, even though he had not had any collisions.

In 1971, there was not yet a treatment for this disease. Dr. Tracy prescribed prednisone which would merely "cushion his tissues," not treat the blood disease. Putting a child with this condition in the hospital, explained Dr. Tracy, would be more of a hindrance than a help, since the frustration of confinement could cause a pre-schooled to bang his head. Best to keep him at home, remove or pad the furniture and stay within 3 feet of Kevin at all times, keeping a careful eye to avert any bumps. Daily blood tests would be done to keep a check on the condition. While I trusted Dr. Tracy, I needed more input. My sister's husband, a medical doctor in New Haven, Connecticut, was horrified by my reports of the numbers from every blood test—so low was the platelet level. Tests for the blood count were done on four or five different days, all showing the same dangerously low number of platelets. The somber concern of my

brother-in-law's response to the numbers frightened me
further.

We decided to consult with another doctor, Marc
Beem, M.D., who was a leading pediatrician at Weyler
Children's Hospital, University of Chicago. I contacted
him and he assured us that Frank Tracy was a highly
respected pediatrician. He said "All you can hope for is
a spontaneous remission; you're in the hands of the
gods." (I found this to be a curious phrase for a man I
had heard was an agnostic). Sometimes children with
this disease do go into remission; with adults it is almost always fatal, he told us. I asked how long it might
be, if we were fortunate enough to have Kevin go into a
spontaneous remission that day, before his platelet count
would allow him to safely play and return to pre-school.
"At least four months," was the reply. Little Kevin had
been a content, relaxed, healthy toddler prior to the
break-up of the structure of my psyche in April of 1971.
How was it that seven months after dramatic changes in
my personality as a result of my break-down, my beloved three-year old, the light of my life during those
months, was now close to death, a month before we
would be getting ready for Santa Claus? Would Christmas even be celebrated in our home this year, or would
we be in deep grief? Somewhere within me I began to
feel that our family energies of the previous months had
culminated in this potentially tragic crisis we were experiencing. Somewhere within me I knew that my sensitive little boy had absorbed the chaotic and negative
energies of our family system during that particularly

difficult year, and manifested them as a life-threatening physical disease.

In 1972 I had not yet heard about the magic of living from the present moment. I did not consciously know that the greatest place to be for peace and healing power was in the body. I had not been informed about the importance of coming into the five physical senses and staying the mind where fear can take over. I seemed to be propelled by Grace into the HERE AND NOW. There I felt no fear, or very little, and was able to take care of him without being gripped by the terror of his life being in great jeopardy.

My mother flew to Chicago to help me take care of Kevin. Having been a nurse prior to becoming a mother, she was excellent help in a crisis. We moved furniture, padded the furniture we could not move and played with Kevin on the carpet for safety's sake, doing puzzles, drawing, keeping him safe from bumping into things. "Why don't you do a little laying on of hands," my mother suggested. Having been most recently in my intellectual, Unitarian phase, I had not given spiritual healing a thought and my association of hands on healing in 1972 was of people in tents in the deep south behaving in ways I had never included in my life. But clearly, I had nothing to lose in secretly trying to heal my son. While he played with puzzles on the floor, I put my hands on his back, said nothing out loud, but simply surrendered to WHATEVER might respond to my heart's desire that Kevin be made restored to full health. My three year old son had no idea what I was doing, not consciously anyway, and I didn't know what I was doing either. I simply found myself squarely in the Here and Now, placing my hands on his back and silently *asking* that if there was a power in the Universe that could make him well, let this happen. I had no faith to speak of, but I remember feeling that he HAD to become well. For me, his death was not an option. It was unthinkable and I knew that I was not up to dealing with such a loss at that period of my life.

The next day our pediatrician called and asked us to take Kevin to Children's Memorial Hospital for a bone marrow test to rule out leukemia. The diagnosis of acute idiopathic thrombocytopenia purpura was certain, validated by several blood tests during the first week of the illness. The diagnosis of leukemia was not as clear. With dread about the bone marrow test, a painful experience for anyone, we took Kevin downtown to the hospital. The hematologist met us and said that before doing the bone marrow test she wanted to draw blood from his arm and look at it under the microscope, even though she had already received the report of the many blood tests done previously. She drew his blood, disappeared for a time and returned to tell us, with astonishment, that his blood was completely normal. After a deep breath or two, I asked her how that was possible, since we had been told that if he had a spontaneous remission it would happen gradually and it would be at least four months before he would be out of danger. She said that she didn't know, that "this is a medical miracle" and cannot be explained.

A week later his bruises had all disappeared and his blood count continued to be normal. This was my introduction to spiritual and energy healing. It was also my awakening to the interconnectedness of the unconscious mind of one person with that of another. A few months after my son's medical crisis I received a phone call from Connecticut. An old high school girl friend called me and said that she had been thinking of me and afraid to call because in November she had a dream in which something terrible had happened to my son, Kevin. My friend, Sheila, had no way of knowing of the medical crisis we were going through for I had not been in touch with any of our high school friends during that time. This mysterious connection was not something I had ever learned about in psychology classes. I needed to know more about this mystery and began searching.

Another aspect of this interconnection of energies came to light ten years after Kevin's blood disease. In my curiosity about all aspects of the human experience, I decided to have astrology charts done for each of the four of us in my nuclear family. It was 1978. I wasn't sure if I "believed in" astrology, having not had a chart done before, but wanted to explore it for I was obsessing about whether or not to remain in my marriage. Kathryn de Jersey, a Chicago astrologer, had drawn up the charts of the four family members, after receiving the dates, exact time of birth and location for each of us. As she reviewed our charts she said, "I don't know what your husband does but if he's not a lawyer he ought to be." I told her he was, indeed, a lawyer. The astrologer said my marriage contained extreme stress and if this was not addressed I could get sick. She told me that I should be a counselor, teacher, writer, lecturer. I told her I was a counselor and teacher. She said that my daughter had a beautiful chart and was a very talented, loving girl. This was certainly true; she is a very unusual person—good as gold and brilliant. When she looked at my son's chart she said, "His chart shows that he would probably move from one area of the country to another when he was two years old." Yes, I said, we had moved from Washington, D.C. to the suburbs of Chicago when he was two. Then she said, "His chart shows that in November of his third year he would have a close brush with death, and that he would have some protection at that time, and that he would have recovered in about four months." Four months was the time frame the doctors had given for recovery *if* Kevin went into a spontaneous remission soon after the illness was first diagnosed. Thus I learned that planetary energies may be part of the mix of things that contribute to, or more likely, *reflect* what we are encountering in our journey.

CONTINUING CURIOSITY

In the early '70's, I found myself fascinated with the emerging perspective of "right brain and left brain" cognition. I also read with excitement and was aided by the work of psychoanalyst Heinz Kohut, creator of Self Psychology.

Personally, I was experiencing thyroid cancer, more depression, serious autoimmune (Rheumatoid Arthritis) and neurological diseases (MS, not conclusively diagnosed because an autoposy was required for this in the early '70's). My health concerns added urgency to my quest for a perspective that could help me become healthy. Reaching out to any and all who might offer me healing, I explored inside and outside the establishment.

I nurtured myself taking classes at the Chicago Theological Seminary and Lutheran School of Theology as a Student-at-Large studying the work of theologian Paul Tillich whose writings had gotten me through a difficult time of depression in the early 1970's. I had also enjoyed reading biographies of Tillich during those years and recall having the thought that this man was both brilliantly analytical and also thoroughly sensuous, according to his biographers. I remember thinking that only the *people who were* at least somewhat *more sensuous than analytical were people I* could fully *trust*. Paul Tillich was one of those. I hadn't yet discovered what I was soon to learn: the body does not lie. Our senses are trustworthy. Somehow, I must have sensed this intuitively.

Andrew Weil, M.D. had just written his first book on holistic healing about the time I was struggling with imbalances in mood and some serious physical health failings—with thyroid cancer, Rheumatoid Arthritis and, for ten years, the frightening symptoms of Multiple Sclerosis. I visited the Medical Clinic of the Association of Research and Enlightenment in Phoenix, Arizona and met with a doctor who himself had MS, hoping for encouragement. He also believed I had MS. My endocrinologist had chosen to not do a spinal tap which could contribute to the diagnosis (this was in 1973, before CAT scans had been invented) because there was nothing that could be done about this awful disease so it was better to not know for certain until it was obvious."

I returned to graduate school in the mid-70's, having previously put my formal education aside to become a mother. My 1977 dissertation was on the Hospice Movement which had barely begun in America. Through my research on this project I became personally acquainted with Dr. Elisabeth Kubler-Ross, the psychiatrist who was also interested in mysterious happenings which did not fit into the conventional paradigm of science.

By the late 70's, I had begun learning about The New Sciences. Quantum Physics particularly intrigued me because the way in which this New Physics viewed reality was much like the perspective held by the many metaphysical teachers I had been meeting and whose psychic structures I was researching.

While working on my dissertation, I recall thinking: the opposite state of polyanna *optimism* and the deflated state of *pessimism* come together at a meeting place where *HOPE* is waiting to be found. This thought excited me. There was an electrical charge that accompanied it. At the time I didn't realize that the subject which I would find to be so compelling from the late 1980's onward, the subject that would become my passion and focus, would be the subject of polarities and balancing these opposite energies, and complementary opposite Realities.

From the time I finished graduate school in 1977 until the mid-1990's I fed my curiosity about the way the life process works by attending literally hundreds of lectures, workshops, programs, classes. I CONSUMED these events! In terms of the paradigm of conventional science and psychology (Reality #2) I fed my oral greed and emotional needs with information and new experiences. In terms of the energy paradigm (Reality #1), I received healing energy, Light and expanded my consciousness (without any more recreational drugs!) during those years.

While stuck in another depression in 1981, I discovered a book which brought me back to aliveness and joy. It was Marilyn Ferguson's *Aquarian Conspiracy.* Once again I felt electrified with the excitement this book brought me. The root of the word "conspiracy" is "conspire" which means to breathe together or to love; in that context she named her book. A new era was about to emerge and I was eager to be a participant.

Another time I felt my heart sing, as it had when I was an adolescent first being bitten with the mental bridge-building bug, was when an outline for a 10-week class appeared in my psyche with the title: A New World View: Incorporating Scientific Insight Into Spiritual Practice. With delight in the early '80's I taught this synthesis of material I had been studying and was eager to share. I began saving evidence of "an Aquarian Conspiracy." Significant scientists such as Rupert Sheldrake and Physicist Fritjov Capra came to town and again I felt enlivened by their sharings, as if I was hearing high truth, something beyond science itself.

With concern about my health threats abounding I continued to learn all I could about the scientific research on spiritual healing. Olga Worrall became part of my life. She was the most legitimate spiritual healer in the country, having been tested in laboratory studies with cloud chambers in the physics laboratory at Stanford University and at the University of London. She was "the real McCoy." A number of contacts with Olga Worral at her healing services in the Methodist Church in Baltimore and at the A.R.E. in Virginia Beach were very beneficial to my health. I also became acquainted with John Lennon's psychic healer from New York, a man named Dean Kraft.[93] If he was good enough for one of the Beatles, he was certainly good enough for me. Whenever he came to Chicago I had a session with him and found his ability to "read my mind" quite amazing.

While I experienced degrees of improvement with each healing session, I still struggled with the symptoms of autoimmune and neurological disease and mood fluctuations; these symptoms gave me good reasons to indulge in healing workshops. In the early 1980's I studied Therapeutic Touch, became a Reiki healer and learned MariEl healing from Ethel Lombardi. I also infiltrated my very conventional (Reality #2) social-activist oriented U.C.C. Church (Congregational/Presbyterian) with ideas about Spiritual Healing. Several kindred spirits at my church joined together to start a monthly Service of Prayer and Healing in 1983, something which many of the Reality #2 dominant parishioners found (and still find) to be a bit irregular in such an intellectually sophisticated, main-stream establishment church. To justify this endeavor I carefully researched scientific research on spiritual healing and taught courses on the subject at my own church and many other churches as well and was interviewed on the subject on television shows.

FED BY MANY

In my journey to heal and grow I've studied with, seen, heard and learned from quite a wonderful assortment of people. I've experienced several of these people on many occasions over the span of a quarter of a century and have watched several of *them* evolve and grow. For a time I secretly considered myself to be " the Ralph Nader of the Human Potential Movement" keeping my eye out for those leaders who might have gaps in their integrity. I found few of those, actually. Most often I noticed compassion and wisdom within the consciousness culture and its leadership; I felt much more spaciousness than anything resembling density or contracted energies within the growing community in America of awakening people.

Here is a list of some (only *some*) of the people whose workshops were especially significant for me during the 1970's and 1980's (a more complete list of workshops in which I participated from the the the early 1970's until the mid 1990's is found in Appendix D): Rev. Morton Kelesy (Jungian) Ph.D., Elisabeth Kubler-Ross, M.D., Jean Houston, Ph.D., Stanley Krippner, Ph.D., Larry Dossey, Olga Worrall, Jack Schwartz, Marilyn Ferguson, Ethel Lombardi, David Spangler,Mark Thustron, PhD., Kenneth Ring,Ph.D., Brugh Joy, M.D., Delores Kreiger (Therapeutic Touch), Ph.D,. Richard Moss,M.D., Ram Dass, Daniel Goldman Ph.D., Daniel Brown, Ph.D.,Gerald Jampolsky, Emmanuel (Pat Rodegast), Judith Skutch (Course in Miracles), Barbara Marx Hubbard, Matthew Fox, Rev. Dr.Martin Marty, Virginia Satir, Ph.D., Bob Shaw, MD, Charles Kramer, M.D., Janette Kramer, Hal Stone and Sidra Winkleman (Voice Dialogue), Carolyn Conger, Ph.D.,Fritjov Capra, Ph.D.,Chogyam Trunpga Rinpoche, M.Scott Peck, M.D., Sondra Ray, Helen Bonney's Guided Imagery with Music (GIM), Marty Grossman, M.D., Jeffery Bland, Ph.D., Donald Pachuta, M.D.,Michael Harner, Ph.D.,(Shamanism), Patricia Sun, Ph.D., Hymayat Imayat Kahn (Sufi), John White, Bernie Seigel,

M.D.,Willis Harman, Lawrence LeShan, PhD., Henry Rucker, Hugh Prather, Gurumayi (Siddha Yoga), Jay Haley, Paul Watzlawick, James Masterson, M.D., Otto Kernberg M.D. (his books), Heinz Kohut via Dr.Wolf and Miriam Elson, Aaron Beck, M.D. and David Burns, M.D. (Cognitive Therapy), Albert Ellis, PhD., Arthur Schwartz, Richard C. Schwartz, Ph.D., Drunvalo Melchizedek, Robert Orienstien and Sobel (Psychoneuroimmunology), Silvano Arieti, M.D., Michael Franz Basch, M.D., Robert Bly, Joseph Campbell (alas, not in person), Ilana Reubenfeld, Harriet Goldhor Lerner,PhD., Rudolph Ballentine, M.D., Jos. Palumbo, Therese Bernardez, M.D.,Lionel Corbett, M.D., Robert O. Becker, M.D., Elmer Green, Ph.D. (Menningers), Jean Goldsmith, Ph.D., Monica McGoldrick, Froma Walsh, PhD., Miriam Reitz, Ph.D., Robin Condro, L.C.S.W., Bob Mark, PhD., James C. Windsor, Ph.D., Donald Klein, M.D.,Richard Gardner, M.D., Leo E. Hollister, M.D.(lecture),George Winokur, M.D., Dr. Upledger, Rupert Sheldrake, Robin Scroggs, D.Div., Rev.Wm. Sloan Coffin, Carl Pfeiffer (Orthomolecular psychiatry which studies the effects of nutrition on mood and mental functioning). There were many others.

Some of the many organizations and training programs which were part of my development in the 1970's and 1980's were these: The Institute for Psychoanalysis in Chicago, Shambhalla Meditation Training, The Inner Peace Movement, The Theosophical Society of America, The Association of Research and Enlightenment, The Association of Humanistic Psychology, Common Boundary, The Family Institute of Chicago (Charles

Kramer, M.D., founder), Omega Institute of Holistic Studies, Institute of Noetic Sciences (especially their studies on the placebo effect), The D.M.A. course, The est Training (1979) and a major Chicago Conference on Meditation Related Therapy in 1977.

ORACLE ABUSE

Divination through oracles fascinated me and, until my personality self grew into greater cohesiveness, I was prone to oracle abuse. Indulging in frequent use of the ancient Chinese oracle, The I Ching, annual Astrology readings, numerology consultations and Tarot card readings became an interesting and compelling part of my life. Meanwhile, I stayed very active as a member of my Congregational (U.C.C.) Church. It was a fine balance, a spectrum of spirituality ranging from the structured world of a church filled with members of "the establishment" to the world of sometimes unusual people who immersed themselves in hidden mysteries (which is what the word "occult" means). While I never became an alcoholic or drug addict, I perhaps fell into "psychic abuse," for I had many, many psychic "readings" in the 1980's. I justified this because I wanted clues about my serious health threats but also because I was fascinated with the psyches of professional psychics I encountered and found that the way they viewed the world made more sense to me than many things which my conventional education offered. Several of the psychics I consulted had Ph.D.'s in psychology. The spectrum of psychics I encountered ranged all the way from those with the degree of structure which most Ph.D.'s represent to gypsy psychics (which I do not recommend). And there were many in between. I spent several years in therapy with one psychic who was attuned to subtle energies and was a Jungian-oriented psychologist.

My own research on what I call Primary Process People, people with a great deal of contact with the realm of the unconscious, was a focus for my curiosity. I felt fortunate that I was able to afford all this "continuing education," some of which was unconventional and much more of which was closely connected to the establishment—providing an additional benefit of "Continuing Education Units." Lots of them. I felt that I wanted to learn all I could and someday synthesize what I had learned for others who may not have had the means to study and glean new insights about life from such a diverse array of "teachers." There was an urge within me to put my curiosity and experiences of healing to good use for others in the future.

In 1982, I also entered a two-year post-graduate training program in Marriage and Family Systems Therapy. Systems Theory made great sense to me and I felt an affinity for it, sensing the dance of energies. The dynamics of families occured to me in a flash. As I prepared to enter this respected and established program of Jeanette and Charles Kramer, M.D., I decided to keep private the fact that I had a secret life as an explorer of all manner of extra-establishment adventures from spiritual healing to dream telepathy[27] (the work of noted parapsychologist Stanley Krippner, PhD. fascinated me in particular). I still didn't think the establishment was ready to have one of its clinicians dabbling in the world of numinous, or "spooky" occurances. Much to my surprise, just as I was starting the formal Family Therapy Training program, I discovered that a man who would be supervising my training was also dabbling in spooky things, for he was a participant in my Reiki healing class that year!

Since the workshops and books of Jungian analyst Morton Kelsey had been so useful to me, I considered becoming a Jungian Analyst but felt it to be too analytical, too mental, and I was impressed by the importance of what the body could reveal about us. Increasingly I turned to the emerging, multi-faceted field of Energy Medicine and what it could teach me.

HEART-IN-HAND

After some years of clinical experience in hospitals and schools I came across the work of Roberto Assiagoli in the A.R.E. bookstore in 1981. Based on what he and Jung, both students of Freud, had done I decided that it was legitimate to focus on the Soul in psychotherapy. I began my private practice in earnest the following year.

I was intentional about opening my heart and working from a place of unconditional love. The greatest inner peace and sense of wholeness was with me in those hours when I was "doing" therapy. I was fully present in the Here and Now when I was with my clients and this was an immense relief to me—like being on vacation while I was working. For counselors and therapists, being who we ARE is more important than anything we DO for our clients in terms of techniques and interventions. It has always felt to me that simply being present, simply being who I AM, is the most important aspect of helping people; I believe this is true for all people in the helping fields.

A logo for my business card appeared in an antique shop where I found an adornment for my office: it was a wooden frame holding a piece of tin into which the image of a hand with a heart in its center had been pierced. Around the heart-in-hand were the words of the old Shaker slogan: "Hands to work, hearts to God." It is a fitting symbol as I've worn hats of both therapist and healer. This warm, welcoming visual image represents the marriage of two paradigms of reality: Reality # 1)—the *heart*'s wellspring of compassion, the energy of simply BEING who we *are* and Reality #2)—the *hand* symbolizing DOING the work of therapy using many techniques from our "bag of tricks," or techniques for "fixing" people.

BEING
Reality #1

DOING
Reality #2

This heart-in-hand logo also represents the energy of healing love which flows from a chakra or energy center in the palm of all of our hands when we intend to serve the healing forces with hands-on energy work.

As my therapy practice quickly grew, I continued to be immersed in the exploration of all things relating to healing. I also enriched my Western Judeo-Christian heritage by studying Eastern religions. This gave me new ways and new words for understanding truths about the Life Process. As I "went East" (while continuing to be active in Western civilization's Christian church), the new spiritual practices I learned became a blessing for me in my healing journey.

LEAP OF FAITH

I took a leap of faith and decided to divorce my good but not-quite-right-for-me-at-the-time husband in 1984, trusting the Life Process on one hand and feeling much insecurity on the other. Prior to assuming this responsibility for myself and its frightening freedom, my identity was so entangled in the life I had been leading that I couldn't know for certain who I really was. I knew I was a Soul but I also wanted to know that I was acquiring a psychological self which would support me consistently enough in the material world. Previously my responsible attorney husband had taken care of me, and I found I would space-out, drop the ball of self-responsiblity and fail to discover that I could function to the degree that life in the physical world requires. I wanted to discover whether or not I could really be the grown-up I appeared to others to already be. Prior to my divorce I had felt like something of a fraud, never haven taken full responsibility for my care and maintanence. In retrospect, I can see that I was working on the separation-individuation process, having not satisfactorily accomplished this psychological task as a two-year old or teenager. As I initiated the divorce I didn't know if my health would hold together, but as I ventured out into the world on my own, my physical health improved dramatically. Since the mid-1980's I have been free of all neurological and autoimmune problems.

Adventures with Energy Medicine and learning new ways to help clients embody their soul has been central to my work and to my own integration. Traditional Chinese Medicine has also provided benefit in balancing polarities of energies within the body for me and for my clients. A marriage of matter and spirit. Living in two Realities is something we all do, whether we realize it or not. Doing it with full awareness of our intention for internal harmony moves us toward health and well-being. Focusing on the body and receiving the energy of spaciousness, light, "chi," into our own earthiness has been the most important aspect of my own healing and appreciation of the wholeness that has been with me all along. Many week-long group energy-intensive experiences have been key to my liberation from density into more expansiveness. Robert Jaffe, M.D., Kathryn Nash, Paul Ditscheit and Alexandra Parness have all been leaders in the field of Energy Medicine who have brought many "light workers" together. I have benefited from their leadership and have been empowered by the collective energy fields of the groups of people they have gathered together. One energy medicine intensive experience which liberated me from the part of my mind that had preferred to stay in control was a "Divine Unity Gathering" in Snowmass, Colorado in 1995. After decades of resistance, the density of my controlling mind was made spacious by an infusion of Soul energy which I finally was able to embody. This degree of surrender into peace did not bring internal silence, however. Quieting my curious mind has been a challenge. Insights and ideas continually occur to me and they bring much pleasure.

One fun flash of insight that came to me in 1989 was the idea that some of the things that look like "unrealistic thinking" could be looked at as a mixed paradigm experience. The rules of the two realities are different and sometimes people get them mixed-up. Untangling this mixed paradigm living, or tangled paradigm thinking, seemed to me to be very important. Equally important to me has been to honor the insight that came to me as I thought of each of the two paradigms of reality: these paradigms are on a continuum with extreme versions of each being widely divergent, highly polarized from the other. The place where they meet in mutual respect for their differences is a place where blessings from Creation abound. I've also found pleasure is playing with the integration of metaphysics into Family System Theory.

ANOTHER FAMILY TRAGEDY

On February 5, 1995 while vacationing with her fiancé and his family in Maui, Hawaii, my daughter was tragically injured when a pick-up truck driver drove through a stop sign into the back of a motorcycle she was riding. She lost half of her leg , had a "hangman's" neck fracture with severe subluxation (dislocation), fractured jaw and had a closed head injury. After seeing her own lost leg on the road, and never losing consciousness, she was helicopter flown from the site of the accident to Honolulu's Queen's Medical Center.

A BIRD'S APPEARANCE

A few days after the accident my daughter's fiance saw me with tears in my eyes in the corridor of the hospital. He is an electrical engineer and thinks in very practical, concrete ways; the polar opposite of a mystic. He said to me, "You know, she is going to be alright." I replied, "Oh, I *know* she is. Her Spirit is SO STRONG." (Some people are stronger than steel and my loving daughter happens to be one of those people). He then said, "Well, I know she will be fine because a couple of days ago I was having dinner outside with her father and a little bird jumped up on the table where we were eating. It kept hopping around the table, chirping happily. I looked at it, did a double take and looked again— I could hardly believe what I was seeing: the bird had one and a half legs, just like she has, and it was singing happily. At that point I knew she was going to be O.K."

This story of synchronicity, so mysterious and wonderful, was a double miracle. It brought hope, showing the mysterious help coming to our family from the compassionate Heart of Heaven. It also showed me that my future son-in-law had a place within him that responds to mystical experience. Such a gift was that bird, and so clear to me it has become that all of nature participates in a dance that says "yes" to life and is ever-ready to help us when we ask for help. And every one of us has a mystical place within our heart.

NECK ALIGNMENT

My daughter's injuries had caused extreme subluxation, misalignment, as well as a fracture to the C2 vertebrae on two sides. Because she was having extreme muscle contractions from the pain throughout her body there was danger of the spinal cord being compromised to such a degree that she could become totally paralyzed or even die. Twenty-five pounds of traction was insufficient to pull her neck into alignment and so the doctors had decided that it would be necessary to fuse the first four vertebra and insert a metal rod in her neck. I had been in Mexico on vacation at the time I learned of the accident so it took me a few days to get to her bedside in Honolulu. I called my many spiritual healer friends for prayers and let my church and other friends know that my daughter had requested that everybody "send energy." As my son and I were preparing to fly to the hospital in Hawaii, one of my psychic healer friends, Susan Willenbrink, said to me, "You have gathered up so much Light from your caring church members and all your friends that you are taking a huge bouquet of Light to your daughter. When you and your son walk into her hospital room, miracles will occur." As we got to the hospital we felt the power of this network of Love. We were told that my daughter's neck fusion surgery would occur the following day (and something deep within me said a loud but silent "NO!" to that surgery). As my friend Susan had said they would, miracles happened that day. My daughter's neck "miraculously" stopped resisting the 25 pounds of traction and came into alignment so that the halo brace was able to be locked in place and no neck surgery was required. Mercifully, she has had no paralysis and a neck which, after five months in a halo brace, was back in good working order.

In terms of the physical-material world's Reality #2, one could say that a deeper peace and relaxation may have occurred within my daughter's neck muscles when her mother and brother showed up. This could certainly account for the change in her neck. In terms of Reality #1, "a bouquet of Light" of great spaciousness was brought into her energy field, prayers were answered and a healing occurred. We honor both realms and are grateful for the the marriage of those paradigms in those moments.

HEART CONNECTION.

In 1998, at the Conference on Consciousness and Science in Albuquerque, New Mexico, I heard Dr. Paul Pearsall, author of *The Heart's Code,* speak about his own miraculous healing in Hawaii. After his talk I shared with him my daughter's experience at the Queen's Medical Center in Honolulu, informing him (I thought) about the Alternative Healing department which makes its services available to patients who request it. I was eager to spread the word about this wonderful hospital. To my surprise, I discovered that the Alternative Healing program which served my daughter had been started by Paul Pearsall himself. It is my hope that such programs will emerge at hospitals in all of these United States. As at Queen's Medical Center, conventionally trained, Reality #2, medical-model paradigm doctors and nurses can work side-by-side with Reality #1, energy paradigm practitioners who do Healing Touch and other forms of energy medicine. When my daughter was in such pain that even the morphine in her intravenous tube would not bring relief, the Healing Touch and Reiki treatments that she received were of immense benefit.

At a Conference on "Creating Integrated Healthcare," the 2nd Annual Alternative Therapies Symposium led by Larry Dossey, M.D. and Jeanne Achterberg, PhD. in 1997, I heard Dr. Gary Schwartz present his fascinating research on the relationship between the heart, the brain and the cellular memory of the body. This kind of leading edge research will bring spirituality and science, Reality #1 and Reality #2, into the partnership longed for at the beginning of this New Millennium.

More useful research about the heart's ways came my way from The Institute of HeartMath Research. In 1999 I began passing along to my clients heartening news from science: meditating on the heart can bring great benefits to the endocrine and cardio-vascular systems. The electrical power of the heart is indeed the sacred heart's flames.

Years earlier Morton Kelsey had suggested to me that God works through electricity somehow. And Hal Stone said that perhaps God could be defined, simply, as energy. As this New Millennium unfolds we have a chance to gather our electrical hearts in community and create great energy fields which can lift the collective energy of humanity to greater lighter heights.

COMMUNITY CONNECTION AND KINSHIP

As life in the 90's brought me to a place of knowing my wholeness more fully than before, I found a need for celebration. My connection to my church continued, yet I wanted celebration and ceremony with kindred spirits who were seeking intimacy and joy around awakening to greater consciousness. I found such opportunities for sharing consciousness in community.

In the early '90's the man who had created the I.F.S. model of therapy, Dick Schwartz, encouraged me to put together and lead a consultation group for therapists to help them use his model. I did so, but soon found myself teaching and sharing the perspectives and approaches I had been using prior to making the acquaintance of I.F.S. In this group we have shared and explored a variety of ways of doing holistic counseling, and we have meditated and prayed together for our clients (without saying their names out loud for the sake of confidentiality) and for ourselves as well. Such experiences are not only supportive but they celebrate the healing and wholeness which can be enhanced in others and in ourselves. This type of community of counselors I strongly recommend for anyone in the helping professions today.

One of the richest experiences of my life was a time of meditation with women, well-developed in their spirituality, on the sacred ground of the Black Hills of South Dakota in 1997. There I felt that I was receiving guidance and direct input from another dimension which validated all the ideas I had been teaching. Yet the ideas came through in a way that was even more simplified and more joyful than my previous thoughts and presentations had been. The three-hour experience was one in which I felt that we, as a culture, needed to shift our style of life and put play and joy into a place more central in our lives while bringing an end to world hunger. And we were to marry the truths of pagan, pre-Christian teachings about the earth *together with* the teachings Jesus had taught about love, peace and justice. The day after this meditation experience I felt the deepest peace, joy and connection with heaven and earth that I had ever known.

Other energetically rich experiences allowed me to conclude the 20th Century in communities of consciousness. Specifically, they were the Warrior-Monk[95] and Enlightenment Intensives.[96] As a sequel to the transformational weekend for men called The New Warriors (also named The Mankind Project) its founder, Bill Kauth, created longer intensive experiences and made them co-educational. These week-long happenings included much meditation, sacred dance and respectful rituals which honored a diversity of spiritual traditions and what I think of as bio-psycho-spiritual clearing experiences which allow the participant to release energy blockages and "baggage" of the past. A "process" of creating one's own reality and then creating the opposite was clearly about seeing and bringing together the opposites which had been my wish for myself for many years. Being able to physically experience the human dichotomies in such a safe and sacred container as such a community creates is something for which I am grateful. Not only were the polarities within my psyche brought forth in all their splendor/horror, but the experience of feeling "one with everything" was and has continued to be felt deeply. While feeling my feet fully on the ground and knowing myself to be a unique, individuated, differentiated, separate individual, I felt something more. As I was awakened by a rooster's crow and the early morning sunshine, I felt "I AM the rooster, I AM the sun." This was not my first experience of an enlightened moment, yet it is a clear and rich memory which I cherish. The Warrior-Monk Intensive deepened my experience of Oneness and of selfhood on every level.

Returning home from the eight day Warrior-Monk experience in 1999 I felt happy, whole, balanced and connected. Two nights later I awakened in the middle of the night and felt the desire to meditate. There was a full moon that night late in May. I recall the moment clearly when I said to myself while "trying" to meditate, "Oh, Nancy Ging, you had a great and enriching time at Warrior-Monk but, let's face it, you are still somewhat divided against yourself; you still are more split than you want to be and so give up, accept the fact that you are someone who will always experience the human condition to such an extent that trusting your wholeness on an on-going basis may be beyond your reach. Too much to expect for one wired up like you are. This is probably as good as integration of personality can get for you, and you may always be, to some degree, a prisoner of faulty wiring in your brain and bio-chemical quirks, personality density, held captive by your gremlin, darkness, your shadow, and still unable to write your book and share what you have to share. Let's face it, Nance, you will never know wholeness as you want to; just accept this." At that precise moment, to my complete surprise, a very palitable warm energy flowed down into my head and surrounded me. I felt immensely loved, throughly accepted "as is." A physical feeling of deep trust in a unified self within me and profound trust in The One beyond my Self/self was present to such a degree that night that it has never left me for a moment since that time.

RESISTANCE DID NOT ENTIRELY DISAPPEAR

Although my experience of trust and wholeness continued to be consistent and profound since the initiation—the gift of grace under the full moon that May—I found I was still capable of resistance to the flow of what felt like my Soul's purpose, my heart's desire. I had a book to finish writing.

I employed a gifted coach named Jeanne Dickerson to support me in getting out of my own way so that I could complete the book I'd been wanting to finish for years. Distractibility had been a dominant trait of my personality. My coach suggested I get a tangible, concrete symbol of my "gremlin," the source of my distrations. I choose from my closet a shawl which was dense, solid black, rough-in-texture with a woven pattern of squares. I recalled, as a child, putting a rough woolen, dark green U.S. Marine Corps blanket with my father's name on it over a coffee table and hiding under this "cozy house" which I had created for myself. This green blanket was a souvenier from my father's service in the Phillipines during World War II. There, under that dark, dense blanket I felt the joyful child in me singing, "Jesus wants me for a sunbeam." Now, decades later, I put a black shawl over my shoulders, a shawl which represented the shadowy gremlin polarity within my personality; it could be quite sinister in its insistence that it would not allow me to finish my book. Beneath the black shawl, the aliveness of my joyful Soul was unmistakably present. It seemed that Jesus *still* wanted me for a sunbean and I wanted to write this book from my heart. On my computer I began a dialogue with my dark side and discovered that something which I had been preaching to others for years was very real and true for me as well.Certainly we teach what we need to learn. This gremlin within me, which had been causing me to procrastinate and fail to finish my book, was wanting only my attention and my respect. I was rediscovering something that the poet Rilke had written:

"Perhaps everything terrible is in its deepest being something helpless that wants help from us."[97]

This difficult energy of distraction, this dense gremlin-like force which had made the manifestation of my book such a struggle for so long, became my partner and friend. I wrote to my dark polarity:

Distraction reigns,
Procrastination pains me
When I forget *your* need,
Your greediness immense,
Your darkness, ever dense.
"Remember me! You say,
"This moment, every day you live.
Away from me you must not bend.
And let us paraphrase your friend:
I AM the way, the truth and the dark/Light split
Words reflecting Nazareth's
Guru Supremo."
We are a duo;
The times which are upon us here
Say this:
When polar opposites appear
Let's welcome the dichotomies,
Let us embrace as partners, these.
My love will honor, now, your rage
Include it in the coming Age,
Tamed within my heart, not far
Away from me, you are
Within these chambers, holding close
The dark and Light, for we are both
Included in the "All That Is"
Complete, connected,
Resurrected wholeness.

IN CONCLUSION

In conclusion, collusion with one's darkness is recommended. Integration of dark and Light arrives for those who seek it. Wholeness is our birthright. We arrive as sensual, joyful infants clearly knowing nothing but this wholeness. We split and break away from knowing wholeness as our complex, diversity of human energy engulfs us. And we can know our wholeness again while we are in our body, before we die and move into the wholeness waiting for us as our Eternal Home. There is still time to play in the Here and Now.

Diversity, a certainity;
Equal we can't be
In terms of energy
Nor talent, beauty;
But equally we share
A Soulful goal,
Our choice
To serve collectively,
Perhaps a duty,
Which is: *to know our wholeness.*
This is ALL we're here for.
We are here for ALL,
Our wholeness, knowing of it
Tells us our totality,
Shows us equally the holy, All That Is.
That is all.
Within ourselves
As it is so
Without—
That is, within the great Beyond.
Simply, this is it—
To know,
Then go
        Enjoy
           It All.

APPENDIX A:

The Narcissistic Line of Development (à la Heinz Kohut)

The Pole of Grandiosity
"Marvelous me!"*

- Infantile, archaic grandiosity
- The Grandiose Self
  - Knows no boundaries
  - A sense of limitlessness

The Pole of Idealization
"Wonderful you!"*

- The idealized parent image
- The omnipotent object is soothing, calming

Movement toward mature self

Idealizing Selfobject

- Parents attunement and calming enables child to lay down structure for child's own goals

The self is developed by means of ① "transmuting internalizations" of the 2 early (mirroring & idealizing) selfobjects and ② optimal frustration.

— Cohesive Self —

Values, ideals mature goals

JOY

Tension Arc

Talents link the 2 poles

and ability to soothe oneself
Ability for enthusiasm
Mature form of admiration for others

Mirroring Selfobject

- Parents adoration, attunement, support for healthy assertiveness

Reasonable ambition normal self-esteem

and empathy
Self-confidence
Wisdom
Humor
Creativity
Acceptance of one's finitude, transience, the sense that one is loveable

From Exhibitionism

To

Movement toward mature self

Mature forms of self-investment

Nancy Ging Chart - 1989
for 1990 AHP Workshop
* Lionel Corbet, M.D., 1988

APPENDIX B:

TEN STRATEGIES FOR DOING HOLISTIC (BIO-PSYCHO-SPIRITUAL) THERAPY

1. Inquire about your client's cosmology and "ultimate concern."

> If they do not have one, suggest this Cosmology of Parts and Whole; Selves, Circles, a Triangle, Poles and Soul:
> Demonstrate diagram with arms of Soul, holding personality partners.
> This one is workable with any of the world's major religions and wisdom traditions.
> It is easy to comprehend and remember when presented.

2. Primary problem to present to clients:

> "Your main problem is a problem with your memory; you need to REMEMBER *who you really are*."

3. "Visualize your Soul as your *totality* of experience, and your *CONTAINER* of experience."
> Stress the primacy of WHOLENESS / SOULNESS, which each person already has.
> Continually reinforce this.

4. Teach clients to consciously balance two Realities and opposites paradigms:

> Remember: Particle (Concrete)—Wave (Energy)
> Remember: Problems & mysteries,
> Inner life & outer life,
> Gradual growth/improvement & instant Wholeness,
> **Experience**(feelings, thoughts) & **Awareness** (not what you *think*)

5. Visualize personality polarities as partners balancing at centered, connected, cohesive self

6. Therapist can provide "Full Spectrum Reality Therapy" with knowledge of some

> 1) Feminine/ Energy/Vibrational/Wave/Creative Therapies
> 2) Masculine/Linear/Concrete Form/Mental (Rational/Cognitive)Therapies
> Note: Some therapies already include both

7. Move energy and honor the body with imagery:

> Exercise: Polarized parts on a see-saw with heart as the fulcrum
>
> Exercise: "On the Other Hand" kinesthetic experience
> Exercise: Sensing the differences (color, tone, texture, movement) of Male and Female sides
>
> Exercise: Inner Male dancing with Inner Female
>
> Exercise: A trio of Figure 8 energy experiences: heaven-heart-earth, past-now-future, right brain hemisphere-corpus callosum-left brain
>
> Exercise: Soul merge; opening crown, inviting essence of one's Soul energy into body
>
> Exercise: Feeling qualities of energy of various feelings, dense and spacious (perhaps using the "Simple Prayer" of St. Francis of Assisi)

8. "Heart-Brain Partnering"

Remember: Compartments and components and their connections:

> Teach clients of the heart's compartments: Strong (Yang-ish): Courage, Joy, etc.
> Tender (Yin-ish) Compassion, Trust, etc.
> Both (YinYang-ish) Gratitude, etc.

Encourage clients to develop love for their brain and learn it's basic masculine and feminine components

9. Teach clients to *be a trinity* 1)Yin Brain, 2)Yang Brain, 3) Heart

10. Rhymes for remembering:

A & E,
1-2-3, a-b-c (aware, balanced, centered/cohesive/connected)

APPENDIX C:

A list of academic institutions, professional and ecclesiastical organizations where the author has presented her material during the past 15 years:

10-week course, "A New World View; Incorporating Scientific Insight into Spiritual Practice," 1st Congregational Church of Western Springs, IL, 1982 and Union Church of Hinsdale, IL, 1984

Workshop Leader, "Incorporating Scientific Insight into Spiritual Practice," at The Family Institute of Chicago (Northwestern University) Conference: Healing the Family's Heart; The Spiritual Dimension of Family Therapy, August 1986

Gave Sunday sermon on "Creation-Centered Spirituality," The Unitarian Church of Winnetka, IL, March 1987

Workshop leader, "Self-Psychology and the New Age Client," Association for Humanistic Psychology, Mid-West Conference, Indianapolis, April 1990

Workshop Leader, Family Institute Alumni Conference, "Therapy with the New Age Client," Northwestern University, November 1990

Presenter, National Association of Social Workers, Fox Valley District, "Embracing our Selves," April 1991

In-Service presentation, DuPage County Human Services Council, "Spirituality in Social Service Settings," 1991

In-Service presentation, Lutheran Social Services, "Spiritual Perspectives for Social Service Settings," 1991

Workshop Presenter, 2nd Annual Internal Family Systems Conference, "Spirituality and I.F.S.," University of Illinois, October 1992

Guest teacher, University of Chicago, Dept. of Human Development, Family Therapy Class, July 1993, July 1994 and August 1995

Presenter to Oncology Social Workers, at Northwestern Memorial Hospital, April 1993

Workshop leader, Family Institute Alumni Conference at Northwestern University, Nov. 6, 1993, "Therapy with the Spiritual or New Age Client."

Presenter, 3rd Annual Internal Family Systems Conference, IJR, University of Illinois, June 1994, "Embodiment of Parts and Self."

Presenter for Association of Research and Enlightenment, "Enhancing our Health by Embracing Our Selves," August 1994

Presenter to Forest Hospital Clinical Staff on "Spirituality and Clinical Practice," DesPlaines, IL. January 1995

Instructor/Workshop Leader, The Family Institute at Northwestern University, two all-day workshops on "Family Systems and Spirituality," March and June 1995

Workshop presenter, "Being Present to Ourselves; Empowerment Through Embodiment," University of Illinois, Institute for Juvenile Research, Dept. of Psychiatry, 7th Annual Conference Family Systems Conference, March 1995

Presenter for National Association of Social Workers and Linden Oaks Hospital Program, "Empowerment through Embodiment," March 1995

Presenter for Common Ground, Chicago and Deerfield, Il. March and April, 1995 "On Parts and Whole, Selves and Soul."

Workshop Presenter, "Embodiment and I.F.S." at the 4th Annual Internal Family Systems Conference, IJR, Dept. of Psychiatry, University of Illinois, May 1995

Presenter for Association of Research and Enlightment at College of DuPage on "Polaraties and Paradoxes" Summer 1995

Workshop Presenter, Alumni Conference, Family Institute at Northwestern University,"Spirituality and Psychotherapy", Nov.'95

Guest teacher, Illinois Benedictine College, Psychology class, on Clinical Hypnosis, Jan. 1996

Oasis Center, Chicago, all-day workshop, "Polarities and Partnerships; Balancing Internal and External Energies," .5 CEU's, Jan 21, 1996

Presenter for MacNeal Hospital Social Service Department, 2.5 CEU's, 3-hour program "Empowerment through Embodiment; Being Present to Ourselves" March 5, 1996

Guest teacher addressing "Spirituality in Social Work Practice," School of Social Work, M.S.W. program, University of Illinois, Champaign-Urbana, April 29, 1996

Oasis Center, Chicago, all-day workship, "Living in two Realities, Dancing with our Dichomoties, Partnering our Polarities, Honoring our Opposites," .5 CEU's, May 4, 1996

5th annual Internal Family Systems Conterence, IJR, Dept. of Psychiatry, U. of Illinois, Presenter, "Internal Family Systems Therapy with the Narcissistically Vulnerable," May 17, 1996

Workshop presenter, "Living in Two Realities. . . ." Annual Conference of the Society for Spirituality and Social Work, July 13-16, 1996, 3 CEU's, University of Nebraska at Omaha

Seminar presenter for Aurora University, George Williams College School of Social Work, Alumni Reunion. Topic: "Spirituality: The All-Embracing System" August 25, 1996

C.S.W.E. (Council on Social Work Education) Panel Member, on Spirituality in Clinical Practice, Chicago, March 6, 1997

INANNA workshop, "Embodiment and Paradigm Bridging," Spring 1997

N.A.S.W., Fox River Valley District Program (half day) leader on "Holistic Social work and Energy Medicine", Copley Memorial Hospital, Aurora, 3 CEU's. IL. March 15, 1997

6th Annual Internal Family Systems Conference, Presenter, "Spirituality, Energy Medicine and IFS," Family Institute, Northwestern University, 3 CEU's, May 15, 1997

3rd Annual Conference of The Society for Spirituality and Social Work, Workshop; "Balancing Life's Two Realities, Dancing with our Dichotomies, Partnering Our Polarities," College of St. Catherine, St. Paul, Minnesota, 3 CEU's, June 30, 1997

7th Annual Internal Family Systems Conference, "Living in Two Realities, Bridging Paradigms," Northwestern University, April 1998

North Chicago V.A. Hospital, 6 hour presentation to Clinical Social Workers, Psychologists, Psych-Nurses,on "Alternative Therapies and Theories for Holistic Social Work," October 1998

Hines V.A. Hosptial, 2 hour presentation to Social Workers on "Paradigm Bridging; Social Workers and Alternative Methods of Healing," March 22, 2000

University of Kansas, 3-hour workshop, "Of Parts and Whole, Selves and Soul: A Unified Theory of the Self and Psych-Spiritual Therapy," at the Society for Spirituality and Social Work, Annual Conference, June 24-27, 2000

National Association of Social Workers, Committee on Cultural and Spiritual Diversity, 2-hour presentation on "Clinical Practice in the Light of Earth-Based Wisdom Traditions." February 11, 2001

Proposed workshop for National Association of Social Workers Conference, Chicago, Illinois, Sept. 2001, "Where Personality Meets Soul: A Unified Theory of the Self"

Proposed workshop at Northwestern University for The Family Institute, Alumni Conference on Sex, Love and Committment, Fall 2001, Workshop title: "Sex and the Unified Self."

APPENDIX D:

AUTHOR'S PERSONAL LOG (from the early 1970's through mid-1997) OF WORKSHOPS, LECTURES, CONFERENCES I ATTENDED or *presented (in italics)* and life-changing events in rough chronological order, including healings and "readings" received; this list is not absolutely complete.

1971-75—Read much Paul Tillich and Karen Horney
 1973—Read Heinz Kohut's Psychoanalytic Study of the Child, *The Ayalysis of the Self*
 1973 The Inner Peace Movement, my 1st parapsychology training

1973 Fall Semester Course, Dr. Don Miller, "The Systematic Theology of Paul Tillich," Bethany Theological Seminary (audited Course) 1974 Winter Semester course (audited) "Social Thought of Paul Tillich," Dr.Franklin Sherman, Luthern School of Theology at Chicago
 1974: Parent Effectiveness Training, (Effectiveness Training Associates) Training workshop to teach PET, 11-27-74

Transactional Analysis Supervision Group led by Dick Tapley, PhD. 1974

Suzanne England Osterbusch, D.S.W. Course at Union Church on Transactional Analysis, 1973 + 74

Other talks and courses in Transational Analysis in late 70'

101 Introductory Course in Transactional Analysis, 1970's

1975-79:

1975-77 MSW Program at GWC; recieved degree June 77

T.A. (Transactional Analysis) Seminar (2-Days) with Muriel James, at Chicago Theological Seminary, April 23 +24, 1976

Laura Epstien seminar on the Task-Centered Model of Therapy, 1976,77 or 78

Virginia Satir Workshop, Oasis

Course by Dr. Robt. A. DeVito, Madden Mental Health Center Director, Fall-Winter (1975-76)"Introduction to Mental Status"

Seminar by Robt. A. DiVito, M.D. on Multiple Personalities, 1976 at Madden Mental Health Center

Lecture (first of several) by Dr. Stanley Krippner at George Williams College, 1976 or 77 on Parapsychology, Dream Telepathy and ESP

Workshop by Dr. Morton Kelsey (first time) March 24, 1976, ECCRV Conference, Toletine Center, Olympia Fields

1977:

Consultations with Elizabeth Kubler-Ross, M.D., at her home in Flossmor, Il. 1-18-77 and 2-1-77

Lecture by Elizabeth Kubler-Ross, M.D. Crystal Lake, Congregational Church/ Crystal Lake Comm. Hospital, 2-23-77
1-day seminar, "Living With A Life-Threatening Illness," Make Today Count, Chicago,—10-77

Ecumenical Center for Culture, Religion and Values (CCRV) Conference on Death, March 21-25, 1977.

Workshop with Joy Johnson on Adolescents, 4-23-77

Hospice Conference, U. of Chicago, April 28, 77

RECEIVED MY M.S.W. Degree from George Williams College, June, 1977

International Congress on Meditation-Related Therapies, June 17-19,'77: Dr. Swearingen,M.D., "Meditation in Medical Practice,"
Phil Nuereberger, PhD. , Norman S. Don, PhD., Barbara Brown, "Biofeedback,", Charles Garfield, PhD., Olga Worrall, June Singer, "Jung, Yogaand Biofeedback," Dr. Stanley Krippner on "Psychic Healing", Robert O. Becker, M.D., Dr. Bernard Grad

Olga Worral, Spiritual Healer, Consultation in Baltimore, 8-11-77

2-day conference, "Beyond the Double Bind",Communication and Family Systems, Theories, and Techniques with Schizophrenics, South Beach Psychiatric Center, N.Y.(held in Chicago) with Gregory Bateson (on video), Murray Bowen, M.D.(live), Jay Haley, John Weakland, Carl Whitaker (live)13 hours, October 14-15, 1977
5-Day Workshop with Elisabeth Kubler-Ross," Life, Death and Transition," Oct 24-28, 1977, North Carolina

Nick Smyre, Oct.19, 1977 Consultant in Joliet job

Lecture by Dr. Elisabeth Kubler-Ross, Harper College, 11-9-77

Seminar by Froma Walsh, PhD.,"Techniques for Working with Severly Disturbed Families," The Family Institute, 7 hours of training, 11-12-77

5-Day Conference with Dr. Morton Kelsey, ECCRV (Ecumenical Center for Culture, Religion and Values), Toletine Center, Feb. 10-15, 1977 Or 78

1-week Workshop:Elizabeth Kubler Ross, on Death and Dying, North Carolina, 1977

Attended two conferences on Child Abuse, IASSW, Cook County Hospital or U. of Illinois., 1976 or 77 or 78

Hospice Conference U. of C.1976 or '77

5-Day Course, University of Chicago 5-day course, S.S.A.on "Child Psychotherapy,"Joseph Palumbo, 1.5 CEU's, June 1978

Seminar by Clark Davis on Narcissism, 2-4-78

Institute for Psychoanalysis course/Extension Program, Edward Kaufman on Diagnosis and Psychotherapy with Children, Une 20-August l,1977

The est Training, June 1978

1979:

5-Day "Conference on Death," ECCRV (Ecumenical Center for Culture, Religion and Values), Tolentine Ctr, Olympia Fields, IL. $100, with Morton Kelsey, (Check this date: Feb. 10-14, 1979 or March 21-25, 19979
   Speakers: Morton T. Kelsey, L.T.D.
   Eliz. Kubler-Ross, M.D.
   John van de Beek, O.S.A., PhD.
   Reneta Glass S.S.J., PhD. Paul Jones, S.J., PhD.

LADSE Institute with Dr Rose, Prof. of S.W. at Wisconsin, on Family Therapy, March 16, 1979

Seminar by Donald Ringsley, M.D.,"Developmental Aspects of Narcissism and Borderline Personality Disorders," Forest Hospital Talk 4-4-79

Program on C.S. Lewis at Wheaton College,4-9-79

Rev. Henry Rucker, program on Dreams, 4-14-79

Spiritual Advisory Council Program, April 26-28, 1979
Jean Houston 1-day workshop? 5-4-79

5-day course at Univ. of Chicago, S.S.A., Dr. Jos. Palombo, "Psychotherapy with Children with Narcissistic and Boreline Personality Disorders," June 25-29, 1979

Holistic Health Conference,"Transforming Energy and Awareness," A.R.E., Sept 15-16, 1979, Pick Congress,Chicago, Speakers, Harmon H. Bro, PhD., Hugh Lynn Cayce, Gina Cerminara, PhD. Drs. Gladys & Wm. McGarey, Rachel Runnels, Mark Thurston, PhD.

Illinois Asso. for School Social Work Conference, Nov. 9+10, 1979

Conference: Wholistic Health, Inc. Annual Conference, Oct. 5, 1979, Speakers, Dr. Granger Westberg, etc.

Riveredge Hospital Lecture, Oct 17, '79

Rev. Henry Rucker Program on Healing, Chicago 10-27-79

IASSW Conference on "Learning disorders in School Age Children,"Speakers: Suzanne Berger, (Insitutite of Pychoanalysis,), Nov.9 '79

Seminar on "Responsive Parenting," LADSE, Kathy Wentling,11-20-79

LADSE Institute, "Consultation of Behavioral Management," LaGrange, IL. Chris Isrealson, Ann Casey, Dec. 7, 1979

Jean Houston Conference 1979 and again in 1980

1980:

Weekend Workshop with Jean Houston, PhD. "New Ways of Winter 1980

Biofeedback training at A.R.E.Holistic Health Clinic, Scottsdale,Arizona Feb. 27-March 1, 1980

Consultation with Ann Bruck, Feb. 27, '80

Hospice Conference, March 1, 1980?

Marriott Conference Fri. March 7+8, 1980

2-day Michael Reese Hospital, Dept. of Psychiatry Conference on "Parenthood as an Adult Experience," March 7-8,1980, Chicago. Speakers included: Daniel Offer, M.D., E. James Anthony, M.D., Marian Tolpin,M.D., Arnold Goldberg, M.D., Joseph Palombo, M.A., Ner Littner, M.D., Anna Ornstein, M.D., Judith Wallerstein, PhD., Daniel Friedman, M.D.,

LADSE Institute, 5-16-80

"Depression and Physical Illness," 6-16-80

Henry Rucker Program on Dreams, 12-13-80

1981:

Became an "A.C.S.W." in 1981

One Day Worskshop on "Dreams" by Rev. Henry Rucker, Chicago, 1-17-81

River Edge Hospital Lecture, 1-14-81

Theosophical Society Lecture, 2-19-81

Lecture: "C.G.Jung," The Theosophical Socitey, 2-26-81

Wholistic Health Center workshop, "Stress Management," Mark Laser, 3-1-81

1-Day Workshop,"Working with Children, Adolescents and Families," Roger Hatcher, PhD.(On The Immature Child)and Robert Shapiro,PhD.,(Working with the Child's Unconscious), Barry Weber, PhD. (On the Over-Indulged Child), Michael A. Partipilo, PhD.,(on NLP) 3-18-81

University of Chicago—3 courses, Summer of 1981

5 Day Course, University of Chicago, Arthur Schwartz,"The Age of Melancholy: Depression in the 80's, June 23-27, 1981, 1.5 CEU Credits

5-(Mornings)Day Course, University of Chicago,S.S.A. Narcissism:Psychology of the Self as applied to Social Casework Treatment," Miriam Elson, 1.5 CEU Credits June 1981

5 (Afternoons)Day Course, University of Chicago, S.S.A."Psychoanalytic Object Relationship Theory," Erika Fromm, 1.5 CEU Credits, June, 1981

1-Week Conference on "Dreams and ESP," Association of Research and Enlightenment, Virginia Beach, Va. July 20-25, 1981
Speakers: Mark Thurston, PhD. Stanley Krippner, PhD.
1-Week Conference, "Attunement for Healing," A.R.E. (Association for Research and Enlightenment),Virginia Beach, Va.July 12-18, 1981
Speakers:Olga Worrall,

3-Day American Imagery Conference, International Imagery Asso. and the Journal of Mental Imagery,"Narcissism and The Self," Speakers included Ernest Wolf, M.D. on Kohut, Dr. Hyman Muslin, M.D., Akhter Ahsen

2-Day Workshop on "Meditation," Jack Schwartz, Personal Stress Institute, Oct. 17+18

Conference, "Healing in our Time," Washington D.C.Nov. 5-8, 1981: List of Speakers:

Luthern General Hospital Course, Oct-Nov.on Family Therapy

Lecture, Brain Research Foundation, University of Chicago

1982:

Two Year Training Program—Family Institute Chicago Aug. 1982-June 1984 Teachers and Supervisors:

Shambhala Meditation Training 3-Days, Chicago, Feb 12-14

Lecture by Margaret Creedon,PhD., "Learned Helplessness," at Little Friends School, 2-18-82

One-Day Workshop Therapeutic Touch, Delores Kreiger, PhD., 2-27-82, Theosophical Society, Wheaton, Illinois

NASW Program on "Adolescent Depression—Clinical Dx and Treatment," Art Delvin "3-17-82

Dr. Margaret Creedon on "Learned Helplessness," at Little Friends School, Naperville, 2-18-82

Dr. Gavaria at Little Friends School, Naperville, on Object Relations Theory and Self-Psychology, 3-7-82 est 3-19-21, 1982 more est, 3-26-82

Muscle toning session with mild electrical stimulation (which aleviated my Wintertime depression!) 3-9-82

Wholistic Health Talk, "Avoiding a Broken Heart," 3-31-82

Suicide Seminar, Hinsdale, IL 4-1-82

Mercy Hospital Conference on Depression, Chicago 4-1-82

Weekend Conference with Herbert Puryear, PhD. 4-30-82, A.R.E. Sponsored, Chicago, on "Discovering your human potential"

Lecture by Dr. Erik Peper, "Visualization, Relaxation, Optimal Performance of the Mind/Body" Theosophical Society, March 14, '82

Dr. Herb Puryear, seminar on C.G. Jung and "The Secret of the Golden Flower," A.R.E., Chicago, April 30-May 1,1982

Family Institute Conference on "Separation, Divorce, Re-Marriage, April 24, '82, Speakers Charles Kramer, M.D., Dr. Richard Gardner, Jean Goldsmith, PhD.

Lecture, Brain-Research Foundation, University of Chicago, 4-27-82

2-Day Seminar, Lawrence LeShan, Ph.D., "Psychotherapy with Cancer Patients, May 21-22, 1982

10-week course at U. of Illinois on Depression, April 1-June 3, 1982 (In children and adults), James Forkeotes

"Depression and Life Crisis"—4-lectures at Forest Hospital: Leo E. Hollister, M.D. "Anti-Depressant Medication—Current Issues" 9-8-82

David D. Burns, M.D., "The Cognitive Therapy of Depression," 2-8-82

Thomas McGlashan, M.D. "Depression in Schizophrenia; Post-Psychotic Depression or Aphanasis"

Rauch Memorial Suicide Conference, Hinsdale Community House 4-1-82, Rev. Dan Staufacher
Family Institute Conference,"Separation, Divorce and Beyond," 4-24-82

Jo Lief and Linda Birnbaum, Saturday morning seminar for women, 6/82
est Seminar on "The Body" June 8,22,29, July 6, 20, Aug 3,17, 24, 31

1-week conference "Transpersonal Approaches to Counseling and Psychotherapy,"A.R.E., Virginia Beach, VA. Speakers: Harmon Bro, PhD., Herbert Puryear, PhD., James C. Windsor, PhD. July 11-16, 1982
est Seminar on "The Authentic Philosophy of Heidigger," July 24, 1982
1st Degree REIKI Course, 4 evenings, July 19-22,' 1982, Ethel Lombardi

Depression Medication Lecture, Forest Hospital, 9-8-82

Lecture by Chogyam Trungpa Rinpoche, (Shambhalla), at Francis Parker School, Chicago, 9-16-82

A.R.E. Conference Sept.24-25,'82 (Herb Puryear, etc.)

Chicago Family Therapy Conference (6th Annual) , Family Institute of Chicago, Oct 15-16, 1982, Speakers included: Monica McGoldrick,Attended Workshops with C.F. Midelfort, M.D., Joy Johnson, Phillip L. Elbaum (Sex Therapy), Charles Kramer, M.D.,

Lecture by Gerald Jampolsky, M.D.,Family Cancer Support Network, Evanston, on "Attitudinal Healing," 10-28-82

7-Day Jean Houston Workshop, Oct 29-Nov.4, 1982 "The Possible Human," Oasis Center, Chicago

Lecture by Rev. Wm. Sloan Coffin, Union Church of Hinsdale, IL11-5-82

Conference on Healing, A.R.E. Nov 6-7, Chicago, '82

Weekend Conference at Union Church of Hinsdale on "Living in a Global Village;The World Rule of Law," Arthur Larson of Duke University, Nov. 11 & 12 (Speaker was our houseguest as well)

Lecture by Albert Ellis, Riveredge Hospital 11-17-82

REIKI Course 4-evenings, Ethel Lombardi, Nov. 16,17,18 19, 1982

Marilyn Ferguson 1-Day Conference, Gestalt Institute and Unity, Evanston, 11-20-82

National Conference on Healing, Oasis Center, Chicago, November 5-7, 1982

> Heard: Lawrence LeShan, Jeffery Bland, David Bresler,PhD., Dr. Upledger

2nd Degree REIKI ($400) Course Dec. 11 + 12, 1982
est Communications Workshop, March 19-21

Association of Research and Enlightment Conference on Transpersonal Psychotherapy, Virginia Beach, Va. 6/24 until ?

Forest Hospital Lecture on New Medication for Depression, 9-8-82

The 6th Annual CHICAGO FAMILY THERAPY CONFERENCE,"The Practice of Family Therapy, Strategies and Techniques.Speakers included: Monica McGoldrick, Joy Johnson, Phillip Elbaum,Charles H. Kramer, M.D.,etc. Oct. 15 + 16, 1982

Albert Ellis,PhD., River Edge Hospital lecture, 11-17-82

4-evening course,REIKI, Ethel Lombardi, Nov. 16-19, '82

David Burns M.D.,at Forest Hopital, "Cognitive Therapy, 12-8-82

Shambhalla Meditation weekend Feb.12-14,'82

1983:

Workshop on "Psychosynthesis," The Gestalt Institute of Chicago, in Evanston, 2-5-83

Psychic Reading (expensive one, $ 175) with Aron Abramhamson, 2-18-83

Rudolph Ballentine, M.D. , lecture, "Nutrition and Your Mind," Himalayan Institute, 3-4-83

I led program, "Wholeness and Wellness: Optimizing Healing in Body, Mind and Soul" Women's Asso. of Union Church, Hinsdale, 3-17-8883

I taught class, "The Aquarian Conspiracy—Hope for the 80's," Francis Parker School, Evening Courses, Mar. 9–Apr. 14
1-Week Course, Connie Newton, "Integrated Awareness, (I.A.)" March 26-30, 1983

Illinois Society for Clinical Social Work Conference, "The Treatment of Eating Disorders,", James C. Sheinin,M.D., Craig Johnson, Ph.D., Froma Walsh, PhD., S.Louis Mogul, M.D.,, John Levitt, Ph.D., 4-15-83
1-Day Workshop A.R.E., Chicago, 4-17-83, Speakers: Jesse Stern, Dr. Stanley Kripner, Helen Wambach, Gladys McGarry, MD,, Mark Thurston, PhD.,
1-day seminar with Larry Feldman, M.D.,, "Marital and 6 hours Family of Therapy of Depression", Family Institute, 3-25-83

Workshop, Bob Shaw, "Contextual Psychotherapy," April 9,1983, Sponsored by The Family Institute of Berkeley, CA., in Chicago ($130)

A.R.E. Conference, Chicago, 4-16-83, Speakers included: Shirley Dunlap, etc.

I co-led with Cindy Bouman, Saturday Seminar, "Death and Grief" and "The Healing Process" Spring, 1983

Consultations with Dr. Theodore TePas, M.D. (Orthomoecular Psychiatry) March-Sept. 1983

1-Day seminar, Froma Walsh, PhD.,"Normal and Dysfunctional Families: Criteria for Assessment and Treatment," Family Institute, May 13,1983 ($45) 6 hours

1-week Course, "Clinical Hypnosis Training," University of Cicago,S.S.A. Instructors: Erika Fromm and Daniel Brown ,PhD., June 16-20, 1983

A.R.E. Va. Beach, 8-26-83

I taught 10-week course, "Healing and Christianity," Union Church, Hinsdale, Fall 1983

Mariel I Course (2nd time taken and hosted), Ethel Lombardi,4 evenings, ending 10-28-83

I Ging gave week seminar on spiritual healing at the First Congregational Church western Springs, IL September 18th thru–Nov, 20th, 1983

I gave meditation/sermon at Service of Prayer and Healing, Union Church of Hinsdale, 11-13-83

Stanley Malestrom, MindBody Consultation, 11-19-83

Healing Training, Psychic Dean Kraft (Beattle's John Lennon's Psychic Healer), 11-29-83

1984:

I co-led with Ellen Carmignani, seminar on "Nutrition, Behavior and Spirituality," Union Church of Hinsdale, Jan. 12

Lecture by M.Scott Peck, M.D., Elgin, Il. (Ecker Mental Health Center at U.C.C. Church), Spring, 1984

Lecture, Brain-Research Foundation, U. of Chicago, 4-11-84

Weekend Workshop on Ericksonian Hypnotherapy by Associate Trainers in Clinical Hypnosis (Anthony Gaito, instructor), May 4 + 5, 1984

2-Day A.R.E.Conference, "Hope for the Future: Visions and Challenges" Chicago, 4-14-84, Speakers: Norman Sheeley, M.D., Talk by Harmon Bro, PhD., Mark Thurston,PhD."Discovering Your Soul's Purpose," Kennith Ring,PhD., Near Death Research, Willis Harman, June Bro, 4-14-84

2-Day Workshop with Virginia Satir, Milwaukee, 4-18+19, 1984

I got divorced from Thomas F. Ging, after 19 years, May 1984

I gave lecture on "Depression in Children" Walker School P.T.A, Clarendon Hills, May (the evening after going to court for my divorce)

Guided Imagery: An Intensive (3-day) Training Program for

Clinicians,Institute for the Advancement of Human Behavior, Martin L.Grossman, M.D., & David Bresler, PhD., June 8-10

1-Day Course on "The I Ching," Ken Saichek, Oasis Center, July 22, 1984

Watched Ramtha Video Tapes July 1984
1-Day Course on "The I Ching and Jungian Psychology," John Gianini, Sponsored by Ruth Berger's New Age Psychic Center, 8-4-84

DMA Course, Dr. David Wright, George Williams College

Lecture by Paul Watzlawick, PhD., "Problems of Change and Change of Problems," Riveredge Hospital Lecture, Oct.17, 1984

Himayat Inayati, seminar, 11-3-84

One-Day Seminar by M.Scott Peck, M.D. for Professionals on "Spiritual images in Pastoral Counseling and Psychotherapy," and "Sexuality and Spirituality: Kissing Cousins." Nov. 8, 1984, Evanston, IL

Lecture on "Overvieew of Affective Disorders in Children and Adolescents," Riveredge Hospital, 11-14-84

Weekend Conference with M. Scott Peck, M.D., Christian Laity of Chicago, Nov. 9-11, 1984

1985:

Lecture by Werner Erhard, 1-13-85
1-day workshop by Juith Citrin, "Opening to our Light," Oasis Center, Chicago, 2-10-85

I co-led weekend retreat with Dr. Robt.O.Shaffer, "Forgiveness: Letting Go and Lightening Up." Sponsored by Union Church of Hinsdale, held at Lake Geneva, Wisconsin, Feb 14-16

Weekend Retreat with Don Tubising, PhD. Lake Geneva, Union Church Sponsored, March 1-3,'85

Lecture, Peter Giovacchini,M.D.,"Psychoanalytic Techniques in the Treatment of Character Disorters, March 20, 1985, Riveredge Hospital,

1-Day Seminar, Illinois Society for Clinical Social Work,"Change Agents in Psychotherapy," April 19, 1985, Speakers: Peter L. Giovacchini, M.D., Robert Rutledge, John Gianini, etc.

Workshop by Betty Bosdell, PhD., "Psychosynthesis and Imagery," 4-23-85, Unity on the North Shore

Lecture by M. Scott Peck, M.D., "Spirituality and Human Nature," and "Psychiatry, Christianity and the Nuclear Arms Race," Oasis Center, May 3, 1985

3-Day Advanced Imagery Workshop, Chicago, June 7-9, '85

Summer School Course at George Williams College, DMA, David Wright, PhD. June 18-Aug. 20, 1985 (10 sessions)

5-day Course, University of Chicago, S.S.A., "Advanced Hypnotherapy," by Erika Fromm and Daniel Brown, PhD., June 1985

DMA Course led by David Wright, PhD. July, 1985

Telephone reading with, Marsha the psychic nutritionist at Aristos Center for Nutritional Sciences, Colorado Springs, Co. July 5,'85

2-Day Workshop with Jay Haley and Cloe Mandanes,"Strategic Marital Therapy," Family Therapy Insitiute, Inc. of Washington, D.C., July 12-13, 1985

Took MARIEL Course for second time (first time in 1883), Ethel Lombardi in Maine, Aug. 26-31, 1985
1 day Seminar with Bernie S. Siegel, M.D., "The Process of Healing", Oasis Center, 10-13-85

Lecture by Dr. O. Carl Simonton, M.D., Gottlieb Memorial Lecture, Oct. 16, 1985

Robert Fritz, author and founder of DMA, 10-22-85, "Creativity"

University of Illinois, Dr. Ashbrook, "Diet + Behavior," 10-29-85

2-Day Workshop, Bob Shaw,M.D., "Contextual Work With Couples" Nov.8+9, 1985, The Family Institute of Chicago
1-day workshop, "The Healing Brain," Robert E. Ornstein, David S. Sobel, M.D., M.P.H., Jon D. Levine, M.D., PhD.,, The Institute for the Study of Human Knowledge (ISHK), 7 hours,
11-25-85

Ramptha Video Tapes, Dec. 1985

1986:

I co-led with nutritionist Ellen Carmignani, a half-day program, "Self-Care for Women in Mid-Life and Beyond" Union Church, Hinsdale, 3rd Sat. in Jan.

I taught a 10-week adult education course, "Creation-Centered Spirituality of Matthew Fox," Union Church of Hinsdale, Winter Quarter

Lecture, Howard Gardner, PhD., "Frames of Mind," Argonne National Laboratories, 2-28-86

Bob Shaw, M.D. Workshop, March 6+7, 1986

Weekend Workshop with Emmanuel/Pat Rodegast, Judith Stanton, Oasis Center for Human Potential, March 22-24, 1986 ($135)
David Sheehan, M.D. from Mass. General Hospital, at River Edge Hospital Lecture on "Panic and Anxiety Disorders: Diagnosis and Management Strategy," 3-16-86

2-day workshop, Emmanuel/Pat Rodegast, Oasis Center, Chicago, March 22, 1986

Ken Wapnick, M.D.,Intensive seminar on "A Course in Miracles," Unity of Chicago, April 25-27, 1986 (I only attended half of the weekend.)

Robert Freedman, M.D.(from U. of Colorado, Dept. of Psychiatry) on

"Depresion in Adolescents and Children," Hinsdale Hospital Lecture, 4-17-86

Gary Oberg, M.D., Lecture on "Orthomolecular Psychiatry," Schizophrenia Ass. of Western Suburbs, May 25,1986

Dr. Jael Greenleaf, "The Alcoholic Family as a Learning System," River Edge Hospital Lecture, May 21, 1986

Dr. Thomas F. Nagy, "Professional Ethics and Mental Health Specialist," Old Orchard Hospital, Dept. of Psychology, 6-19-86

One-Week Course, GIM (Guided Imagery and Music), Institute for Consciousness and Music (ICM) June 22-27, 1986

Weekend Conference with Fritjov Capra, PhD, "The Planetary Vision Quest," series, The Institute of Cultural Affairs, July 4-6, 1986

Weekend Workshop, "Healing the Family's Heart; The Spiritual Dimension in Family Therapy," The Family Institute of Chicago, at Lake Geneva, Wis., Charles H. Kramer, M.D. and Ken McAll, M.D.,

I presented a workshop:"Incorporating Scientific Insight into Psycho-Spiritual Practice with Families," at the above conference of The Family Insititue, August 15-17

Lecture by June Singer, "The Creativity of Wm. Blake," Jungian Insitute, Oct 10 or 11, 1986
1-Day Workshop with Patricia Sun, Ph.D., Unity on the North Shore, 11-8-86

An Evening with Ram Dass, The Seva Foundation, Nov. 9, 1986, Chicago at The Peoples Church (U.C.C.)

2-Day Conference, "Personality Disorders: Facing the Challenge", Mental Health Division, DuPage County Health Dept., Nov. 20-21,1986, Speakers: James Masterson, M.D., David Shapiro, Ph.D., Joy Johnson, M.A., etc.

1987:

Weekend Intensive with Carolyn Conger, PhD.at Lake Geneva, GWC Campus, Jan 15-18, l987

Meditation/Study group with Darrel Greenwood, PhD., LaGrange,Il. Winter, weekly?

Two-Day workshop, Robert Shaw, M.D., "Constructing Therapeutic Realities for Individuals, Couples and Families," Forest Institute of Professional Psychology, The Forest Hospital Foundation and the Chicago Instutute for the Study of Context, Jan. 23-24, l987

1-Day workshop, Edwin H Friedman, "Paradox:A way in therapy, and a way in life," I.J.R.'s Family Systems Program, Feb.9,l987

IJR Program Feb. 9, l987

Meditation Retreat for U.C.C. Clergy, Program leader, Myself
Feb.14, '87 (Rev. Stifler, of Villa Park, Co-ordinator) (check year on this, may have been '77)
Therapeutic Touch Program, Delores Kreiger, PhD., Feb. 28, 1987

I gave Discourse (a.k.a. Sunday sermon) on "Creativity-Centered Spirituality" on March 15, 1987 at Th Lake Shore Unitarian Society, Winnetka, IL

Weekend Workshop,"Journeys to the Spirit"—Pat Rodegast, Judith Stanton, & Emmanuel", Oasis Center, (CEU's: 1) March 20,21,22,l987

Maxine Jones, M.A. Program at Wellspring, Wheaton 4-26-87
1-Day program for Professionals with Morton Kelsey, "The Sacrament of Sexuality," Evanston, IL. April 30, '87

Weekend Workshop with Rev. Morton Kelsey,"A Time to Begin; Encountering God in Everyday Life," Union Church of Hinsdale and Christian Laity of Chicago, May 1-3, 1987

3-Day Intensive Guided Imagery Training (19 contact hours), American

Imagery Institute and The Medical College of Wisconsn, Donald Pachuta, M.D., Anees Shiek, PhD.,Errol Korn, M.D.,June 5-7, 1987
1-Day Workshop with Maggie Scarff, "Intimate Partners," Women's Health Resources, Illinois Masonic Medical Center, Chicago, June 15, 1987

One-day workshop on "Marital Therapies for Depression", AFTA (American Family Therapy Association, I.J.R., and Family Institute sponsored): Carol Anderson, PhD., James Coyne, PhD., Neil Jacobson, PhD., 6-17-87

Siddha Yoga Meditation Weekend, Chicago, with Gurumayi, June 19-21, 1987

Lecture at Manic-Depression Asso. Meeting, August 3,1987, by Margaret Diederick, M.D.

7-Day Meditation Retreat with Ram Dass, at Omega Institute, Rhinebeck, N.Y. August 19-26, 1987

2-evening MariEl (Advanced Class), Ethel Lombardi, Aug 26+27, 1987

Lecture, "Free Inquiry," (Anti-Spirituality, Rational Humanists), at Northeastern University, Chicago, Sept. 1987

3-Day Workshop, "Agenda for the 21st Century," at Omega Institute, Rhinebeck, N.Y., Sept 5-7, 1987. Speakers: Fritjof Capra, Willis Harman, etc.

1-Day Workshop, Bill O'Hanlon, M.S., "An Erickson Approach to Working with Adolescents," Asso. of Illinois Township Committees on Youth, Oct. 8, 1987

Lecture by Peter E. Sifneos, M.D., River Edge Hospital, "The Process of Short-Term Dynamic Therapy," 10-21-87
1-Day workshop, Judith Siegel, PhD., Alumni Asso. of The Family Insitiue of Chicago, "Object Relations Therapy: Bridging Self and Other, Past and Present," Nov. 13,

3-Day Common Boundry (Between Psychotherapy and Spirituality) Conference, (7th annual conference), "Reawakening the Inner Child," Nov. 19-21, 1987, Washington, D.C., Speakers included: Edith Sullwold,

Emmanuel/Pat Rodegast, Robert Bly, Charles L. Whitfield, M.D.,Roger Wollger,PhD., Carol Ann Bush, Louis M.Savery, etc.

Lecture by Jenna Eisenberg on Applied Kinesiology, 1987

I became a NASW Diplomate in Clinical Social Work in l987

1988:

Lecture by Rev. Wm.Sloan Coffin, sponsored by West Suburban Inter-faith Peace Initiative, Hinsdale, IL 1-17-88

Warrenville Cenacle Meditation & Journaling Workshop/Retreat,Sister Joyce Kemp of the Chicago Cenecle, Feb 13, l988

Lecture by Hugh Prather, 2-17-88

Father Bob Sears Weekend at Union Church (I was onlPlanning Commit-tee), Family Therapy and Spirituality, March 4-6, Class on Joseph Campbell (on film) 3-17-88

3-day seminar, "The Church is a Healing Community," Ecumenical Heal-ing Mission, St. Bede's Cpiscopal Church & Peace U.C.C., Bensenville and Wood Dale Community United Methodist Church, May 19-22

I led workshop, "Scientific Insight and Spiritual Practice," on May 21, at 3-day workshop, "The Church is a Healing Community" (see above) at Wood Dale Community United Methodist Church, May 19-22

Weekend seminar, Dr. Michael Franz Basch, M.D.,"Freud, Kohut and Daniel Stern and the Development of Affect in Infants," Mentor Series, Central Partners, Evanston, June 4+5, l988

Sunday School class on Isreali-Palestinian relations, taught by R.O. Shaffer, PhD, Summer Sunday mornings, July, Aug.

Weekend workshop, Brugh Joy,M.D."A Touch of Joy: Healing Seminar," Oasis, July 22-24,l988
l week, Independent study of Roberto Assigioli at The Clearing in Door County, Sept 11-17, 1988

Lecture—Stuart Udofsky, M.D., new chief of psychiatry, University of Chicago, Brain Research Foundation Program, 9-20

2-Day seminar, Loyola University—Institute of Pastoral Studies, "A Christian Spirituality of the Negative Emotions," James Zullo, Evelyn Whitehead and James Whitehead, Sept 23 +24, 1988

Lionel Corbett, M.D. (Jungian Analyist and Clinical Director of Psychiatry at Rush Pres. St. Lukes Hospital): "Jungian Psychology and Kohut's Self Psychology" at Loyola Univ. Sponsored by C.G. Jung Institute, Oct 8-9, 1988

Alumni Conference, Family Institute of Chicago, "Successful Therapy with Families: Looking Toward the Nineties," Oct. 21-22, 1988

Became a Diplomate in Clinical Social Work with the American Board of Examiners on 10-28-88

Course sponsored by the Institute for Advanced Perception, (Harold S. Schroeppel's material) 1988

1989:

Telephone Psychic Consultation with psychic Janice Lowell in Maine, 1-23-89

Carolyn Conger, PhD. (Spiritual/Psychic Healer) Weekend Workshop, Lake Geneva, Jan.13-15, 1989

1-day workshop, "Healing the Wounded Child Within," David Grove Seminars (find out exactly WHEN it was)

John White,"Highest States of Consciousness," at The Theosophical Society, 2-2-89

Adlerian Family Counseling, Oscar C. Christensen, D.Ed., The Alfred Adler Institute of Chicago, 2-8-89

Froma Walsh, PhD., "Promoting Healthy Couples Functioning," Center for Family Studies/The Family Institute of Chicago, 2-24-89
David E.Scharff, MD, from Georgetown Univ.Dept of Psychiatry, "Object Relations and Family Therapy", April 21, 89, Center for Family Studies/ The Family Institute of Chicago

Took new licencing exam, became an "LCSW" in l989

I taught class on "Stress and Weight Control," at The Diet Center, Hinsdale, 4-12-89

Program at River Edge Hopital on "Sexual Abuse Issues," Barbara Stock, PhD., 4-28-89

ISCSW Licensing Exam Review Course, 6-10-89
 l-day seminar with Lionel Corbett, PhD., "Psychotherapy as Spiritual Practice (or Discipline) C.G. Jung Institute at Loyola Univ. 7-24-89

4-Day Conference: "Choas and Change in Organizational Life: The Role of the Unconscious in the Workplace," (Choas Theory, Organizational Dynamics and Jungian Psychology), Sponsored by NTL Institute and C.G. Jung Institute, July 26-30, l989
        Worshops and talks attended:

Dr. Murry Stein (Jungian Analyst and author): "Organizational Life as Spiritual Practice."
James Hall "Using the Unconscious in the Workplace"
Thomas Patrick Lavin, "A Primer on Jungian Psychology"
John Giannnini, The Narcissistic Ground for Workaholism: A Jungian Healing Response"
Peter Mudd,PhD., "Fantasy, the Playful Worker: The Creative Unconscious at Work"
John and Joyce Weir, "Projections of the Self
Lionel Corbett, M.D., "Projection and Transference: Factors Disturbing Human Relations"
Fred Nader, "A Primer on Organization Development"
Earl Kruse: "The Shadow: Understanding the Dynamics of the Dark Side"
Lecture by Dr. Murray Stien, "The Myth of Relationship," Jungian Institute of Chicago, 10-6-89

Jim Kinney lecture at Common Ground, "Convergence: The Center of the Wheel," 1 9-25-89

Jim Kinney lecture at Common Ground: "The Devil, You Say" Common Ground, Chicago 10-2-89

Space,Time,and Native American Spirituality 10-30-89

Jane Lukehart, M.A. on "Synchronicity,"10-16-89

Common Ground Chicago, Numerous evening lectures by Jim Kinney:

I gave presentation at the Union Church in Hinsdale, "The Service of Reconciliation and Healing," March 5
1-day Conference, "Waging Peace in the Middle East," Robt O. Shaffer, PhD., Samuel W. Lewis Union Church of Hinsdale, Nov. 4

Michael Harner, PhD., Weekend Workshop Dec 2 + 3, 1989 "The Shamanic Journey, Power and Healing: An Experiential Exploration," Oasis Center of Chicago

1990:

More Common Ground Lectures by Jim Kinney & Co.
Titles: The Gaia Hypothesis, 4-16-90 The Presence of the Past, R. Sheldrake 2-5-90 More On Rupert Sheldrake 1-15-90

1-Day, University of Chicago, S.S.A. Seminar,Judith Nelsen,"Working with Couples in Conflict," 2-2-90

I taught class at The Diet Center, Hinsdale, 2-19-90

Fr.Matthew Fox, on "Creation Spirituality", Call to Action—Midwest Conference, 2-4-90

Lecture, Harriet Goldher Lerner,PhD.,"Women and Intimacy," Womanspace, Rockford, Il. 2-13-90

Evening Lecture, "The Dance of Intimacy," Harriet Goldher Lerner, Womanspace, Rockford, IL. 2-19-90

Lecture, Right Livelihood: Religion and Economics, 4-23-90

1-Day, University of Chicago, S.S.A. Seminar,"Advanced Self-Psychology," Miriam Elson, 3-2-90

1-day workshop, "Cancer; The more you know the better your chances are." American Internal'l Hosp, Zion, IL, in Oakbrook, IL. 3-13-90
> Heard presentations by:
> Michael Partipilo
> Burton Siegel
> Oscar Rasmussem
> Richard Stephenson
> Robt. Mayo
> R. Michael Williams

I taught class on Joseph Campbell and the Power of Myth at Union Church of Hinsdale, Sundays March 4-May 13

I taught class at The Diet Center, Hinsdale, Apr.9

1-Day, University of Chicago, S.S.A. Seminar, "Winnocott as Clinician," William Bordon, Phd., 4-20-90

I read a book which was important to me: *The Chalice and the Blade by Riane Eisler*

Weekend Workshop, Association of Humanistic Psychology, Midwest Annual Conference, Indianapolis, March 29-April 1, 1990. Speakers Included: George Leonard, Charles Whitfield, M.D.

Attended Pre-Conference Institute with Illana Reubenfeld on Body Therapy

I had breakfast with author Charles Whitfield, M.D. conversation about some of my theories; he was very validating, came to my workshop

I presented workshop, "Therapy with the New Age Client", March 30, at Asso. for Humanistic Psychology Midwest Annual Conference, Indianapolis, March 30

Lecture, Ram Dass, Seva Foundation Benefit, Chicago, 5-3-90

Serge King, PhD.,(a Hawaiian shaman trained in the Huna tradition) on "Mastering Your Hidden Self,"Theosophical Society Program, Sunday, 5-6-90

1-Day seminar-Theresa Bernardez M.D. and Harriet Goldher Lerner,PhD., LifeCycle Seminars; "Mothers, Daughters and Intimacy", Chicago, June 24

Evening lecture by Mary Alice Bernadin, "Spirituality and Art," Theosophical Society, May 24

Geneen Roth Workshop on "Breaking Free of Compulsive Eating," Asso. Humanistic Psychology, June 28-29, 1990
1-week seminar, Daniel Levinson, PhD.and Judy Levinson;"Adult Development in Men and Women," Door County Summer Institute,at Egg Harbor, Wisconsin, Dept. of Psychiatry at the Medical College of Wisconsin and Columbia Hospital, Aug. 4-10
1-week Seminar, by Menninger Clinic psychiatrist, Theresa Bernardez. M.D.,"Mothers and Daughters:The Powerful Connection" Seminars for Professional Advancement, Get Away Seminars on Cape Cod, Aug.20-24

Stuart Udolfsky, M.D. Chief of Psychiatry at University of Chicago. and Beth Udolfsky, M.D. Lecture, "New Developments in Psychiatry" for the Woman's Board of the Brain Research Foundation. Sept 25

Domeena Renshaw, M.D. (Prof. of Psyychiatry, Loyola Univ. and Director or Loyola's Sexual Dysfunction Clinic), Seminar: Sex Therapy Today, CPC Old Orchard Hospital, 1-day, Oct.90 , 3 credit hours, Category I, AMA

Lecture by Hyman Muslin, M.D. "Self-Psychology," 10-26-90
The Chicago Psychological Asso and The Institute for Clinical Social Work

Alumni Conference, Family Instutute—Nov 16 & 17, Northwestern Univ. (I presented a workshop)

1991:

Program on "Children of Fast Track Parents; Raising Self-Sufficient and Confident Children in an Achievement Oriented World," by Andree Brooks, Feb 20

I led Lenten Meditation/Prayer/Imagery, Lenten Service at Union Church of Hinsdale, 3-13-91

Certified as a Qualified Clinical Social Worker to continue to be included in the NASW Register of Clinical Social Workers

4-Day Workshop with Stan and Christina Grof, New Orleans, LA Holotropic Breathwork, March 28-31

1-day seminar on "The Immune System and the Mind-Body Connection," Steven Keller, Asso. Prof Psychiatry and Neurosciences, April 3

May 17-24, California study/pleasure trip, (my daughter's U.C.L.A., Law School Graduation May 19) Visited Oaji, CA., Kirshnamurti Center

1-day Program by Dr. Claudia Black, "Adult Children from Troubled Families," NASW, Chicago, June 7

1-day NASW Leadership Workshop (for Board Members), Gary Labranche, Chicago, July 13

Week-long course in Sante Fe, New Mexico, on Self-Psychology and "Creativity and Madness," July 28-August 5

Month long study/pleasure trip to France: Sept 28–Oct 29: 1 week in Paris, 1 week-long Bicycle trip of Dordonne Valley, 1+ week in Provence

Telephone conversation with Rev. Henry Rucker, local Chicago) psychic healer friend, 11-19-91

Weekend Conference, Family Institute of Chicago, Nov 22-23 Olga Silverstien, "Gender and Intimacy" Robert Rutledge, "Object Relations with Severaly Disturbed Couples" Robin Condro, "Therapy with Lesbian Couples"

Dick Schwartz led Internal Family Systems Consultation Group, University of IL, Chicago, 2 times a month, 2 ½ hours, November through end of year and on

Consultations with Dr. Miriam Reitz, 2-4 times per monthly May-Dec.

Larry Lanoff, CSA Associates (Don Kollmar) "Attunement" session

1992: (not entirely complete yet)

I led evening program at Hinsadle Hospital for Cancer Patients, "How a Family can be a Healing System," Date:

Body Therapy at Akiyama Institute, Oak Part Jan 5 and 11

I presented a program to Lutheran Social Services on Parts Psychology, 1-17-92

Denver, Colorado trip, Peace March in honor of Martin Luther King, Jr. Birthday (and the Klu Klux Klan showed up!), Jan 18-22

Wrote Noah's Ark story, Jan 20

Common Ground Chicago Lecture, 1-27-92

Common Ground Chicago Lecture by J. Kenney on *Flow*, 2-10-92

Anne Firestone workshop, "Experiencing The Dark Side," Oasis Center, Feb. 16

Astrology Chart Reading with Jane Larkin Lukehart, Feb '92

3-day Richard Moss, M.D.'s Oasis workshop, "Coming Home:The Energetics of Intimacy," Chicago, Feb 21-23, 1.5 C.E.U's

Dick Schwartz led Internal Family Systems Consultation Group, at U. of IL., Chicago, 2 times a month, Jan–March

I gave presentation that was video taped at A.R.E. Heartland, New Orient Media, on "Parts and Self," 3-21

Weekend Workshop, "Self Acceptance Training", Dick Olney, at Central Partners, March 24 & 25, 12 C.E.U.'s

I presented a workshop at Internal Family Systems Annual Conference, April 3

Weekend A.R.E, Holistic Health Expo, Chicago, April 10-12 Norman Shealy, Carolyn Myss

I present a workshop at the A.R.E. (Association for Research and Enlightenment) Holistic Health Expo in Chicago, entitled "Finding Your Great Self and Healing Your Little Selves," April 11

Qi Gong, Sessions, Consultations, with Dean Deng, M.D. Lake Forest, IL

I moved to Oak Park, on Mother's Day, May 1992

Weekend Meditation Intensive with Gurumayi, Milwaukee, May 20 through the 24th

Monthly Transformational Attunement sessions with Paul Ditchiet throughout 1992 +

Weekend Common Ground Retreat, Woodstock, IL. Jim Kenney and Ron Miller, "Many Ways—One Path," July 24-26, 1992

Common Ground Chicago Lecture on HABITS OF THE HEART; Committment in a Time of Individualism" by Bob Spatz, 7-29-92

Weekend workshop by Duncan Scribner on A.H. Almaas, The Diamond Approach, in Chicago Sept. 12-13, 1992 (held at my condo in Oak Park, sponsored by Jane Lukehart)

I taught 3 hour long sessions of a 5-week course (Carol Jacus, LCSW taught the 2 others) Sept 20 through Oct 18, 1992, Glenview Community Church on "Spiritual Healing, Energy Medicine", etc. Sept 20 Through Oct 18

Common Ground Chicago Lecture by Ron Miller on Martin Buber, 10-4-92

Internal Family Systems weekend Conference, I.J.R, University of Illinois, Oct. 30

I co-led with Nancy Hill, L.C.S.W., her "Dare To Dream" all-day workshop, Nov 7

3-Day 12th Annual Common Boundary Conference, "Invisible Threads," Washington, D.C. Nov. 13-15

Weekend on "The Shamanic Journey:An Experiential Exploration," Michael Harner (I took this a few years earlier, too) Oasis Center, Chicago, Nov. 21-22

1993:

I gave Career Day Program at Lyon's Township High School on "A Career in Social Work," March 18

I gave a presentation "Embracing Our Selves:/Enhancing our Wellness," Wellness House, Cancer Support Center, April 24, 1993

Weekend Workshop, "Embracing Our Selves: Voice Dialogue," led by Bob Sigmon at Oasis Ctr. Chicago, May 22-23,

I was a guest teacher, University of Chicago, Dept of Human Development, July 26

Week-long Parliment of the World's Religions, Chicago Leaders I heard: The Dali Lama, Louis Farrakhan, Cardinal Bernadin, Charlene Spretnak, Swami's: , Charles Tart, Dr. James Forbes, Thomas Berry, August 28-Sept 5

Thich Nhat Hanh Day-long retreat, Sept. 5, St. Mary of the Lake, Mundaline, IL.

3-Day Workshop, "Quantum Consciousness" S. Wolinsky, Chicago, Sept 17-19

"Reading" with Diane Swenson (of Watertown, WI) in Chicago, Sept 20

"Reading" with psychic AstroPhysicist Prof. Dhruv, of India, (follower of Kirshnamurti) who said I had significant original ideas which I needed to write about, Sept.29

Telephone "Reading" with Mark Schoofs in California, Oct. 8

Weekend Conference Nov 5-6, Annual Family Institute of Chicago Conference;

I presented a workshop on "Therapy with the Spiritual Client," Sat Nov. 6, at Family Insititue of Chicago

Mark Schoofs, Evening Program on Spiritual Healing, Nov 12, Oasis Center, Chicago

Dr. Reedy, M.D. Medical Director of Rehab, New Day Ctr. Morning Lecture on Alcoholism, Hinsdale,IL.Nov.14

8-day workshop, Dr. Robt. Jaffee, M.D. and Sandra Parness, Energy Mastery, Woodstock, New York, Nov. 15-22

I gave Meditation/sermon at Service of Prayer and Healing, Union Church of Hinsdale, evening, Nov. 14

I co-taught 11 week course (with Maria Coyne and Pam Knecht) on "Healing and the Mind," Union Church of Hnsdale, December '93 through–March '94

Christmas in San Francisco with family and friends in Sausalito

1994: (Incomplete)

New Years in Connecticut with family of origin

Monthly sessions "Transformational Attunement" with Paul Ditchiet all year and next year

Weekly sessions with Energy Healer Susan Willenbrink

Cranial-Sacral work with Jodi Pattee, Doctor or Chinese Medicine, Healing Arts Center, Oak Park

I led consultation group for therapists all year

I participitated in a client's Soul Retrieval led By Annette Hulefeld, Jan. 8

I led Wellness House (Cancer Support group) Evening program, (volunteer/donation of time) Jan. 17

Illinois Society for Clinical Social Work Program, Feb. 13

1-Day workshop: Hal Stone, PhD. and Sidra Stone, PhD. "Working with Realtionships; A Professional Training Workshop in Voice Dialogue," Oasis Center, Feb 21 .5 CEU's.

I led Oncology Social Workers Program at Northwestern Memorial Hospital, March 23

I led Wellness House (Cancer Support group), on "Awareness", March 24

I co-led 10-week adult sunday school class on Healing (I taught research on Spiritual Healing, A Path with Heart (Kornfield), Healing Hypnosis and Pain, etc., Union Church of Hinsdale, Spring quarter

Member of special committee of Alumni Asso. Geo. Williams College School of Social Work at Aurora University, Manny Jackson Scholarship fund raising program for student diversity

Common Ground Chicago lecture, Jim Kenney, "The Evolution of Consciousness—Robt. Orenstien" April 4

I led Wellness House Cancer Support group Apr. 18

Buddhist-Native American Program, (Dr. Penchamp and Peter Catches) Thai Buddhist Temple, Chicago, April 23

April 28-May 3, Robt. Jaffee M.D. Workshop at The Advanced School of Energy Mastery, Sedona, Arizona

I led Wellness House Support Group, May 9

River-Edge Hospital, Program Opening Adolescent Program, May 13

Lecture by Jan Ola and Laura Glabb, M.D. of Carl Pfeiffer Center, on nutrition and holistic psychiatry, 5-22-94

Trip to Madison, WI. Visit with Healer/Friends there May 22-23

Trip to Colorado and New Mexico, Durango, Ouray, Sante Fe (Stayed at Ghost Ranch one night) June 8-14

I led Wellness House Support Group, June 20

NASW Program, Chicago June 17

2-Day Oasis workshop on "Energy Medicine", Speakers: Robt Jaffee M.D., Caroline Myss, Donna Eden, Sharry Edwards, Leonard Laskow, M.D., Medicine Grizzlybear Lake, June 25-26

Dinner with Anne Firestone, author, psychic "Wolf Spirit Readings" and friend since 1976 when we did medical social work at Resurrection Hospital together, July 3

Darshan with East Indian Saint, Mata Amritanandamayi, "Amachi" in Chicago area July 5, 6, 7

Evening Program, Andrew Harvey, "Dialogues with a Modern Mystic," Oasis Center, July 15

I led program Wellness House, "The Perfectionist" July 18

All day program, Allerton Hotel, Chicago, July 22

Weekend Retreat, Common Ground, Woodstock, IL, Ron Miller and Jim Kenney, "The New Story" July 29-31

I was a guest teacher U. of Chicago, Dept. of Human Development, August 1st

Lecture, Common Ground Chicago, Ron Miller on "What the Buddha Never Taught," August 8

Breakfast with Caroline Myss in Oak Park; shared my ideas and my writing with her, August 14

I led Support group, Wellness House on "The Victim/Passive Pessimist", August 15

I gave presentation for A.R.E. at College of DuPage, "Partnering Polarities, Dancing with Dichotamies, Honoring Opposites," August 26 (Video taped)

Lecture, Common Ground, Chicago August 29

Evening lecture by Wm Brooks, Reincarnation group, DesPlaines, Sept 9

I co-led a 10-week adult Sunday school class with Dan Cherry on M. Scott Peck's book, Further Along the Road Less Traveled, Fall Quarter, Union Church

Internal Family Systems Booster Workshop (I noticed that my Inner Child's relationship with my Self had healed) Sept 16, 4 CEU's

During session with spiritual healer Susan Willenbrink, a traumatic bodily held memory of George Richardson surfaced, Sept 18

Session with Henry Rucker, spiritual healer, Sept 19

4-day Energy Mastery Workshop, Sandra Parness, Madison, WI, Sept 22-25

Energy Healing/Body Focused Session with Kathrine Nash, Sept 25, (I physically FELT an energy around me and, when I asked Katherine about the energy which felt like it was holding my feet she said she "saw" a 10 foot high angel helping with the healing); prior to this experience I didn't exactly believe in angels

Theresa McNeely, psychic telephone consultation Sept 26

I led Wellness Support Group, Sept 26

Half-day program, "Spirituality and Psychotherapy, Cathedral Counseling Center, Chicago, Presenters: Ernest Kurtz, Katherine Amato von Hermat, Sept 30 3 CEU's

Common Ground lecture, Chicago, Oct 3

I evening program for A.R.E. CHicago Heartland office, Oct 9

Canceled trip to Gay and Kathlyn Handricks training in Portland, Oregon to stay home and integrate a sexual abuse trauma which had surfaced during a session with psychic healere, Susan Willenbrink

Theresa McNeely, Oct 12 (she told me to sell A.R.E. video)

EMDR sessions by Gail Dreas, L.C.S.W., Oct 19 + 31, Nov 21, Dec 5, 14, 21

Full Moon Drumming, Wilmette, Oct 21

Schamanic Journey Session with Annette Hulefeld, Oct 24

I led Wellness House Support Group, Oct 24 1-Day NASW Program, Janet Williams, on DSM IV, Oct 27

Evening Program by Author Brezedon, Christ Church Oak Book on Sexual Abuse, Nov 1

Weekend Workshop, "Conscious and Superconscious Healing," by Mark Schoofs, Intuitive Healer, Oasis Center, Chicago Nov. 4-6

I led Service of Prayer and Healing, Union Church, Nov.13

Common Ground Chicago Lecture, Jim Kenney, "From Existentialsim to Zen," 11-21-94

Brunch with Carolyn Myss, Nov 27

I led Wellness House Support Group, Nov 28

Swami Netra, Bodywork, at Spectrum Center, Nov 30 also Dec 12, Dec 19, Dec 26

Session with Theresa McNeely, Dec 1

Evening Program with Spiritual Healer, Delores "Mama" Lucas from Columbus, Ohio, in Chicago suburbs, Dec. 2 Session with Delores Lucas, Dec 4

Hana Kuna bodywork healer, Joe Mina, session Dec 5

Evening Lecture, Clarisa Pinkolas Estes, *Women Who Run With The Wolves*, Anderson's Book Store, Elmhurst, IL. Dec 6

Il. Society for Clinical Social Work Meeting, M.A. Jung's

Internal Family Systems Booster, all day program Dec 9

Network Chiropractic, Dr. Diane Murad, Dec 13 I presented a program at Forest (Psychiatric) Hospital, Des Plaines, IL. on Psychotherapy and Spirituality/Energy Medicine, Dec 19

Cardiovascular stress tests/EKG, Hinsdale Hospital for Heart (Chakra) Pains of several weeks, Dec 27 (Note, for several weeks prior to my daughter's nearly fatal accident on 2-5-95) I had heart pains which totally disappeared which the accident happened and the pain became consciousness; I believe my body may have known ahead of time what was coming; this possibility was suggested to me later by an energy medicine teacher). During the four weeks prior to the accident I was "cat sitting" for a friend's two cats. One of them voluntarily slept on my heart as I lay on my back in bed at night, perhaps in an effort to be of healing help).

1995:

Common Ground Weekend Retreat, "CARE OF THE SOUL" (Thomas Moore's book, Jan 27-29, 1995

Trip to Mexico. Last day of trip learned of daughter's nearly fatal accident (with traumatic leg amputation, broken neck (C2) with severe subluxation, severely broken jaw), on Feb 5 while daughter was vacationing in Maui, Hawaii

Went to Queen's Hospital, Honolulu to be with daughter for two weeks; met Kahuna healers, Healing Hands nurses working with conventional western trained doctors; this was the Alternative Therapy program of Dr. Paul Pearsall

I presented workshop "Being Present to Ourselves; Empowerment Through Embodiment" at Insititute for Juvenile Research Conference, Family Therapy Dept.,, University of Illinois, March 3, 1995

I presented a talk, "Parts and Whole, Selves and Soul" for Common Ground, Chicago, Program, 3-6-95

I again presented "Parts and Whole, Selves and Soul, Common Ground, Deerfield, IL. ,3-8-95

I presented a workshop for a National Association for Social Worker's Program,"Being Present to Ourselves; Empowerment Through Embodiment," Linden Oaks Hospital, Naperville, 3-17-95

Went to Philadelphia, Jefferson Hospital to be with daughter, met Healing Touch nurses, March 19-26

I presented an all-day workshop, "Spirituality and Family Systems" for The Family Institute at Northwestern University, Evanston, IL. 3-31-95

Evening Program, Sufi Llewellyn Vaughn-Lee, PhD. Oasis Center, Chicago, April 7

2-day Hypnosis Workshop, American Academy of Medical Hypnoanalysts, Dr. Zelling, Chicago, April 29-30, 1995, 14 CEU's

2-day Retreat on Spiritual Healing, Rev. Ron Roth, Lake Forest, IL. May 5-6, 1995

Common Ground Anniversary Program, Lake Forest, May 7, 1995

Susan Willenbrink, Oak Park, IL. weekly spiritual healing consultations

Katheryn Nash, Sedona Arizona, several energy healing consultations

Theresa McNeely "readings"

I presented workshop, "Embodiment of Parts and Self," and attended 2-day Annual Conference of Internal Family Systems, May 19-20, '95

Joseph Mina, Body Therapy Consultations, Oak Park, *I presented an all-day workshop "Spirituality and Family Systems" for The Family Institute, at Northwestern University, 6/9/95*

Astrology telephone "reading" with Jane Larkin, 6-15-95

Common Ground Chicago lecture by Tom Hoberg of University of Chicago on T.S. Eliott and Robt Frost and The Holy Grail," 6/19

Charles Lo, M.D. Chinese Medicine Consultations

Paul Ditchiet, R.N., M.S. of Madison, WI. "Transformational Attunment" Consultations, Monthly 90 minute sessions in Chicago

Susan Willenbrink, spiritual energy healing sessions, weekly 2-3 hour sessions

2-day Oasis Center, Conference on Energy Medicine," The Healing Journey," Chicago, June 24-25
        Heard: Jeanne Achterberg
        Helen Bonny
        Rosalyn Bruyere
        Luci Capacchione
        Jacob Liberman
        John Thie (Touch for Health)

Program on Plant Spirit Medicine, by Eliot Cowan at Triton College, June 26, 1995

Program on Research of Dr. Valerie Hunt of UCLA, "Infinite Mind" at K. Noreen's, Elmhurst, IL. 6-29-95

9-day Divine Unity Gathering, Devra West, in Snowmass, CO. July 7-15

1-day Training in "Body-Systems Therapy: Humanistic and Spiritual Approaches," Sheldon Kramer, The Family Institute, Chicago, July 21, 6 1/2 CEU's

Common Ground evening program by Ron Miller on Andrew Harvey, "Confessions of a Modern Mystic," July 24, 1995

Common Ground Weekend Retreat, Woodstock, IL. on Thomas Merton and Rabbi Heschel, led by Ron Miller and Jim Kenney, July 28-30, 1995

I presented 3-hour class "Body-Centered Parts and Self; Energy Medicine, Concrete and Spacious Realities" University of Chicago, Dept. of Human Development, Family Therapy graduate class of Dr. Dan Freedman, August 7, 1995

Telephone "Reading" with Theresa McNeely of Virginia, 8-8-95

Dr. Louis Del Aguila of California, Breathwork and Spiritual Healing, Consultations, Chicago, August, 1995

I lead/taught 2-hr. consultation group meetings on "Integrating Psychotherapy and Spirituality", Hinsdale,IL, once or twice per month

Internal Family Systems all-day Retreat, Chicago, Sept 9, 1995

Program on "The Celestine Prophecy," led by Rev. Greg Skiba, Union Church, Hinsdale, IL. Sept 10, 1995

Program by Ron Miller, Common Ground, Chicago, 9-11-95

Loretta Glowaty, Astrology "reading," Downers Grove, IL 9-12-95

I led Meditation-Prayer Group for Psychotherapists

Monet Exhibit and Program, Art Institute, Chicago 9-14-95

Program on Bagavaad Gita, Common Ground, Chicago 9-18-95

D.O.C.C, University of the South, School of Theology, Sewanee, Tennessee, Weekly Group Meetings at Union Church, Hinsdale, IL (Sept '95-April '96)

CityQuest Program, speaker Dr. Arun Ghandi, grandson Mahatma Gandhi, speaker, Indian Hill Country Club, Winnetta, 9-23-95

Monthly Consultations/Supervision with R.E. Damptz, M.D., Psychiatric Consultant to my private practice since 1981

2-day Workshop, Rev. Roselyn Bruyere, of Calif. on Energy Healing, Chicago, Oct 7-8, 1995

Evening Program, Sonia Choquette, "The Psychic Pathway, at Anderson's Book Store, Downers Grove, Oct. 10

2-day Retreat with Rev. Ron Roth, Lake Forest, IL. Oct 14-15, 1995

Weekend Program on "Genetic, Ethological and Evolutionary Perspectives on Human Development," A Festschrist to Honor Dr. Dan Freedman, U. of Chicago, Oct 27-29, 1995

Weekend Conference, 17th Annual Family InstituteConference, (Jean Baker Miller, keynote) Nov 17-18

I presented workshop "Bridging Developmental Psychology with Spirituality," at above Family Therapy conference, Nov. 18

Kerigma Class, weekly, for 5 months, led at Union Church of Hinsdale, IL. by Rev. Dr. Greg Skiba

Pam Hogan, Taos, N.M. Telephone "reading" 11-20-95

Hypnosis class (I taught it) Illinois Benedictine College, 11-27-95 or 12-5-95

Weekend Retreat called a "Woman's Advance" at Barbara Schuppe's haven, Union Pier, MI. Twice in 1995

Attended Tazie (ecumenical) Services, monthly, Ascension Catholic Church, Oak Park, IL

1996:

I presented an OASIS CENTER all-day Workshop,"Partnering Polarities, Balancing Realities," 1-21-96

Dr. Guo, Chinese Medicine Consultations, Westmont, IL, 1/96

Common Ground Chicago 2-hr program, by Ron Miller on Thich Nhat Hanh on *LIVING BUDDHA, LIVING CHRIST*, 1-22-96

I gave a presentation at Union Church of Hinsdale, Service of Prayer and Healing, "Healing Power of Community," 2-4-96

Evening Program, Maya Angelou, at Elmhurst College, Feb. 11 (VERY SPECIAL, "Take me with you," she told everyone)

Common Ground Chicago, 2-hr program, 2-12-96

Common Ground Chicago, program, Jim Kenney on "Anthropology and the Evolution of Morality," Feb. 19

Weekend Conference "Men in Community" 5th Chicago Men's Conference, Feb 24-25, 1996
        Heard: John Lee
        Robtert Moore
        Bob Mark, Buddy Portugal
        Jon McCrae
        And others

I co-taught with Dan Cherry, 10 week course on "Experiencing Prayer" (book by Tom Sampson) Union Church of Hinsdale, IL, Winter-Spring 1996

I taught workshop at McNeal Hospital, Berwyn, IL for Social Workers,Chaplins, Nurses, (was paid honorium $250) March 5

EMDR Level I 2-day Training, Certified, March 31, 1996, Indianapolis, Indiana

I led all-day workshop at Oasis: "Balancing Realities, Dancing with Dichomotomies, Partnering Polarities," May 4, 1996

2-Day 5th Annual Internal Family Systems Conference, U.of Illinois, 12 CEU's, May 16 & 17, 1996

I presented a workshop at above conference on May 16, "Healing Narcissistic Injuries with IFS" May 16

3-day Weekend Intensive with healer Rosalyn Bruyere, "Reawakening The First Chakra," Chicago, June 7-9, 1996

4-day Conference, Society for Spirituality & Social Work, Univ. of Nebraska at Omaha (at Dana College, Blair,NE)

I presented a workshop of "Living in Two Realities, Partnering our Polarities," for Society for Spirituality & Social Work, Dana College, Blair, NE) July 13-17

I was invited to be on the National Board for SSSW, 6-18-96

Week-long conference on "Socially Engaged Buddhism and Christianity," The Society for Buddhist-Christian Studies, DePaul Univ., Chicago, July 27-Aug.3

Heard:

> H.H.The Dali Lama,
> Rosemary Radford Ruether,
> Prof. Ewert Cousins
> Sr. Jose Hobday

Weekend Seminar, James Hillman and Michael Meade,"Character, Fate and Destiny," Institute for the Study of Imagination, Chicago, Sept 6-7

2-Day EMDR Level II training, Francine Shapiro, PhD. Sept 28-29, Chicago

Women's Weekend Retreat, (a.k.a. " Women's Advance") Schupee Haven, Union Pier, MI, Nov. 22-24

1997:

2-Day Level I training, TFT (Thought Field Therapy), Dr. Jeffery Santee, 1/11 + 12/ 97

Spontaneous stop at a Psychic Fair for a 15 minute reading with Theresa Ozakewski, 1-12-97

Telephone Reading with local Chicago area psychic healer, Zandee Zebella, 1-28-97

Lecture by Trappist Monk, Wayne Teasdale on "The Speculative Mystics, Meister Eckhart and Jan van Ruysbroek" Common Ground Chicago, Feb 3

Evening Program, Steven Vasquez, "Colored Light Therapy," at Mariott Oak Brook, Feb. 12

Astrology consultation with psychic Diana Yoksas, Downers Grove, IL, late Feb, 1997

I was a member of a panel on "Spirituality in Social Work;Clinical Issues" at CSWE (Council on Social Work Education) Conference, Chicago, March 6, 1997

I hosted Women's Retreat for members of National Board of Society for Spirituality and Social Work, March 7-8

National board meeting for SSSW, Chicago, March 8, (I was given the job of being the "process person for the Board")

I led panel and gave a presentation on "Holistic Social Work and Energy Medicine," N.A.S.W. Fox River Valley District Program, Copley Hospital, Aurora, IL , March 14, 1997

Attended Program by Rev Ron Roth, Spiritual Healer on "Spirituality, Prayer and Healing," Lake Forest College, March 23

Evening Program by Andrew Weil, M.D. on" 8-Weeks to Optimal Health" at Transitions, Chicago, March 29 1-day seminar, "First Things First," Steven Covey Leadership Corp. Oak Brook, IL. April 10

2nd Annual Alternative Therapies Symposium, "Creating Integrated Healthcare, Orlando, Florida, April 16-19, 1997
Speakers Heard: Beverly Rubik
       Matthew Fox
       Larry Dossey
       Jeanne Acterberg
       Frank Lawlis, M.D.
       George Carpenter, D.O.
       Gary Schwartz
       Etc.

1-day seminar, "The Aging of the Brain, The Aging of the Mind" Mind Seminars, Bruce Quinn, M.D. PhD., Countryside, IL. May

Qi Gong workshop, Univ. Of Arizona, Tucson, AZ. May 24, 1997

Dinner with Gary Schwartz of U. Of Arizona and his wife Linda at their home in Tucson, shared my favorite theoretical ideas with them; (they are doing very important research on the heart-brain connection)

2-Day 6th Annual Internal Family Systems Conference, on Internal Family Systems Therapy at Northwestern University, May 16-17

I presented 3 hr. workshop on "Spirituality, Energy Medicine and IFS" at 6th Annual Internal Family Systems 2-day, Conference, May 16-17

Weekend workshop, "The Art of Healing," Mark Earlix, Chicago, CEU's, July 5 & 6

Evening Lecture, Common Ground, "T.S. Eliott, Robt. Frost and the Holy Grail, by Tom Hoberg, University of Chicago Enlish Prof.

APPENDIX E:
RELATED READING:

Resources for Paradigm-Bridging and Balancing
Realities in Life and in Holistic Studies
Compiled (mainly) between Janurary 1995 and July
2000 by Nancy S.B.Ging, LCSW

The New Sciences:

Bohm,D, WHOLENESS AND THE IMPLICATE ORDER, NY:Routledge, 1980

Capra, Fritjof and Steindl-Rast, David, BELONGING TO THE UNIVERSE: Explorations on the Frontiers of Science and Spirituality, HarperSanFrancisco, 1991

Capra, Fritjov, THE TAO OF PHYSICS, Boulder,CO:Shambhala, 1975

Gribbin, John, IN SEARCH OF SCHRODINGER'S CAT; Quantum Physics and Reality, NY:Bantum Books, 1984

Hunt, Valerie V. INFINITE MIND: Science of the Human Vibrations of Consciousness, CA:Malibu Pub. 1989, 1996

Herbert, Nick, QUANTUM REALITY; Beyond the New Physics, NY:Anchor, 1985

Hofstadter, Douglas R, GODEL, ESCHER, BACH; An Eternal Golden Braid, NY:Basic Books, 1979

Hall, Nina (Editor) EXPLORING CHOAS; A Guide to the New Science of Disorder, NY:Norton, 1994

Jones, Roger S., PHYSICS FOR THE REST OF US, Chicago:Contemporary Books, 1992

Jones, Roger S., PHYSICS AS METAPHOR, NY:Meridian, 1982

LeShan, Lawrence & Margenau, Henry, EINSTEIN'S SPACE & VAN GOGH'S SKY, NY:Macmillian, 1982

Toben, Bob, SPACE, TIME AND BEYOND, NY:Dutton, 1975

Waldrop, Mitchell, COMPLEXITY;The Emerging Science at the Edge of Order and Choas, NY:Touchtone/Simon and Schuster, 1992

Wilbur, Ken, QUANTUM QUESTIONS, Boston:Shambhala, 1984

Wilbur, Ken, THE HOLOGRAPHIC PARADIGM and other paradoxes, Boston:New Science Library, 1982

Wolf, Fred Alan, THE EAGLE'S QUESTY; A physicist's Search for Truth in the Heart of the Shamanic World, NY:Summit, 1991

Wolfson, Richard Prof., Middlebury College, "Einstein's Relativity and The Quantum Revolution: Modern Physics for Non-Scientists, 12 Lectures," VA, Springfield:The Teaching Company, 1995

Zukav, Gary, THE DANCING WU LI MASTERS; An Overview of The New Physics, NY:Morrow Quill, 1979

New Paradigm/World View:

Anderson, Walter Truett, REALITY ISN'T WHAT IT USED TO BE; Theatrical Politics, Ready-to-Wear Religion, Global Myths, Primitive Chic, and other wonders of the PostModern World, SF:Harper & Row, 1990

Dossey, Larry, M.D., TIME, SPACE and MEDICINE, Boulder,CO:Shambhala, 1982

Dossey, Larry, M.D. RECOVERING THE SOUL: A Scientific and Spiritual Search, NY:Bantam 1989

Grof, Stanislav, M.D., THE HOLOTROPIC MIND; The Three Levels of Human Consciousness and How They Shape Our Lives; HarperSanFrancisco, 1990

Shlain, Leonard, M.D. ART AND PHYSICS, Parallel Visions in Space, Time and Light, NY:Wm Morrow, 1991

Consciousness Studies:

Anshen, Ruth Nanda, THE MYSTERY OF CONSCIOUSNESS; A Prescription for Human Survival, Wakefield,R.I & London:Moyer Bell, 1994

Brucke, R.M., COSMIC CONSCIOUSNESS, ARKANA, 1991 (originally published by Innes, 1901)

Bateson, Gregory, STEPS TO AN ECOLOGY OF MIND, NY:Ballantine, 1972

Laszlo, E., Grof, S. and Russel, Peter,THE CONSCIOUSNESS REVOLUTION, Boston, MA: Element, Inc. 1999

Wilbur, Ken, THE SPECTRUM OF CONSCIOUSNESS, Wheaton,IL:Quest, 1976

Human Evolution:

Wilbur, Ken, SEX, ECOLOGY, SPIRITUALITY; The Spirit of Evolution, Boston:Shambhalla, 1995

Wilbur, Ken, UP FROM EDEN, A Transpersonal View of Human Evolution, 1996 (New Edition) Wheaton, IL:Quest Books

Wilbur, Ken, A BRIEF HISTORY OF EVERYTHING, Boston:Shambhalla, 1996

Body/Energy/Consciousness perspectives:

Dienstfrey, Harris, WHERE THE MIND MEETS THE BODY, NY:HarperCollins, 1991

Genlin, Eugene, FOCUSING, NY:Everest House,1978

Goswami, A., THE SELF-AWARE UNIVERSE; How Consciousness Creates the Material World, NY:Tarcger/Putnam, 1993

Grof, Stanislav, M.D. HOLOTROPIC MIND, NY:Harper Collins,1990

Hendricks, G. and K, AT THE SPEED OF LIFE; A New Approach to Personal Change through Body-Centered Therapy, NY:Bantam, 1993

Johnson, Don Hanlon, and Grand, Ian, Editors, THE BODY IN PSY-CHOTHERAPY; Inquiries in Somatic Psychology, Berkeley, CA:North Atlantic Books, 1998.

Keleman, Stanley, EMOTIONAL ANATONY, Berkeley,CA;Center Press, 1985

Johanson, Greg and Kurtz, Ron, GRACE UNFOLDING; Psycho-therapy in the Spirit of the Tao-te ching, NY:Bell Tower, 1991

Wilson, Robert Anton, QUANTUM PSYCHOLOGY, New Falcon Pub. 1993

Wolinsky, S., PhD. QUANTUM CONSCIOUSNESS;The Guida to Experiencing Quantum Psychology, CT;Bramble,1993

Heart and Brain:

Amen, Daniel, M.D. CHANGE YOUR BRAIN, CHANGE YOUR LIFE, New York:Times Books, 1998

Pearsall, Paul,PhD. THE HEART'S CODE, New York:Broadway Books,1998

Childre, D. and Martin,H., THE HEARTMATH SOLUTION, HarperSanFrancisco, 1999

McArthur, D. & McArthur, B. , THE INTELLIGENT HEART, Virginia Beach,VA: 1997

Fogarty, Robin, BRAIN COMPATIBLE CLASSROOMS, Arlington Heights, IL: Skylight Publishing, 1997

Vibrational Medicine:

Gerber, Richard, M.D., VIBRATIONAL MEDICINE; New Choices for Healing Ourselves, Sante Fe, NM:Bear & Co, 1988

Hutchinson, Michael, MEGA BRAIN POWER; Transform Your Life with Mind Machines and Brain Nutrients, NY:Hyperion, 1984

Energy Healing, Energy Medicine & The Chakra System:

Bruyere, Rosalyn, WHEELS OF LIGHT, NY:Fireside/Simon and Schuster, 1989

Brennan, Barbara, HANDS OF LIGHT; A Guide to Healing Throught the Human Energy Field; NY:Bantam, 1987

Brennan, Barbabra, LIGHT EMERGING; The Journey of Personal Healing, NY:Bantam, 1993

Carlson, Richard and Shield, Benjamin, HEALERS ON HEALING, L.A.,CA:Tarcher, 1989

Chopra, Deepak, M.D. QUANTUM HEALING; Exploring the Frontiers of Mind/Body Medicine, NY:Bantam, 1989

Eden, James M.D., ENERGETIC HEALING:The Merging of Ancient and Modern Medical Practices, NY:Plenum Press, 1993

Epstein, Donald, D.C., THE 12 STAGES OF HEALING; a Network Approach to Wholeness, San Rafael, CA:New World Library, 1994

Kreiger, Delores, THERAPEUTIC TOUCH, NJ:Prentis Hall, 1979

Laskow, Leonard, M.D., HEALING WITH LOVE, The Art of Holoenergetic Healing, HarperSanFrancisco, 1992

Locke, Steven, M.D., and Colligan, Douglas, THE HEALER WITHIN; The New Medicine of Mind and Body, NY:Mentor, 1987

Myss, Carolyn, ANATOMY OF SPIRIT; NY:Random House, 1996

Schwartz,Gary and Russek,Linda, THE LIVING ENERGY UNIVERSE, Charlottesville, VA:Hampton Roads, 1999

Shealy, Norman, M.D., and Myss, Carolyn, THE CREATION OF HEALTH, Walpole, NH:Stillpoint, 1993

The Healing of Marital and Family Systems:

Eisler, Riane and Loye, David, THE PARTNERSHIP WAY; New Tools for Living and Learning, Healing Our Families, Our Communities, and Our World; A Prictical Companion for "The Chalice and The Blade," HarperSanFrancisco, 1990

Haley, Jay, ORDEAL THERAPY, SanFranciscoCA:Jossey-Bass Pub. 1984

Hendricks, G. and K, CONSCIOUS LOVING, The Journey to Co-Committment; NY:Bantam, 1990

Levine, Stephen and Ondrea, EMBRACING THE BELOVED; Relationship as a Path of Awakening, NY:Doubleday, 1995

McAll, Kenneth, M.D., HEALING THE FAMILY TREE, London:Sheldon Press, 1982

Moseley, Douglas & Naomi, DANCING IN THE DARK; The Shadow Side of Intimate Relationships,Georgetown,MA:North Star Publications,1994.

Prather, High and Gayle, A BOOK FOR COUPLES, NY:Doubleday, 1988

Satir, Banmen, Gerber, Gomori, THE SATIR MODEL, Palo Alto,CA:Science and Behavior Books, 1991

Schwartz, Richard, INTERNAL FAMILY SYSTEMS THERAPY, NY:Giliford, 1995

Taub-Bynum, E. Bruce, THE FAMILY UNCONSCIOUS; "An Invisible Bond" Wheaton,IL.;Quest, 1984

Welwood, John, AWAKENING THE HEART, East/West Approaches to Psychotherapy and the Healing Relationship, Boston & London:New Science Library, 1983

Welwood, John, JOURNEY OF THE HEART, NY:Harper Collins, 1990

Welwood, John, LOVE AND AWAKENING; Discovering the Sacred Path of Intimate Relationship,NY:HarperCollins, 1996

"Parts" Psychololgy:

Assiagoli, Roberto, PSYCHOSYNTHESIS, A Manuel of Principles and techniques. London:Turnstone Press, 1975 (originally published in 1965 by Arkana)

Schwartz, Richard C. INTERNAL FAMILY SYSTEMS THERAPY, NY:Guiliford, 1995

Goulding, R. and Schwartz, Richard C. THE MOSAIC MIND; Empowering the Tormented Selves of Child Abuse Survivors, NY:Norton, 1995

Rowan, John, SUBPERSONALITIES; The People Inside Us, NY:Routledge, 1990

Sliker, Gretchen, MULTIPLE MIND;Healing the Split in Psyche and World, Boston & London:Shambhalla, 1992

Stone, Hal and Winkelman, Sidra; EMBRACING EACH-OTHER; Relationship as Teacher, Healer and Guide, CA:New World Library, 1989

Stone, Hal and Stone, Sidra, EMBRACING YOUR INNER CRITIC;Turning Self-Criticism into a Creative Asset, NY: Harper Collins/ Harper SF, 1993

Ferrucci, Piero, WHAT WE MAY BE; Techniques for Psychological and Spiritual Growth, L.A.,CA:Tarcher/Houghton Mifflin, 1982

Transactional Analysis:

Harris,T.A. I'M OK—YOU'RE OK, New York:Harper & Row, 1967.

James, Muriel, THE POWER AT THE BOTTOM OF THE WELL; T.A. and Religious Experience, NY:Harper & Row, 1974

Polarities:

Levinson, Daniel, THE SEASONS OF A MAN'S LIFE, NY:Ballentine, 1978, Chapters 14 and 15, pgs 209-244.

Will:

Assiagoli, Roberto, THE ACT OF WILL, NY:Penguin, 1973

Thurston, Mark, PARADOX OF POWER; Balancing Personal and Higher Will, VA:ARE PRESS,1987

Narcissism:

Kernberg, Otto, BORDERLINE CONDITIONS & PATHOLOGICAL NARCISSISM, NY:Jason Aronson, 1975

Kohut, Heinz, THE PSYCHOANALYTIC STUDY OF THE CHILD;the Psychoanalytic Treatment of Narcissistic Personality Disorders, NY:International University Press, 1968

Kohut, Heinz, ANALYSIS OF THE SELF, NY:International University Press, 1971

Cognitive Therapy:

Beck, Aaron T., Rush, A.J., Shaw, B.R., Emery, G., COGNITIVE THERAPY OF DEPRESSION, NY:Gilford Press, 1979

Burns, David, FEELING GOOD;The New Mood Therapy, NY:Wm Morrow & Co., 1980

Object Relations and Spirituality:

Almaas, A.H. THE PEARL BEYOND PRICE, Integration of Personality into Being: An Object Relations Approach, Berkeley,CA:Diamond Books, 1988

Almaas, A.H. THE VOID; A Psychodynamic Investigation of the Relationship between Mind and Space, Berkeley,CA:Diamond Books, 1986

Almaas, A.H., ESSENSE, The Diamond Approach to Inner Realization, ME:Samuel Weiser, 1986

Almaas, A.H., THE ELIXIR of ENLIGHTENMENT, Maine:Sameul Weiser, 1989

Almaas, A.H., DIAMOND HEART, Book One, Elements of the Real Man, Berkeley,CA:Diamond Books, 1987

Transformational Psychology:

Hillman,James, REVISIONING PSYCHOLOGY,NY:Harper & Row, 1975

Houston, Jean, THE POSSIBLE HUMAN, L.A.CA:Tarcher, 1982

Moss, Richard, M.D., HOW SHALL I LIVE, Transforming Health Crisis into Greater Aliveness, CA:Celestial Arts, 1985

Moss, Richard, THE BLACK BUTTERFLY; An Invitation to Radical Aliveness, CA:Celestial Arts,1986

Nelson, John E., M.D. HEALING THE SPLIT: Integrating Spirit Into Our Understanding of the Mentally Ill, Albany:State University of NY Press, 1994

Small, Jacquelyn, TRANSFORMERS; Therapists of the Future, CA:DeVorss,1982

Thurston, Mark, DISCOVERING YOUR SOUL'S PURPOSE, VA:ARE Press, 1984

Edinger, Edward, EGO AND ARCHETYPE, Boston:Shambhalla, 1972

The Enneagram:

Palmer, Helen, THE ENNEAGRAM, NY:Harper Collins, 1988

Storytelling:

Kurtz, Ernest and Ketcham, K., THE SPIRITUALITY OF IMPER-FECTION; Storytelling and the Journey to Wholeness, NY:Bantam, 1992

Popular Reading in Spirituality:

Chopra, Depak, M.D. THE SEVEN SPIRITUAL LAWS OF SUCCESS, San Rafael,CA:Amber-Allen and New World Library, 1994

Fields, Rick, with Taylor, Weyler, Ingrasci, CHOP WOOD, CARRY WATER, A Guide to Finding Spiritual Fulfillment in Everyday Life; L.A.,CA.:Tarcher,1984

Grabhorn, Lynn, EXCUSE ME, YOUR LIFE IS WAITING, Charlottesville, VA:Hampton Roads, 2000

Hillman, James, THE SOUL'S CODE; In Search of Character and Calling, NY:Random House, 1996

Miller, Ronald S., and the Editors of New Age Journal, AS ABOVE, SO BELOW; Paths to Spiritual Renewal in Daily Life, L.A.,CA.:Tarcher,1992

Moore, Thomas, CARE OF THE SOUL, NY:Harper Collins, 1992

Norwood, Robin, WHY ME, WHY THIS, WHY NOW, NY:Carol Southern Books, 1994

Peck, M. Scott, M.D., THE ROAD LESS TRAVELED, NY:Simon & Schuster, 1978

Redfield, Jas., CELESTINE PROPHESY, NY:Warner, 1993

Williamson, Marianne, RETURN TO LOVE; Reflections on the Principles of "A Course in Miracles," NY:Harper Collins, 1992

Zukav, Gary, THE SEAT OF THE SOUL, NY:Simon & Schuster, 1990

Mysticism and Psychotherapy:

Brunton, Paul, THE SENSITIVES; Dynamics and Dangers of Mysticism, NY:Larson, 1987

Deikman, Arthur, M.D., THE OBSERVING SELF; Mysticism and Psychotherapy; Boston:Beacon, 1982

Emerson, Ralph Waldo, FIVE ESSAYS ON MAN AND NATURE, Edited by Robert E. Spiller, NY: Appleton-Century-Crofts, Inc., 1954

Bortoft, Henri, THE WHOLENESS OF NATURE; Goethe's Way Toward A Science of Conscious Participation in Nature, New York:Henri Bortoft, 1996

Mabry, John, GOD AS NATURE SEES GOD; A Christian Reading of the Tao Te Ching, Rockport, MA:Element,Inc., 1994

Carroll, L. Patrick and Dyckman, Katharine, INVITING THE MYSTIC, SUPPORTING THE PROPHET; An Introduction to Spiritual Direction, Paulist Press, 1981

Carse, James, BREAKFAST AT THE VICTORY: The Mysticism of Ordinary Experience, CA:HarperSanFrancisco, 1994

Shadow and Evil (these are not necessarily synonyms):

Fedorschak, VJ, THE SHADOW ON THE PATH, Prescott, AZ: Hohn Press, 1999.

Johnson, Robert A., OWNING YOUR OWN SHADOW; Understanding the Dark Side of the Psyche, HarperSanFrancisco,1991

Pierrakos, Eva and Thesenga, Donovan, FEAR NO EVIL; The Pathwork Method of Transforming The Lower Self, Madison,VA:Pathwork Press, 1993

Woodruff and Wilmer, Editors, FACING EVIL; Light at the Core of Darkness; LaSalle,IL:Open Court Press, 1988

Forgiveness:

Smeedes, Lewis; FORGIVE AND FORGET, NY:Harper & Row, 1984

A Course in Miracles:

Inner Peace Foundation, A COURSE IN MIRACLES, NY:Coleman Graphics, 1975

Wapnick, Kenneth, M.D. THE OBSTACLES TO PEACE, Crompond, NY: Foundation for "A Course in Miracles," 1987

Singh, Tara, HOW TO LEARN FROM A COURSE IN MIRACLES; NY:Harper & Row, 1985

Williamson, Marianne, RETURN TO LOVE: Reflections on the Principles of "A Course in Miracles," NY:Harper Collins, 1992

New Works on Dying/Death:

Doore, Gary, Editor, WHAT SURVIVES? Contemporary Explorations of Life After Death, L.A.,CA:Tarcher, 1990

Kubler-Ross, Elisabeth & Kessler, David, LIFE LESSONS, NY:Scribner, 2000

Levine, Stephen, WHO DIES? An Investigation of Conscious Living and Conscious Dying, NY:Anchor, 1982

Levine, Stephen, HEALING INTO LIFE AND DEATH, NY:Anchor, 1987

Ring, Kenneth, LIFE AT DEATH; A Scientific Investigation of the Near-Death Experience, NY:Morrow, 1980

Sogyal Rinpoche, THE TIBETAN BOOK OF LIVING AND DYING, HarperSanFrancisco, 1992

Shamanic Counseling:

Doore, Gary, Editor, SHAMAN'S PATH, Boston:Shambhala, 1988

Ingerman, Sandra, SOUL RETRIEVAL; Mending the Fragmented Self, NY:HarperCollins, 1991

Wolf, Fred Alan, THE EAGLE'S QUEST; A Physicist's search for Truth in the Heart of the Shamanic World, NY:Summit/Simon & Schuster, 1991

Spiritual Emergency/Emergence:

Grof, Stanaslov, M.D. and Grof,Christina, Editors, SPIRITUAL EMER-GENCY, When Personal Transfomation Becomes a Crisis, L.A.,CA:Tarcher, 1989

Depossession Therapy/Spiritual Releasement

Baldwin, William, D.D.S. SPIRIT RELEASEMENT THERAPY, Human Potential Foundation Press, 1993

Hickman, Irene, D.O. REMOTE DEPOSSESSION, 1994

Stages of Spiritual and Moral Development:

Fowler, James, STAGES OF FAITH; The Psychology of Human Development and the Quest for Meaning, ST:Harper, 1981

Lickona, T., Moral Development & Behavior; Thoery, Research and Social Issues, (Lawrence Kohlberg's 6 stages of moral development) NY:Holt, Rinehart and Winston, 1976

Peck, M. Scott, M.D.. FURTHER ALONG THE ROAD LESS TRAVELED; The Unending Journey Toward Spiritual Growth; Edited Lectures, NY:Simon & Schuster, 1993

Dreams, Dream Telepathy and Jungian Psychology:

Jung, Carl, MEMORIES, DREAMS AND REFLECTIONS, NY: Randon House, 1961

Kelsey, Morton, Dreams a WAY TO LISTEN TO GOD, NY:Paulist Press, 1978

Sanford, John, DREAMS; GOD'S FORGOTTEN LANGUAGE, NY:Harper Collins, 1968

Ullman, Montague, Krippner, Stanley, Vaughan, Alan. (1989). DREAM TELEPATHY:EXPERMENTS IN NOCTURAL ESP (Second Edition). Jefferson,MC:McFarland Publishers, 2001.

Wolf, Fred Allen, THE DREAMING UNIVERSE; a mind-expanding journey into the realm where psyche and physics meet; NY:Simon and Schuster, 1994

Synchronicity:

Bolen, Jean Shinoda, THE TAO OF PSYCHOLOGY: Synchronicity and the Self, NY:Harper & Row, 1979

Coelho, Paulo, THE ALCHEMIST; A Fable About Following Your Dream, Originally published in Portuguese in 1988; English version, HarperSanFrancisco, 1993,

Combs, Allan and Holland, Mark, SYNCHRONICITY, Science, Myth, and the Trickster, NY:Paragon House, 1990

Peat, F. David, SYNCHRONICITY;The Bridge Between Matter and Mind, NY:Bantam, 1987

Thurston, Mark, SYNCHRONICITY as Spiritual Guidance, Virginia Beach,VA:A.R.E. Press, 1997

Meditation:

Kelsey, Morton, THE OTHER SIDE OF SILENCE; A Guide to Christian Meditation (Jungian perspective), NY:Paulist Press, 1976

Kornfield, Jack, A PATH WITH HEART; A Guide Through the Perils and Promises of Spiritual Life, NY:Bantam, 1993

Levine, Stephen, GUIDED MEDITATIONS, EXPLORATIONS AND HEALINGS, NY:Anchor/Doubleday, 1991

Satir, Virginia, MEDITATIONS & INSPIRATIONS, Berkeley:Celestial Arts, 1985

Thurston, Mark, THE INNER POWER OF SILENCE; A Universal Way of Meditation, VA:Inner Vision, 1986

Thich Nhat Hanh, PEACE IS EVERY STEP; The Path of Mindfulness in Everyday Life, NY:Bantam, 1991

Ram Dass, JOURNEY OF AWAKENING; A Meditator's Guidebook; NY:Bantam, 1978

Prayer:

Dossey, Larry, M.D., HEALING WORDS; The Power of Prayer and the Practice of Medicine; CA:HarperSanFrancisco, 1993

Michael, Chester and Norrisey, Marie, PRAYER AND TEMPERMENT; Different Prayer Forms for Different Personality Types, Charlottesville, VA:The Open Door, 1991

Norris, Kathleen, THE CLOISTER WALK, NY:Riverhead Books, 1996

Williamson, Marianne, ILLUMINATA; Thoughts, Prayers, Rights of Passage, NY:Random House, 1994

Roth, Ron, Rev. PRAYER AS ENERGY MEDICINE, NY:Harmony Books, 1997

Rupp, Joyce, osm, PRAYING OUR GOODBYES, IN:Ave Maria Press, 1988

Sampson, Tom, EXPERIENCING PRAYER, TN:James Winston Pub. Co. 1995

Jewish Spirituality:

Buber, Martin, I AND THOU, A new translation by Walter Kaufmann, NY:Chas.Scribner & Son's, 1970

Buber, Martin, THE LEGEND OF BAAL-SHEM, Read by Theodore Bikel, Berkeley, CA:Audio Literature, 1992

Kushner, Lawrence, HONEY FROM THE ROCK; Ten gates of Jewish Mysticism, NY:Harper & Row, 1977

Kushner, Lawrence, GOD WAS IN THIS PLACE & I, I DID NOT KNOW; Finding Self, Spirituality and Ultimate Meaning, Woodstock, VT:Jewish Lights Pub., 1991

Christian Spirituality and Theology:

Borg, Marcus, J. THE GOD WE NEVER KNEW; Beyond Dogmatic Religion to a More Authentic Contemporary Faith, NY:HarperCollins, 1997

Church, Forrester, F.,(Editor) THE ESSENTIAL TILLICH; An Anthology of the Writings of Paul Tillich, NY:Collier, 1987

Fox, Matthew, ORIGINAL BLESSING, A Primer in Creation Spirituality, Sante Fe:Bear & Co. 1983

Eddy, Mary Baker, SCIENCE AND HEALTH, Boston, MA: The First Church of Christ, Scientist, 1875

Fox, Matthew, THE COMING OF THE COSMIC CHRIST, NY:Harper & Row, 1988

Kelsey, Morton, CHRISTO-PSYCHOLOGY, NY:Crossroads, 1982

Tillich, Paul, THE COURAGE TO BE, New Haven:Yale University Press, 1952

Welch, John, SPIRITUAL PILGRIMS, Carl Jung and Theresa of Avila, NY:Paulist Press, 1982

Hinduism:

Rama, Swami, THE PERRINEAL PSYCHOLOGY OF THE BAGAVAD GITA Honesdale, PA:Himilayan Publishers, 1985

Buddhism:

Asthma, Stephen, BUDDHA FOR BEGINNERS, NY:Writers & Readers Pub., 1996

Suzuki, Shunryu, ZEN MIND, BEGINNER'S MIND, Weatherhill, 1970

Thich Nhat Hanh, ZEN KEYS, NY:Doubleday, 1974

Thich Nhat Hanh, LIVING BUDDHA, LIVING CHRIST, NY:Riverhead Books, 1995

Tulku, Tarthang, SKILLFUL MEANS; Gentle Ways to Successful Work, Berkeley,CA:Dharma Pub., 1978

Trungpa, Chogyam, SHAMBHALA:The Sacred Path of the Warrior, Boston & London:Shambhala Press, 1988

Taoist Perspectives:

Bolen, Jean Shinoda, M.D., THE TAO OF PSYCHOLOGY: Synchronicity and the Self, NY:Harper & Row, 1979

Johanson, Greg, and Kurtz, Ron, GRACE UNFOLDING; Psychotherapy in the Spirit of the Tao-Te Ching, NY:Random House, 1991

Mabry, John, GOD AS NATURE SEES GOD; A Christian Reading of The Tao Te Ching, Rockport, MA:Element, Inc, 1994

Islam:

Kahn, Pir Valiat (Sufi teacher)

Rumi, WE ARE THREE, New Rumi Translations by Coleman Banks, Athens, GA:Colman Barks, 1987

Bly, Robert, THE KABIR BOOK, Forty-Four of the Ecstatic Poems of Kabir, Versions by Robert Bly, NY:Beacon, 1971

Native American:

Steiger, Brad, INDIAN MEDICINE POWER, MA:Para Research,1984

Steiger, Brad, KAHUNA MAGIC, MA:Para Research, 1971

King, Serge, KAHUNA HEALING, Wheaton,IL:Theosophical Pub.

Feminine Spirituality, Goddess Tradition:

Fischer, Kathleen, WOMEN AT THE WELL; Feminist Perspectives on Spiritual Direction, NJ:Paulist Press, 1988

Sjoo, Monica and Mor, Barbara, THE GREAT COSMIC MOTHER; Rediscovering the Religion of the Earth, NY:Harper & Row, 1987

Religionless Culture:

Coupland, Douglas, GENERATION X, Tales for An Accelerated Culture, (A Novel) NY:St Martin's Press, 1991

Coupland, Douglas, LIFE AFTER GOD, NY:Pocket Books/Simon & Schuster, 1994

Anthropological, Sociological, Historical Perspectives:

Armstrong, Karen, A HISTORY OF GOD, NY:Ballatine, 1993

Cambell, Joseph, THE INNER REACHES OF OUTTER SPACE: Metaphor as Myth and as Religion, NY:Harper & Row, 1886

Eisler, Riane, THE CHALICE & THE BLADE, Our History, Our Future, NY:Harper & Row, 1987

Smith, Huston, THE WORLD'S RELIGIONS, HarperSanFrancisco, 1958

Spretnak, Charlene, STATES OF GRACE; The Recovery of Meaning in the Postmodern World, NY:Harper Collins, 1991

Guru Studies:

Gopi Krishna, LIVING WITH KUNDALINI; The Autobiography of Gopi Krishna, Boston & London:Shambhala, 1993

Osborne, Arthur, Editor, THE TEACHINGS OF RAMANA MAHARSHI ME, York Beach:Samuel Weiser, Inc. 1996

Ram Dass, MIRACLE OF LOVE, Stories about Neem Karoli Baba, NY:Dutton, 1979

Yogananda, Paramahansa, AUTOBIOGRAPHY OF A YOGI, L.A.,CA.: Self-Realization Fellowship 1946

Muktananda, Swami, THE PERFECT RELATIONSHIP, S. Fallsburg, N.Y.:SYDA Foundation, 1980

Critique of the New Age:

Spangler, David and Thompson, Wm. Irwin, REIMAGINATION OF THE WORLD; A Critique of the New Age, Science, and Popular Culture, Sante Fe,NM:Bear & Co.,1991

Ferguson, Marilyn, THE AQUARIAN CONSPIRACY; Personal and Social Transformation in the 80's, L.A.CA:Tarcher, 1980

Furguson, Duncan, Editor, NEW AGE SPIRITUALITY, An Assessment Louisville,KY:Westminister/John Knox, 1993

Channeled books (a sampling of many):

Bartholomew, I COME AS A BROTHER; A Remembrance of Illusions, Taos,NM:High Mesa Press, 1986

Hicks, Jerry and Ester, (Abraham-Hicks material) San Antonio, TX: Hicks, 1996

Huffines, LaUna, BRIDGE OF LIGHT, Tiburon, CA:H.J. Kramer,Inc., 1993

Kirkwood, Annie, MARY'S MESSAGE to the World, NY:Putnam 1991

Kyron, THE END TIMES, New Information for personal peace, Dek Narm CA:The Kyron Writings, 1993

Marciniak, Barbara, BRINGERS of the DAWN, Teachings from the Pleiadians, Sante Fe,N.M:Bear & Co., 1992

Rodegast, Pat and Stanton, Judith, EMMAMUEL'S BOOK, Weston,CT:Friends Press, 1985

Roman, Sanaya, SPIRITUAL GROWTH, Tiburon, CA: H.J. Kramer, Inc., 1989

Walsch, Neale Donald, CONVERSATIONS WITH GOD (Book I, 1995) and BOOK 2,1997) Charlottesville, VA:Hampton Roads Publishing Co.

Edgar Cayce:

Puryear, Herbert, THE EDGAR CAYCE PRIMER;Discovering the Path to Self-Transformation, NY:Bantam, 1982

Sugrue, Thomas, THERE IS A RIVER; The Story of Edgar Cayce, NY:Holt, Rinehart & Winston, 1942

McArthur, David and Bruce, THE INTELLIGENT HEART; Transform Your Life with the Laws of Love (Combines the wisdom of Edgar Cayce with the science of HeartMath, Virginia Beach,VA:ARE PRESS, 1997

Reincarnation and Past Life Regression Therapy:

Fiore, Edith, M.D., YOUR HAVE BEEN HERE BEFORE, NY:Ballentine, 1978

Lucas, Winifred Blake, REGRESSION THERAPY: A Handbook for Professionals, 2 Volumes

Wambach, Helen, LIFE BEFORE LIFE, NY:Bantam, 1979

Weiss, Brian, M.D. MANY LIVES, MANY MASTERS, NY:Simon & Schuster,1988

Oracles and Carl Jung:

Anthony, Carol, THE PHILOSOPHY OF THE I CHING, Stow, MA:Anthony Pub, 1981

Anthony, Carol, A GUIDE TO THE I CHING, Stow, MA:Anthony Pub.,1982

Nichols, Sallie, JUNG AND TAROT; An Archetypal Journey, York Beach, Maine:Samuel Weiser,1980

Astrology:

Arroyo, Stephen, ASTROLOGY, PSYCHOLOGY & THE FOUR ELEMENTS; An Energy Approach to Astrology and Its Use in the Counseling Arts, Sebastopol, CA:CRCS Pub., 1975

Numerology:

Campbell, Florence, YOUR DAYS ARE NUMBERED; A Manual of Numerology for Everybody, Marina del Rey,CA:DeVorss & Co.,1931

Jordan, Juno, NUMEROLOGY;The Romance in you Name, Marina delRey,CA:DeVorss & Co.,1965

Sacred Geometry:

Frissell, Bob, NOTHING IN THIS BOOK IS TRUE, BUT IT'S EXACTLY HOW THINGS ARE, Berkeley,CA:Frog, Ltd., 1994

Melchizedek, Drunvalo, THE ANCIENT SECRET OF THE FLOWER OF LIFE, Volumes 1 & 2, Flagstaff,AZ:Light Technology Publishing Co.,1990 & 2000

ALTERNATIVE/HOLISTIC THERAPIES:

Kinesiology:

La Tourelle, Maggie, THORSONS PRINCIPLES OF KINESIOLOGY, SanFrancisco:Thorsons/HarperCollins, 1992

Smart Drugs:

Dean, Ward, M.D., Morgenthaler, John, Fowkes, Steven Wm., SMART DRUGS II; The Next Generation, Menlo Park,CA:Health Freedom Publications, 1993

Chinese Medicine:

Beinfield, Harriet, Korngold, Efrem, BETWEEN HEAVEN AND EARTH, A Guide to Chinese Medicine, NY:Ballentine Books, 1991

Haas, Elson,M.D. STAYING HEALTHY WITH THE SEASONS; Berkeley,CA:Celestial Arts, 1981

Kaptchuk, Ted J. THE WEB THAT HAS NO WEAVER, Chicago:Cogdon & Weed, 1983

Flower Essences and Aromatherapy:

Higley, Alan and Connie, & Leatham, Pat, AROMATHERAPY A-Z, Carlsbad, CA:Hay House, Inc. 1998

Harvey, Clare andd Cochrane, Amanda, THE ENCYCLOPAEDIA OF FLOWER REMEDIES, San Francisco:Thorsons/HarperCollins, 1995

Kaminski, Patricia and Katz, Richard, FLOWER ESSENCE REPERTORY, Nevada City,CA:Flower Essence Society, 1986, 1987, 1992, 1994, 1996

McIntyre, Anne, FLOWER POWER; Flower Remedies for Healing Body and Soul Through Herbalism, Homeopathy, Aromatherapy, and Flower Essences, NY:Henry Holt & Co,1996

Mazzarella, Barbara, BACH FLOWER REMEDIES FOR CHILDREN; A Parents' Guide, Rochester,VT:Healing Arts Press, 1994

Scheffer, Mechthild, BACH FLOWER THERAPY;Theory and Practice, Rochester,VT, Healing Arts Press, 1988

Scheffer, Mechthild, MASTERING BACH FLOWER THERAPIES; A Guide to Diagnosis and Treatment, Rochester, VT: Healing Arts Press, 1996

Wright, Machaelle Small, FLOWER ESSENCES; Reordering Our Understanding and Approach to Illness and Health, Jeffersonton, VA: Perelandra, Ltd, 1988

NOTES

1 Teresa of Avila, *Interior Castle* (1571), Trans. K. Kavanaugh and O. Rodriguez (New York: Paulist Press, 1979).

2 Joseph Campbell, "The Transformation of Myth Through Time," video-tape, Wm. Free Productions., 1989).

3 Ram Dass, at meditation retreat at Omega Institute in Rhinebeck, N.Y. 1986

4 Ralph Waldo Emerson, referred to "the Over-Soul, the lap of immense intelligence." *The American Mind,* Warfel, Gabriel, Williams, Vol. 1, pp 520, (NY:American Book Co., 1937).

5 Jungian Analyst Lionel Corbett, M.D. shared this metaphor of medical model scientists notion of consciousness.

6 The Old Testament, Book of Exodus, Chapter 3, 14-15

7 Stanley Keleman, *Emotional Anatomy*, pp 150-151,(Berkeley, CA: Center Press, 1985).

8 Stanley Keleman, *Emotional Anatomy*, p xi, (Berkeley, CA:Center Press, 1985.

9 Stanley Keleman, *Emotional Anatomy,* p 146, (Berkeley, CA:Center Press, 1985).

10 Daniel Amen, M.D. is a Marin County, California neurologist and psychiatrist who is masterful at using the SPECT brain scan for all kinds of brain quirks, large and small.

11 Daniel Amen, M.D. *Change Your Brain, Change Your Life*, (New York:Times Books, 1998).

12 F. Shapiro, *Eye Movement Desensitization and Reprocessing*, (New York:Guilford, 1995).

13 Teilhard De Chardin, Pierre, *Toward the Future*, 1934, from "The Evolution of Chastity" p. 86 (NY:Harcourt Brace Jovanovich,1975).

14 The first line of my poem is a phrase created by Alan Jones who Marcus Borg quoted at a weekend seminar at Union Church of Hinsdale, IL. In 1998.

15 The computer program from HeartMath is named *"Freeze Framer"*. Childre, D. And Martin, H. *The HeartMath Solution*, (HarperSanFrancisco, 1999).

16 Paul Pearsall, *The Heart's Code*, (New York:Broadway Books, 1998).

17 The Bible, New Testament, The Book of Matthew, Chapter 6:33

18 This figure eight image I learned in an "Energy Mastery," workshop in Madison, Wisconsin led by Sandra Parness, Sept.22-25, 1994 . What I added to the two infinity symbols was the smaller one, like a pinwheel at the top of the head, bring into partnership the left and right brain hemispheres. Later I discovered the same thing in a book by Julianne Everett, *Heart Initiation* (Diamond Light Foundation, 1994).

19 Paul Tillich, *The Eternal Now*, (New York: Charles Scribner's Sons, 1963).

20 C. G. Jung, *Memories, Dreams, Reflections*. Recorded and edited by Aniela Jaffe. (NY:Pantheon Books, 1963).

21 J. Wagner, (1986) Stage Play "The Search for Signs of Intelligent Life in the Universe,"staring Lily Tomlin

22 Wayne Dyer, in a talk given in Chicago in the mid-1990's.

23 D. Bohm, audio cassette "Parts Of a Whole," (Boulder, CO:Soundstrue/ New Dimensions, 1988).

24 In The Holotropic Mind, Stanislav Grof, M.D., pg 8 the author speak of the "implicate (enfolded) order and the explicate (unfolded) order which David Bohm, wrote about in *Wholeness and the Implicate Order*,(London, Routledge and Kegan Paul,1980).

25 Sigmund Freud, (1915) "The Unconscious," a paper published in The Collected Works of Sigmund Freud, Standard Edition, Vol. 14, P.s. 186-188, (London:Hogarth Press,1974).

26 Paulo Coelho, *The Alchemist* p 140 (NY:HarperCollins, 1993).

27 Joseph Campbell, "The Transformation of Myth Through Time," videotape (Wm Free Productions, 1989).

28 Blanche Gallagher, *Meditations with Teilhard de Chardin*, p 81, (Sante Fe, N.M.: Bear & Co, 1988).

29 Jane Lukehart provided me with the longest basic list of *traditional* Yin and Yang qualities during her 1993 presentation at Common Ground, Chicago

30 G. Marcel *The Philosophy of Existentialism*,(New York:Philosophy Library, 1956).

31 Maya Angelou spoke at Elmhurst College, Elmhurst, IL. on Feb. 11, 1996

32 J. Krishnamurti, The idea of introspection being judgmental and different from awareness I learned from a video taped interview (early 1980's) of this great guru, produced by the Theosophical Society of America.

33 Gabriel Marcel *The Philosophy of Existentialism*,(New York:Philosophy Library, 1956).

34 Ron Miller, Professor of Religion at Lake Forest College spoke of God as Preposition at a Common Ground Lecture, 1995

35 Martin Buber, *I and Thou,* A new translation by Walter Kaufmann, (NY:Chas. Scribner & Son's, 1970).

36 Brother Lawrence, *Practicing the Presence of God*, 14th Century. (Orleans, MA: Paraclete Press, 1985).

37 *Poems by Gerard Manly Hopkins*, "God's Grandeur," (Oxford University Press, Second Edition, 1930).

38 W. Blake, "Auguries of Innocence" lines # 1-4, p 338, Under, L. And O'Connor, We. *Poems for Study* (NY:Rinehart, 1953).

39 W. Blake, "Auguries of Innocence" beginning lines # 1-4, p 338, Under, L. and O'Connor, We. *Poems for Study*, (NY:Rinehart, 1953).

40 L. Unger, and We. O'Connor, *Poems for Study*, pg 343, (NY: Rinehart, 1953).

41 W. Blake, "Auguries of Innocence," last lines of poem 125-132, p 341, Under, L and O'Connor, We. *Poems for Study*, (NY:Rinehart,1953).

42 Marcus Borg, *The God We Never Knew,* Ch. 1, p 12, (Harper SanFrancisco, 1998).

43 Jerry and Ester Hicks, *A New Beginning II*, Ch. 11, "Law of Attraction,"pp 101-105, (TX:SanAntonio:Jerry and Ester Hicks, 1996).

44 Jerry and Ester Hicks, *A New Beginning II*, Ch. 15, "Law of Allowing," pp 137-144, (TX:SanAntonio:Jerry and Ester Hicks, 1996; First Printing, 1991).

45 Visionary and author David Spangler shared this perspective of the three alleged Christs at Ypsilanti State Hospital during a workshop sponsored by the Association for Research and Enlightenment in Chicago in the mid-1980's.

46 Oprah Winfrey made this comment on her Television show, "OPRAH" on May 21, 1996.

47 Emily Dickenson, THE COMPLETE POEMS OF EMILY DICKENS ON, Edited by Thomas H. Johnson, "Hope is the thing..." p 116,(Boston, MA: Little, Brown & Co. 1955).

48 S. Kramer, and S. Akhtar, (1994) *Mahler and Kohut*, Northvale, NY: Aronson.

49 Anna Freud, *The Ego and The Mechanisms of Defense*, NY: International Universities Press, 1966.

50 Daniel Levinson, *Seasons's Of A Man's Life*, Ch. 14 and 15, pgs 209-244(New York:Ballentine, 1978).

51 Heinz Kohut, M.D., *Analysis Of The Self*, (New York:International University Press, 1971).

52 Lionel Corbett, M.D. Workshop on Jung and Cahoot, 1986, Chicago

53 T.A. Harris, *I'm OK—You're OK*, (New York:Harper&Row, 1967).

54 F. Shapiro, (1995) *Eye Movement Desensitization and Reprocessing*, New York:Guilford

55 Roberto Assiagoli, *Psychosynthesis,* (London:Turnstone Press, 1975).

56 Hal Stone, interviewed by Jeffery Mishlow, PhD. "The Total Self," Video for the InnerWork collection, (Oakland,CA:Thinking Allowed Productitons,1989).

57 Richard C. Schwartz, *Internal Family Systems Therapy*,(NY:Guilford Press, 1995).

58 I took the est Training in 1978 and was exposed to the wonders of paradox where I learned of the What's so/So what? paradox which was part of that seminar.

59 Joseph Mina is a Hana Kuna healer, formerly administrator of a Philadelphia law firm, who now travels around the country giving energy healing sessions.

60 See *The Collected Poems of W.B. Yeats,* "The Second Coming," p 185 (NY:Macmillian Co., Definitive Edition, 1956).

61 Virginia Satir, *The New Peoplemaking*,(Mountain View, CA:Science and Behavior Books 1988).

62 Jay Haley and Cloe Mandanes of the Family Therapy Institute in Washington, D.C., presented a workshop/training program on "Strategic Marital Therapy, " in Chicago, July 12-15, 1985 in Chicago where I heard Jay Haley speak about "ordeal therapy." *Ordeal Therapy*, (San Francisco:Jossey-Bass Publishers 1984).

63 Sigmund Freud, (1915) "The Unconscious," a paper published in The Collected Works of Sigmund Freud, Standard Edition, Vol. 14, Pp 186-188, (London;Hogarth Press 1974).

64 Kenneth McAll spoke of this phenomenon during his keynote address at the Family Insititute Conference, "Healing the Family's Heart," August 15-17, 1986; See also, McAll, Kenneth, M.D., *Healing The Family Tree,* (London:Sheldon Press, 1982).

65 Jim Kinney, Common Ground retreat at Woodstock, IL, July 29-31,1994, referred to some New Agers as "New Age Fundamentalists."

66 M. Scott Peck, M.D., *Further Along the Road Less Traveled ,*Ch. 5., pp 87-89, NY:Simon & Schuster, 1993).

67 Harmon Bro led a workshop at the Association for Research and Enlightenment (Edgar Cayce) in Virginia Beach, VA..in 1982 for counselors and psychotherapists wanting to integrate spirituality into their work.

68 Dr. Martin Marty, University of Chicago Divinity School professor of Religious History shared this thought during a presentation at Union Church in the 1970's.

69 Nora and Delia Ephron, (1996) Screenplay, *Michael*, Turner Pictures Worldwide,Inc.

70 D.H. Lawrence, Selected Poems, "We Are Transmitters," pg 105 (NY;Compass Books, 1959).

71 D.H. Lawrence, Selected Poems, "The Deepest Sensuality," p 116 (NY:Compass Books, 1959).

72 M.Scott Peck, M.D. and Rev. Dr. Morton Kelsey both referred to the close relationship between sex and spirituality, calling them "kissing cousins" at lectures I attended by each of these men in the 1980's.

73 The New Testament, Chapter: John 21: 15-17

74 Abraham Maslow's hierarchy of needs can be found in *Religions, Values and Peak Experiences* (Cleveland:State Univ. Of Ohio, 1964).

75 The New Testament, Chapter: John 14:6

76 The New Testament, Chapter: John 10:30

77 Andrew Cohen is the Founder of Enlightenment Magazine www.wie.org

78 The Bible, Old Testament, The Book of Exodus, Chapter 3: 13-14.

79 The Wheel of Religions with esoteric and exoteric levels of each religion is something I learned from a teacher, Jim Kinney of Common Ground, Chicago. (A book by Charlene Spretnak in the Bibliography, *States of Grace*, speaks of every religion having something it does best.)

80 Morton Kelsey is an Episcopalian priest, Jungian psychoanalyst, teacher and author of numerous books about meditation, dreams and healing. I attended a number of his workshops from 1977 through 1988, learning about scientific research on spiritual healing. In 1979 I taught adult Sunday School classes on his book, *Dreams, A Way to Listen to God.*

81 David Burns, M.D. *Feeling Good; The New Mood Therapy*, pp 40-41, (NY:Signet,1980). pg 40-41,1980.

82 All or nothing thinking is intimately related to perfectionism; those who use this type of thinking think of themselves as being either perfect or worthless.

83 I learned this formula from corporate psychologist Robert O. Shaffer, PhD of R.H.R.& Co.

84 Matthew Fox, Original Blessing, A Primer in Creation Spirituality,(Sante Fe:Bear & Co. 1983).

85 Ted Peters 1988 article about Matthew Fox in the Christian Century Magazine.

86 Non-ordinary reality is the name shamanic healers and counselors use for the reality out of which they do their trance work; I studied this type of healing in a few weekend workshops with Michael Harner and Sandra Ingerman.

87 Richard Gerber, M.D. Vibrational Medicine,(Sante Fe, N.M.:Bear & Co.,1988).

88 B. Breiling, *Light Years Ahead*, (Tiburon, CA:Light Years Ahead Publishing, 1996).

89 Kay Wahlgren is the artist from Glen Ellyn, Illinoi s who created "15th Century Thought" in 1983.

90 This is included in the HeartMath exercises.

91 O. Hobart Mowrer, *The Crisis In Psychiatry and Religion*,(Princeton, N.J: D.Van Nostrand, 1961).

92 Paul Tillich, *The Courage to Be*, pg 34, (on being embracing non-being) (New Haven:Yale University Press, 1952).

93 Dean Kraft, *Portrait of a* Psychic *Healer*, (NY:Berkley Books, 1981).

94 Montague Ullman, Stanley Krippner, and Alan Vaughan, *Dream Telepathy: Experiments in Nocturnal ESP* (Second Edition). (Jefferson, NC: McFarland Publishers, 1989).

95 Warrior-Monk intensives are still being offered and can be found on the Internet

96 The leader for The Enlightenment Intensive experience was Wayne "Bhava" Hicks, who resides in Albuquerque, New Mexico

97 Rainer Maria Rilke, Rilke on Love and Other Difficulties, Translations and Considerations by John J.L. Mood, p 99 (NY:W.W. Norton & Co., 1975).